P9-DBT-640

Also by Christina Hoff Sommers

*One Nation Under Therapy: How the Helping
Culture Is Eroding Self-Reliance*

Who Stole Feminism? How Women Have Betrayed Women

The War Against Boys

How Misguided Policies Are Harming Our Young Men

Christina Hoff Sommers

Simon & Schuster

New York   London   Toronto   Sydney   New Delhi

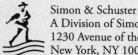 Simon & Schuster
A Division of Simon & Schuster, Inc.
1230 Avenue of the Americas
New York, NY 10020

This Simon & Schuster hardcover edition August 2013

SIMON & SCHUSTER and colophon are registered trademarks of Simon & Schuster, Inc.

For information about special discounts for bulk purchases, please contact Simon &
Schuster Special Sales at 1-866-506-1949 or business@simonandschuster.com.

The Simon & Schuster Speakers Bureau can bring authors to your live event. For more
information or to book an event contact the Simon & Schuster Speakers Bureau at
1-866-248-3049 or visit our website at www.simonspeakers.com.

Designed by Aline C. Pace

Manufactured in the United States of America

10   9   8   7   6   5   4   3   2   1

Library of Congress Cataloging-in-Publication Data
Sommers, Christina Hoff.
    The war against boys: how misguided policies are harming our young men / Christina
Hoff Sommers.—New and Revised Edition.
       pages cm
    Includes bibliographical references and index.
    1. Teenage boys—United States. 2. Teenage boys—United States—Psychology.
3. Feminism—United States. I. Title.
    HQ797.S6 2013
    305.235'1—dc23
          2012051639

ISBN 978-1-4516-4418-0
ISBN 978-1-4391-2658-5(ebook)

For Tamler and David Sommers

Contents

The War Against Boys

Preface to the New Edition

When the first edition of *The War Against Boys* appeared in 2000, almost no one was talking about boys' educational and social problems. Now it's hard to open a newspaper without stumbling upon references to the multiple books, articles, studies, and documentaries highlighting boys' academic, social, and vocational deficits. So is the war over? Not yet.

Although many educators recognize that boys have fallen far behind girls in school, few address the problem in a serious way. Schools that try to stop the trend, through boy-friendly pedagogy, literacy interventions, vocational training, or same-sex classes, are often thwarted. Women's lobbying groups still call such projects evidence of a "backlash" against girls' achievements and believe they are part of a campaign to slow further female progress.

The recent advances of girls and young women in school, sports, and vocational opportunities are cause for deep satisfaction. They should not, however, blind us to the large and growing cohort of poorly educated young men in our midst, boys who are going to be lost in our knowledge-based economy. To address the problem, we must acknowledge the plain truth: boys and girls are different. Yet in many educational and government circles, it remains taboo to broach the topic of sex differences. Gender scholars and experts still insist that the sexes are the same and argue that any talk of difference only encourages sexism and stereotypes. In the current environment, to speak of difference invites opprobrium, and to speak of boys' special needs invites passionate, organized opposition. Meanwhile, one gender difference refuses to go away: boys are languishing academically, while girls are soaring.

In the first edition of *The War Against Boys*, I focused primarily on how groups such as the American Association of University Women, the Wellesley Centers for Women, and the Ms. Foundation were harming our nation's young men. These organizations and their doctrines are still very much with us. But in this revised edition, I describe the emergence of additional boy-averse trends: the decline of recess, punitive zero-tolerance policies, myths about juvenile "superpredators," and a misguided campaign against single-sex schooling. As our schools become more feelings centered, risk averse, competition-free, and sedentary, they move further and further from the characteristic sensibilities of boys.

However, in the fourteen years since *The War Against Boys* was first published, England, Australia, and Canada have made concerted efforts to address the boy gap. In these countries, the public, the government, and the education establishment have become keenly aware of the increasing number of underachieving young males. In stark contrast to the United States, they are energetically, even desperately, looking for ways to help boys achieve parity. They have dozens of commissions, trusts, and working groups devoted to improving the educational prospects of boys. Using evidence and not ideology as their guide, these education leaders speak openly of male/female differences and don't hesitate to recommend sex-specific solutions.

Success for Boys, for example, is an Australian program that has provided grants to 1,600 schools to help them incorporate boy-effective methods into their daily practice.[1] In Great Britain, ten members of Parliament formed a Boys' Reading Commission and published a comprehensive report in 2012.[2] It offers educators a "tool kit" of successful practices. Paul Capon, president of the Canadian Council on Learning, acknowledges the political temptation to avoid or deny the problem of male underachievement. Still, he says, "You have to ask what is happening, and you have to ask why. It's a head-in-the-sand, politically correct view to say there's no problem with boys."[3] In the United States, our education establishment remains paralyzed with its head in the sand.

The subtitle of the first edition was "How Misguided Feminism Is Harming Our Young Men." The emphasis on *misguided*—I did not intend to indict the historical feminist movement, which I have always seen as one of the great triumphs of our democracy. But some readers took the book to be an attack on feminism itself, and my message was lost on them. In this edition, I have sought to make a clearer distinction between the humane and progressive women's movement and today's feminist lobby. That lobby too often acts as a narrow, take-no-prisoners special interest group. Its members see the world as a zero-sum struggle between women and men. Their job is to side with the women—beginning with girls in the formative years of childhood.

Most women, including most equality-minded women, do not see the world as a Manichean struggle between Venus and Mars. The current plight of boys and young men is, in fact, a women's issue. Those boys are our sons; they are the people with whom our daughters will build a future. If our boys are in trouble, so are we all.

In the war against boys, as in all wars, the first casualty is truth. In this updated edition, I give readers the best and most recent information on "where the boys are." I say who is warring against them and why; I describe the best scientific research on the issues in debate; and I show readers the high price we will pay if we continue to neglect academic and social needs of boys. I also suggest solutions.

This book explains how it became fashionable to pathologize the behavior of millions of healthy male children. We have turned against boys and forgotten a simple truth: the energy, competitiveness, and corporal daring of normal males are responsible for much of what is right in the world. No one denies that boys' aggressive tendencies must be mitigated and channeled toward constructive ends. Boys need (and crave) discipline, respect, and moral guidance. Boys need love and tolerant understanding. But being a boy is not a social disease.

To appreciate the growing divide between our educational establishment and the world of boys, consider this rare entity: a boy-friendly American school. In June of 2011, I visited the Heights School, an all-male Catholic academy outside Washington, DC. As I approached, I saw a large banner that said "Heights School: Men Fully Alive."

The school is thriving. There is new construction and a population of 460 fully engaged male students, grades three through twelve. Competition is part of the everyday life of the students, and awards and prizes are commonly used as incentives—but this competition is deeply embedded in an ethical system. The younger boys (ages eight to ten) attend class in log cabins filled with collections of insects, plants, and flowers. They memorize poetry and take weekly classes in painting and drawing. At the same time, the school makes room for male rowdiness.

The day of my visit, the eighth-grade boys were reenacting the Roman Battle of Philippi in 42 BC, which they had studied in class. The boys had made their own swords and shields out of cardboard and duct tape, emblazoned with dragons, eagles, and lightning bolts. For more than an hour, they marched, attacked, and brawled. At one point, a group of warriors formed a classic Roman "tortoise"—a formation with shields on all sides. Another battalion charged full-speed into the tortoise. Younger boys gathered on the sidelines and catapulted water balloons into the fray.

I asked the principal if the boys ever get hurt. Not really, he said. Anyway, one of his first lectures to parents concerns the "value of the scraped knee." There weren't even scraped knees in the battle I observed—just boys having about as much fun as there is to be had.

The Heights School is an outlier. Sword fights, sneak water balloon attacks, and mock battles hold a special fascination for boys, but most of today's schools prohibit them. Play swords and shields? Those, even in miniature, invite suspension. Boys charging into each other? Someone could get hurt (and think of the lawsuits). Young males pretending to kill one another? A prelude to wife abuse. Gender scholars have spent the past twenty years trying to resocialize boys away from such "toxic" masculine proclivities. And a *boys* school? The American Civil Liberties Union has recently joined forces with a group of activist professors to expose and abolish the injustice of such invidious "segregation." For them, what I saw at the Heights School is not "men fully alive"—it is gender apartheid.

The war against boys is not over. It is fiercer than ever. But the stakes have risen, the battle lines have become clearer, and here and there one sees signs of resistance and constructive action. My second edition is dedicated to inspiriting the forces of reason and, eventually, reconstruction.

1

Where the Boys Are

Aviation High School in Queens, New York, is easy to miss. A no-frills, industrial-looking structure of faded orange brick with green aluminum trim, it fits in comfortably with its gritty neighbors—a steel yard, a plastics factory, a tool supply outlet, and a twenty-four-hour gas station and convenience store. But to walk through the front doors of Aviation High is to enter one of the quietest, most inspiring places in all of New York City. This is an institution that is working miracles with students. Schools everywhere struggle to keep teenagers engaged. At Aviation, they are enthralled.

On a recent visit to Aviation, I observed a classroom of fourteen- and fifteen-year-olds intently focused on constructing miniaturized, electrically wired airplane wings from mostly raw materials. In another class, the students worked in teams—with a student foreman and crew chief—to take apart a small jet engine and then put it back together in just twenty days. In addition to pursuing a standard high school curriculum, Aviation High students spend half of the day in hands-on classes learning about airframes, hydraulics, and electrical systems. They put up with demanding college preparatory English and history classes because unless they do well in them, they cannot spend their afternoons tinkering with the engine of a Cessna

411 parked outside on the playground. The school's two thousand pupils—mostly Hispanic, African American, and Asian from homes below the poverty line—have a 95 percent attendance rate and an 88 percent graduation rate, with 80 percent attending college.[1] The New York City Department of Education routinely awards the school an "A" on its annual Progress Report.[2] And it has been recognized by *U.S. News & World Report* as one of the best high schools in the nation.[3] Aviation High lives up to its motto: "Where Dreams Take Flight." So what is the secret of its success?

"The school is all about structure," Assistant Principal Ralph Santiago told me. The faculty places a heavy emphasis on organization, precision workmanship, and attention to detail. No matter how chaotic students' home lives may be, at Aviation, they are promised five full days per week of calm consistency. The school administrators maintain what they call a "culture of respect." They don't tolerate even minor infractions. But anyone who spends a little time at the school sees its success is not about zero-tolerance and strict sanctions. The students are kept so busy and are so fascinated with what they are doing that they have neither the time nor the desire for antics. Many who visit the school are taken aback by the silent, empty hallways. Is it a holiday? Where are the kids? They are in the classrooms, engaged in becoming effective, educated, employable adults. "Do you have self-esteem programs?" I asked, just for the fun of it. "We don't do that," replied the principal.

Study groups from as far away as Sweden and Australia have visited and are now attempting to replicate Aviation in their home countries. It would appear to be a model of best practices. But there are very few visits from American officials. No one from the US Department of Education has visited or ever singled it out for praise. Aviation High is, in fact, more likely to be investigated, censured, and threatened by federal officials than celebrated or emulated. Despite its seventy-five-year history of success, and despite possessing what seems to be a winning formula for educating at-risk kids, it suffers from what many education leaders consider to be a fatal flaw: the school is 85 percent male.[4]

The women students at Aviation High are well respected, hold many of the leadership positions, and appear to be flourishing in every way. But their numbers remain minuscule. They know their passion for jet engines makes them different from most girls—and they seem to enjoy being distinctive. One soft-spoken young woman whose parents emigrated from India told me she loves the school, and so do her parents: "They like it because it is so safe." She is surrounded by more than seventeen hundred adolescent males in a poor section of Queens, yet she couldn't be safer.

Principal Deno Charalambous, Assistant Principal Ralph Santiago, and other administrators have made efforts to reach out to all prospective students, male and female, but it is mostly boys who respond. From an applicant pool of approximately three thousand junior high pupils from across the five New York City boroughs, the school makes about 1,200 offers and fills 490 seats in its entering ninth-grade class. Admission is open to all, and the school admissions committee looks at grades and test scores. But, says Santiago, "our primary focus is on attendance." Give us students with a good junior high attendance record and an interest in all things mechanical, he says, and Aviation can turn them into pilots, airplane mechanics, or engineers.

"Why did you choose Aviation?" I ask Ricardo, a ninth grader. "I liked the name." The world of aviation—and classes with a lot of hammering, welding, riveting, sawing, and drilling—seems to resonate more powerfully in the minds of boys than girls. At the same time, it is girls who are the overwhelming majority at two other New York City vocational schools: the High School of Fashion Industries and the Clara Barton High School (for health professions) are 92 percent and 77 percent female, respectively. Despite forty years of feminist consciousness-raising and gender-neutral pronouns, boys still outnumber girls in aviation and automotive schools, and girls still outnumber boys in fashion and nursing. The commonsense explanation is that sexes differ in their interests and propensities. But activists in groups such as the American Association of University Women and the National Women's Law Center beg to differ.

The National Women's Law Center has been waging a decade-long battle against New York City's vocational-technical high schools—with Aviation High at the top of its list of offenders. In 2001, its copresident, Marcia Greenberger, along with two activist lawyers, wrote a letter to the then–Chancellor of the New York City Board of Education, claiming that girls' rights were being violated in the city's vocational public schools and demanding that the "problem be remedied without delay."[5] The letter acknowledged that girls prevailed by large margins in four of the schools, but such schools, they said, do not prepare young women for jobs that pay as well as the male-dominated programs. "The vocational programs offered at these schools correspond with outmoded and impermissible stereotypes on the basis of sex." The letter noted that "even the names assigned to vocational high schools send strong signals to students that they are appropriate only for one sex or the other."[6]

In 2008, prompted by the National Women's Law Center, the public advocate for the City of New York, Betsy Gotbaum, published a scathing indictment entitled *Blue School, Pink School: Gender Imbalance in New York City CTE (Career and Technical Education) High Schools*. Why are there so few girls in vocational schools for automobile mechanics, building construction, and aviation? The report offered a confident reply: "Research shows that the reluctance of girls to participate in such programs is rooted in stereotypes of male and female roles that are imparted early in childhood."[7] In fact, the literature on gender and vocation is complex, vibrant, and full of reasonable disagreements. There is no single, simple answer.

I asked Charalambous, Santiago, and other administrators whether Aviation High had received any official complaints. They were vaguely aware of the 2001 letter and 2008 report, but were confident that the stunning success of their school, especially one serving so many at-risk kids, would allay doubts and criticism. The educators at Aviation define equity as "equality of opportunity"—girls are just as welcome as boys. They were frankly baffled by the letters and threats and seemed to think it was just a misunderstanding. But the activists at the National Women's Law Center, as well as the authors of the *Blue School, Pink School* report, believe that true equity means equality of participation. By this definition, Aviation falls seriously short. There is no misunderstanding.

We must all be "willing to fight," exclaimed Marcia Greenberger at a 2010 White House celebration of the Title IX equity law.[8] To an audience that included Secretary of Education Arne Duncan, Assistant Secretary for Civil Rights Russlynn Ali, and White House senior advisor Valerie Jarrett, she noted that Title IX could be used to root out sexist discrimination in areas "outside of sports." Said Greenberger, "We have loads of work to do!" She singled out Aviation High School as an egregious example of continuing segregation in vocational-technical schools. Ms. Jarrett concluded the session by assuring everyone in the room that "We are hardly going to rest on our laurels until we have absolute equality, and we are not there yet."

Before Ms. Jarrett or the secretary of education or other education officials join Ms. Greenberger and her colleagues at the National Women's Law Center in their pursuit of absolute equality, they need to consider Aviation High School in the larger context of American education and American life.

Boys and Girls in the Classroom

In 2000, the Department of Education (DOE) published a long-awaited report on gender and education entitled *Trends in Educational Equity of Girls and Women.*[9] The research was mandated by Congress under the Gender Equity in Education Act of 1993.[10] Women's groups such as the National Women's Law Center and the American Association of University Women lobbied heavily for the 1993 law and DOE study. Their own research showed that girls were being massively shortchanged and demoralized in the nation's schools. The AAUW, for example, called the plight of adolescent young women "an American tragedy."[11] It was because of such claims that Congress was moved to pass the Gender Equity in Education Act, categorizing girls as an "underserved population" on a par with other discriminated-against minorities. Hundreds of millions of dollars in grants were awarded to study the plight of girls and to learn how to overcome the insidious biases against them. Parents throughout the country observed Take Your Daughter to Work Day; the Department of Health and Human Services launched a self-esteem enhancing program called Girl Power!; and, at the United Nations Fourth World Conference on Women in Beijing in 1995, members of the American delegation presented the educational and psychological deficits of American girls as a pressing human rights issue.[12]

In 2000, women's groups eagerly awaited the DOE study. It promised to be the most thorough assessment of gender and education yet. Solid and unimpeachable statistics from the federal government would be a great boon to their campaign on behalf of the nation's young women.

But things did not go as planned. The shortchanged-girl movement rested on a lot of unconventional evidence: controversial self-esteem studies,[13] unpublished reports on classroom interactions,[14] and speculative, metaphor-laden theories about "school climates" and female adolescent malaise.[15] Here, for example, is a typical pronouncement: "As the river of a girl's life flows into the sea of Western culture, she is in danger of drowning or disappearing."[16] Those portentous words were uttered in 1990 by feminist psychologist Carol Gilligan, a leader of the shortchanged-girl movement. The picture of confused and forlorn girls struggling to survive would be drawn again and again, with added details and increasing urgency. By 1995, the public was more than prepared for psychologist Mary Pipher's bleak tidings in her bestselling book, *Reviving Ophelia: Saving the Selves of Adolescent Girls*. According to Pipher, "Something dramatic happens to girls in early adolescence. . . . They crash and burn."[17]

The DOE's *Trends in Educational Equity* report was based on more straightforward criteria: grades, test scores, and college matriculation. By those standards, girls were doing *far better* than boys. The DOE's National Center for Education Statistics (NCES) analyzed forty-four concrete indicators of academic success and failure. About half of the indicators showed no differences between boys and girls. For example, "Females are just as likely as males to use computers at home and at school," and "Females and males take similar mathematics and science courses in high school." Some favored boys: they do better on math and science tests, and they enjoy these subjects more and demonstrate greater confidence in their math and science abilities than girls. *Trends in Educational Equity* found that the math and science gaps were narrowing, but they still singled them out as areas of concern. On the whole, however, girls turned out to be far and away the superior students. According to the report, "There is evidence that the female advantage in school performance is real and persistent."[18] As the study's director, Thomas Snyder, told me almost apologetically, "We did not realize women were doing so well."

A few sample findings:

- "Female high school seniors tend to have higher educational aspirations than their male peers."

- "Female high school seniors are more likely to participate in more after-school activities than their male peers, except for participation in athletics."

- "Female high school students are more likely than males to take Advanced Placement examinations."

- "Females have consistently outperformed males in reading and writing."

- "Differences in male and female writing achievements have been relatively large, with male 11th graders scoring at about the same level as female 8th graders in 1996."

- "Females are more likely than males to enroll in college."

- "Women are more likely than men to persist and attain degrees."

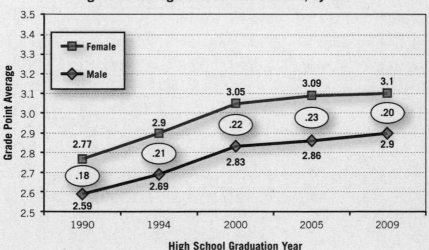

Figure 1: Average GPA of 12th Graders, by Sex

Source: US Department of Education, Institute of Education Sciences, National Center for Education Statistics, *High School Transcript Study (HSTS), 2000, 1998, 1994, 1990.*

Contrary to the story told by the girl-crisis lobby, the new study revealed that by the early 1990s, American girls were flourishing in unprecedented ways. To be sure, a few girls may have been crashing and drowning in the sea of Western culture, but the vast majority were thriving in it: moving ahead of boys in the primary and secondary grades, applying to college in record numbers, filling the more challenging academic classes, joining sports teams, and generally outperforming boys in the classroom and extracurricular activities. Subsequent studies by the Department of Education and the Higher Education Research Institute show that, far from being timorous and demoralized, girls outnumber boys in student government, honor societies, and school newspapers. They also receive better grades,[19] do more homework,[20] take more honors courses,[21] read more books,[22] eclipse males on tests of artistic and musical ability,[23] and generally outshine boys on almost every measure of classroom success. At the same time, fewer girls are suspended from school, fewer are held back, and fewer drop out.[24] In the technical language of education experts, girls are more academically "engaged."

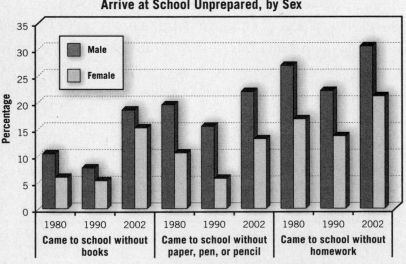

Figure 2: Percentage of High School Sophomores Who Arrive at School Unprepared, by Sex

Source: National Center for Education Statistics, *The Condition of Education 2007*, Indicator 22.

If all the data from the Department of Education had to be condensed into a single anecdote, it could be this one about a parent-teacher conference in a middle school in New Jersey in 2010:

> A sixth-grade boy, whose mother asks he be identified as Dan, squirms as his teacher tells his parents he's not trying hard enough in school. He looks away as the teacher directs his parents to a table of projects the class has done on ancient Greek civilization. Some projects are meticulous works of art, with edges burned to resemble old parchment. Dan's title page is plain and unillustrated, and he's left an "e" out of "Greek." "You'll never get anywhere if you don't try," says Dan's father as they leave the classroom. "I don't understand," says Dan's mother, whose two older daughters got straight A's in school without her intervention.[25]

But Don't Boys Test Better?

Boys do appear to have an advantage when it comes to taking tests like the SAT. They consistently attain higher scores in both the math and verbal sections, though girls are well ahead in the recently added essay section.[26] But according to the College Board, the organization that administers the SAT, the boys' better scores tell us more about the selection of students taking the test than about any advantage boys may enjoy. Fewer males than females take the SAT (46 percent of the test takers are male) and far more of the female test takers come from the "at risk" category—girls from lower-income homes or with parents who never graduated from high school or never attended college. "These characteristics," says the College Board, "are associated with lower than average SAT scores."[27]

There is another factor that skews test results. Nancy Cole, former president of the Educational Testing Service, calls it the "spread" phenomenon. Scores on almost any intelligence or achievement test are more widely distributed for boys than for girls—boys include more prodigies and more students of marginal ability. Or, as the late political scientist James Q. Wilson once put it, "There are more male geniuses and more male idiots." The boys of marginal ability tend not to take the SAT, so there is no way to correct for the high-achieving males who show up in large numbers.

Suppose we were to turn our attention away from the highly motivated, self-selected two-fifths of high school students who take the SAT and consider instead a truly representative sample of American schoolchildren. How would girls and boys then compare? Well, we have the answer. The National Assessment of Educational Progress, mandated by Congress in 1969 offers the best measure of achievement among students at all levels of ability. Under the NAEP program, 120,000 to 220,000 students drawn from all fifty states as well as District of Columbia and Department of Defense schools are tested in reading, writing, math, and science at ages nine, thirteen, and seventeen. In 2011, eighth-grade boys outperformed girls by 1 point in math and 5 points in science. But in 2011 and 2007 respectively (the most recent year for this data), eighth-grade girls outperformed boys by 9 points in reading and 20 points in writing. (Ten points are roughly equivalent to one year of schooling.[28])

The math and science gap favoring boys has been intensely debated and analyzed. In 1990, at the beginning of the shortchanged-girl campaign, young women were even further behind. (Seventeen-year-old females, for example, were then 11 points behind males in science.) It is likely that the women's lobby was helpful in drawing attention to the girls' deficits and in promoting effective remedies. But what is hard to understand is why the math and science gap launched a massive movement on behalf of girls, and yet a much larger gap in reading, writing, and school engagement created no comparable effort for boys. Just as hard to explain is the failure by nearly everyone in the education establishment to address the growing college attendance gap. Today, women in the United States earn 57 percent of bachelor's degrees, 60 percent of master's degrees, and 52 percent of PhDs.

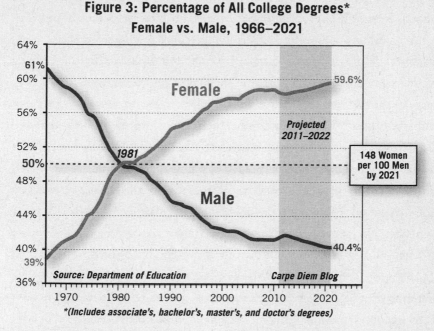

Figure 3: Percentage of All College Degrees*
Female vs. Male, 1966–2021

(Includes associate's, bachelor's, master's, and doctor's degrees)

Graph by Mark Perry (University of Michigan and American Enterprise Institute).
Data from Department of Education, ECLS-K (Early Childhood Longitudinal
Study—Kindergarten, 1998–1999 cohort).

According to DOE projections, these male-female disparities will only become increasingly acute in the future. As a policy analyst for the Pell Institute once quipped, only half in jest, "the last male will graduate from college in 2068."

Where Have all the Young Men Gone?

Trends in Educational Equity was a serious study carried out by an unimpeachable source—highly regarded, apolitical statisticians at the Department of Education's National Center for Education Statistics. But it flatly contradicted the shortchanged-girl thesis. Yes, it showed that young women needed special attention in certain areas such as their performance on standardized math and science tests; at the same time, it exposed the folly of calling them "under-served" or "shortchanged." How did the women's groups react?

Initially, they ignored it. But so did most journalists, educators, and public officials. The Education Department wasn't comfortable with its own findings and gave them little publicity. (One official told me, off the record, that some of the staff worried that it would deflect attention away from worthy women's causes.) A few months after the study appeared, I asked its director, Thomas Snyder, why the Department of Education had not alerted the public to its findings. After all, the misleading AAUW report *How Schools Shortchange Girls* generated hundreds of stories by journalists and newscasters across the country. Shouldn't *Trends in Equity in Education* have received more publicity? "We were probably more guarded than necessary," he said, "but we are a government agency. . . . In retrospect, we should have done more."

So what finally slowed down the girl-crisis parade? Reality struck. The "left the 'e' out of 'Greek'" phenomenon became impossible to ignore. Teachers observed male fecklessness and disengagement before their eyes, day after day in their classrooms. Parents began noticing that young women were sweeping the honors and awards at junior high and high school graduations, while young men were being given most of the prescriptions for attention deficit/hyperactivity disorder.[29] College admissions officers were baffled, concerned, and finally panicked over the dearth of male applicants. A new phrase entered the admissions office lexicon: "the tipping point"— the point at which the ratio of women to men reaches 60/40. According to insider lore, if male enrollment falls to 40 percent or below, females begin to flee. Officials at schools at or near the tipping point (American University, Boston University, Brandeis University, New York University, the University of Georgia, and the University of North Carolina, to name only a few) feared their campuses were becoming like retirement villages, with a surfeit of women competing for a tiny handful of surviving men. "Where Have All the Young Men Gone?" was a major attraction at a 2002 meeting of the National Association of College Admission Counseling.

Throughout the 2000s, stories of faltering schoolboys appeared in almost every major magazine and newspaper in the country. My own book

The War Against Boys was published in 2001, accompanied by a cover story in *The Atlantic*, "Girls Rule: Mythmakers to the Contrary, It's Boys Who Are in Deep Trouble." These were followed a few years later by articles in *Newsweek, BusinessWeek, The New Republic*, and *U.S. News & World Report*. Programs such as *60 Minutes* and *20/20* dramatized the plight of boys, as did data-filled books such as *Why Boys Fail* and *The Trouble with Boys*.[30] In addition to this steady flow of news stories and books, various state commissions and policy centers issued reports on the precarious state of schoolboys.[31] In 2006, for example, the Rennie Center for Education Research and Policy, a nonpartisan Massachusetts think tank on education, released *Are Boys Making the Grade?* Initially, its researchers wondered if the media stories about disadvantaged boys were exaggerated. They asked, "[I]s the picture as one-sided as the media portray?" Their final answer: a resounding, unequivocal yes. "The gender gap is real and has a negative effect on boys."[32] With obvious surprise at their own findings, the Rennie researchers reported, "In Massachusetts, the achievement of girls not only exceeds the achievement of boys in English language arts at all grade levels, girls are generally outperforming boys in math as well."[33] The study concluded, "Boys are struggling in our public schools." It suggested several reforms such as more experimentation with single-sex classrooms, a heightened focus on male and female learning styles in teacher training programs, and special attention to black, Hispanic, and other subgroups of boys.

The same year, 2006, the California Postsecondary Education Commission (a group of business leaders, educators, and public policy experts that advises the governor) published *The Gender Gap in California Higher Education*. It showed women from all major ethnic groups moving well ahead of men throughout the University of California (UC) system.[34] In the professional schools, once dominated by men, women were earning 57 percent of degrees in law, 62 percent in dentistry, 73 percent in optometry, 77 percent in pharmacy, and 82 percent in veterinary medicine. Just like Thomas Snyder in the Department of Education and the Rennie researchers in Massachusetts, the California Postsecondary Education Commission authors seemed both surprised and alarmed by their findings. "The magnitude of the issue [of male disadvantage] is large."[35] And they noted the potential harm the growing gap could wreak in the US workforce and in the nation's "competitiveness in the global economy."[36]

By the middle of the 2000s, the precariousness of boys and young men in American schools was one of the most thoroughly documented phenomena in the history of education. Groups like the National Women's Law Center and the AAUW might have been expected to return to the drawing board to look for ways to address the special needs of girls, while acknowledging the considerable vulnerabilities of boys. That did not happen.

The Empire Strikes Back

In 2008, Linda Hallman, the AAUW executive director, announced her organization's determination to continue to "break through barriers" for women and girls and not to allow "adversaries" to obstruct their mission:

> Our adversaries know that AAUW is a force to be reckoned with, and that we have "staying power" in our dedication to breaking through the barriers that we target. . . . We ARE **Breaking through Barriers.** We mean it; we've done it before; and we are "coming after them" again and again and again, if we have to! All of us, all the time.[37] [AAUW emphasis.]

This powerful and influential organization saw the new focus on boys as part of an organized backlash against the gains of women. A few weeks before Ms. Hallman's declaration of war, the AAUW issued a 103-page study refuting the idea that boys were disadvantaged. According to *Where the Girls Are: The Facts About Gender Equity in Education,* the boy crisis was a hoax. This study, said Ms. Hallman, "debunks once and for all the myth of the 'boys' crisis' in education."[38] She described it as "the most comprehensive report ever done on the topic."[39] As we shall see, it did not come close to *Trends in Educational Equity*, or dozens of other studies, in objectivity, soundness, or comprehensiveness. But it did garner masses of publicity, including respectful treatment in places such as the *New York Times*, *Washington Post*, *Wall Street Journal*, and *NewsHour with Jim Lehrer*.[40] On its blog, the AAUW urged its more than 100,000 members around the country to "Build Buzz on *Where the Girls Are*." There was no buzz machine behind the research on boys. What did the AAUW find?

Chapter 1 of *Where the Girls Are* begins with a comment on the motives of authors (this author included) who write about the plight of boys:

> Many people remain uncomfortable with the education and professional advances of girls and women, especially when they threaten to outdistance their male peers. . . . From the incendiary book *The War Against Boys* . . . to more subtle insinuations such as the *New York Times* headline, "At Colleges, Women Are Leaving Men in the Dust," a backlash against the achievement of girls and women emerged.[41]

The report flatly rejects the idea that boys as a group are in trouble. In fact, it asserts that young men are faring better today than ever before. Today's young men, say the authors, are graduating from high school in record numbers. "More men are earning college degrees today in the United States than at any time in history."[42] Men have not fallen behind; it is simply that females "have made more rapid gains."[43] The report does not deny that there are serious inequities in education, but attributes them to race and class—not gender. It calls for a refocused public debate on the deep division among schoolchildren by race and family income. Finally, it emphatically reminds readers of the real world that awaits young men and women once they leave school: "Perhaps the most compelling evidence against the existence of a boys' crisis is that men continue to outearn women in the workplace."[44]

It is hard to know how to respond to the suggestion that those of us who write about the plight of boys are "uncomfortable with the advances of girls." The AAUW gives no evidence for it. The same charge was made by two professors, Rosalind Chait Barnett, a senior scientist at the Women's

Studies Research Center at Brandeis University, and Caryl Rivers of Boston University, in their 2011 book, *The Truth About Girls and Boys:* "The fact that girls are succeeding academically touches a wellspring of psychic fear in some people." They called the boys' crisis "manufactured"—part of a "backlash against the women's movement."[45] Soon after the 2008 release of *Where the Girls Are*, Linda Hallman told the *New York Times* that "conservative commentators" were behind the "distracting debate" over allegedly disadvantaged boys.[46]

But alarm over the plight of boys comes from parents, educators, writers, research institutes, and commissions from across the political and social spectrum. What we share is a concern for all children, along with an awareness that boys appear to need special help right now. That is not backlash; it is reality and common sense.

What about the claim that boys are doing better than ever? According to the AAUW report:

> More men are earning college degrees today in the United States than at any time in history. During the past 35 years, the college-educated population has greatly expanded: The number of bachelor's degrees awarded annually rose 82 percent, from 792,316 in 1969–70 to 1,439,264 in 2004–05.[47]

It is true that in absolute terms more boys were graduating from high school and going to college in 2005 than in the previous forty years. But that is because the population of college-age males was much larger in 2005 than in the previous forty years. In 1970, men earned 451,097 BA degrees; by 2009, the number was 685,382—a 52 percent increase. In the same time period, BA degrees conferred to women went from 341,219 to 915,986—a 168 percent increase.[48] Good news all around, says the AAUW. But was it? The picture changes when you control for population growth and consider the *rate* of improvement. Males stalled in the mid-1970s while females rapidly advanced (see Figure 4).

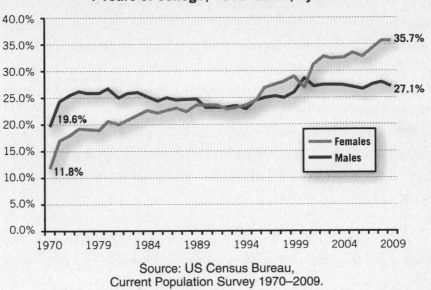

Figure 4: Percentage of Population Ages 25–34 with 4 Years of College, 1970–2009, by Sex

Source: US Census Bureau,
Current Population Survey 1970–2009.

The AAUW researchers point out that even if men are not keeping up with women, they are doing better than in the past. As Linda Hallman explained during a PBS online discussion, "[I]n the percentage of boys graduating from high school and college, boys are performing better today than ever before."[49] Technically true, but thoroughly misleading. In 2008, for example, US Census data shows that among women and men ages twenty-five to twenty-nine, 34 percent of women had a bachelor's degree—compared with 26 percent of men.[50] The number of women with college degrees had increased by 14 percent from 1978; the men, by less than 1 percent (0.77 percent, to be precise). If the facts were reversed and young men soared while women stalled, Ms. Hallman and her colleagues would have a different outlook.

Most of the news stories conveyed the AAUW's message that there is no serious *gender* achievement gap in education—the problem is race and social class. As one AAUW author told the *Washington Post*, "If there is a crisis, it is with African American and Hispanic students and low-income students, girls and boys."[51] But here the AAUW obscures the fact that the gender gap favors girls across all ethnic, racial, and social lines. Young black women are twice as likely to go to college as black men; at some of the prestigious historically black colleges the numbers are truly ominous—Fisk is now 64 percent female; Howard, 67 percent; Clark Atlanta, 72 percent.[52]

When economist Andrew Sum and his colleagues at the Center for Labor Market Studies at Northeastern University examined gender disparities in the Boston Public Schools, they found that for the class of 2007, among blacks, there were 191 females for every 100 males attending a four-year college or university. Among Hispanics the ratio was 175 females for every 100 males. For white students the gap was smaller, but still very large: 153 females to every 100 males.[53]

The facts are incontrovertible: young women from poor neighborhoods in Boston, Los Angeles, or Washington, DC, do much better than the young men from those same neighborhoods. There are now dozens of studies with titles like "The Vanishing Latino Male in Higher Education," "The Latino Male Dropout Crisis," and "African-American Males in Education: Endangered or Ignored?"[54] When the College Board recently studied *The Educational Experience of Young Men of Color*, its conclusions were dismaying: "There is an educational crisis for young men of color in the United States. . . . Collectively, [our] data shows that more than 51 percent of Hispanic males, 45 percent of African American males, 42 percent of Native American males, and 33 percent of Asian American males ages 15 to 24 will end up unemployed, incarcerated or dead. It has become an epidemic, and one that we must solve by resolving the educational crisis facing young men of color."[55]

What about those middle- and upper-middle-class white—or young men of color from comfortable backgrounds? Clearly, they are not in the same predicament as boys living near or below the poverty line. But even these males are performing well below their female counterparts. Consider, for example, the female advantage when it comes to honor societies, enrollment in AP classes, and earning A's.[56] Judith Kleinfeld, a professor of psychology at the University of Alaska, Fairbanks, analyzed the reading skills of white males from college-educated families. Using Department of Education data, she showed that at the end of high school, 23 percent of the white sons of college-educated parents scored "below basic." For girls from the same background, the figure was 7 percent. "This means," Ms. Kleinfeld writes, "that one in four boys who have college-educated parents cannot read a newspaper with understanding."[57]

Gender is a constant. Kleinfeld found that 34 percent of Hispanic males with college-educated parents scored "below basic," compared to 19 percent of Hispanic females. Isn't it possible—or even likely—that if we found ways to inspire poor black boys to read, those methods might work for Hispanic boys or poor white boys—or even white middle-class boys?

What Motivates the Women's Lobby?

It is not hard to understand why women's groups have invested so much effort in thwarting the cause of boys. When they look at society as a whole, they see males winning all the prizes. Men still prevail in the highest echelons of power. Look at the number of male CEOs, full professors, political leaders. Or consider the wage gap. As the AAUW says, "the most compelling evidence against the existence of a boys' crisis is that men continue to outearn women in the workplace."[58] Why worry about boys doing better in school when they appear to be doing so much better in life?

This is an understandable but seriously mistaken reaction. First of all, most men are not at the pinnacle of power. The "spread" phenomenon we see in testing shows up in life. There are far more men than women at the extremes of success and failure. And failure is more common. There may be 480 male CEOs of Fortune 500 companies (20 women), 438 male members of Congress (101 women), and 126,515 full professors (45,571 women). But consider the other side of the ledger. More than one million Americans are classified by the Department of Labor as "discouraged workers." These are workers who have stopped looking for jobs because they feel they have no prospects or lack the requisite skills and education. Nearly 60 percent are men—636,000 men and 433,000 women. Consider also that that more than 1.5 million (1,500,278) men are in prison. For women the figure is 113,462.[59]

Finally, a word about the infamous "wage gap," which represents one of the most long-standing statistical fallacies in American policy debate. The 23-cent gender pay gap is simply the difference between the average earnings of all men and women working full-time. It does not account for differences in occupations, positions, education, job tenure, or hours worked per week. When mainstream economists consider the wage gap, they find that pay disparities are almost entirely the result of women's different life preferences—what men and women choose to study in school, where they work, and how they balance their home and career. A thorough 2009 study by the US Department of Labor examined more than fifty peer-reviewed papers on the subject and concluded that the wage gap "may be almost entirely the result of individual choices being made by both male and female workers."[60] In addition to differences in education and training, the review found that women are more likely than men to leave the workforce to take care of children or older parents. There were so many differences in pay-related choices that the researchers were unable to specify even a residual effect that might be the result of discrimination.

Wage-gap activists at the AAUW and the National Women's Law Center say no—even when we control for relevant variables, women still earn less. But it always turns out that they have omitted one or two crucial variables. Consider the case of pharmacists. Almost half of all pharmacists are female, yet as a group, they earn only 85 percent of what their male counterparts earn. Why should that be? After all, male and female pharmacists are doing the same job with roughly identical educations. There must be some hidden discrimination at play. But according to the *2009 National Pharmacies Workforce Survey*, male pharmacists work on average 2.4 hours more per week, have more job experience, and more of them own their own stores.[61] A 2012 *New York Times* article tells a similar story about women in medicine: "Female doctors are more likely to be pediatricians than higher-paid cardiologists. They are more likely to work part time. And even those working full time put in seven percent fewer hours a week than men. They are also much more likely to take extended leaves, most often to give birth and start a family."[62] There are exceptions, but most workplace pay gaps and glass ceilings vanish when one accounts for these factors. And as economists frequently remind us, if it were really true that an employer could get away with paying Jill less than Jack for the same work, clever entrepreneurs would fire all their male employees, replace them with females, and enjoy a huge market advantage.

Women's groups do occasionally acknowledge that the pay gap is largely explained by women's life choices, as the AAUW does in its 2007 *Behind the Pay Gap*.[63] But this admission is qualified: they insist that women's choices are not truly free. Women who decide, say, to stay home with children, to become pediatricians rather than cardiologists, or to attend the Fashion Industry High School rather than Aviation High are driven by sexist stereotypes. Says the AAUW, "Women's personal choices are . . . fraught with inequities."[64] It speaks of women being "pigeonholed" into "pink-collar" jobs in health and education. According to the National Organization for Women, powerful sexist stereotypes "steer" women and men "toward different education, training, career paths," and family roles.[65] But is it really sexist stereotypes and social conditioning that best explain women's vocational preferences and their special attachment to children? Aren't most American women free and self-determining human beings? The women's groups need to show—not dogmatically assert—that women's choices are not free. And they need to explain why, by contrast, the life choices they promote are the authentic ones—what women truly want, and what will make them happier and more fulfilled. Of course, these are weighty philosophical questions unlikely to be resolved anytime soon. But surely, one thing should be clear: ignoring boys' educational deficits is not the solution to the wage and power gap. And whatever women's problems may be, they should not blind us to the growing plight of marginally educated men.

In 2006, the *Portland Press Herald* ran an alarming series of reports about the educational deficits of boys in Maine.[66] Among its findings: "High school girls outnumber boys by almost a 2:1 ratio in top-10 senior rankings," and "Men earn about 38 percent of the bachelor's degrees awarded by Maine's public universities." According to the report, boys both rich and poor had fallen seriously behind their sisters. But the director of Women's Studies at the University of Southern Maine, Susan Feiner, expressed frustration over the sudden concern for boys. "It is kind of ironic that a couple of years into a disparity between male and female attendance in college it becomes 'Oh my God, we really need to look at this. The world is going to end." [67]

I can sympathize with the professor's complaint. Where was the indignation when men dominated higher education, decade after decade? Maybe it is time for women and girls to enjoy the advantage. That is an understandable but misguided reaction. It was wrong to ignore women's educational needs for so long and cause for celebration when we turned our attentions to meeting those needs. But turning the tables and neglecting boys is not the answer. Why not be fair to both?

In feminist Betty Friedan's celebrated 1963 book, *The Feminine Mystique*, she said that American women suffered from severe domestic ennui—"the problem that had no name." Today the problem Friedan described hardly exists. For most American women, especially young women, the problem is not the futility and monotony of domestic life; it is choosing among the many paths open to them. Finding male partners as ambitious and well educated as they are is another challenge. Life for women may be difficult, but the system is no longer rigged against them. The new problem with no name is the economic and social free fall of millions of young men.

Thomas Mortenson, a policy analyst at the Pell Institute for the Study of Opportunity in Higher Education, began to notice negative trends for young men twenty years ago. He was certain that journalists, educators, and political leaders would pick it up and run with it. When that did not happen, he wrote about it himself in a 1995 fact sheet entitled "What's Wrong with Guys?" [68] He noted that the women surpassed men in the rates at which they graduated from college in 1991, acknowledging that the gender gap was "widening." He asked, "When the labor market offers such rich rewards for the college educated—both men and women—why have only women responded?" Mortenson foresaw the profound negative effects of male underachievement on the American economy and the family. He also noted the high psychological toll it would exact from men themselves. As he told an education reporter, "Most men define themselves by their work and must be productively engaged." [69]

Unfortunately, Mortenson sounded the alarm during a period when the media, the education establishment, and the government were focused on the AAUW-engineered girl crisis. Congress had just passed the Gender Equity in Education Act, the Department of Health and Human Services had launched Girl Power!,[70] and *Reviving Ophelia* was on the bestseller lists.[71] No one was paying attention to boys, and the problem that has no name went unnoticed. Mortenson, a mild-mannered, just-the-facts-ma'am Joe Friday from Iowa, was no match for the girl advocates and their buzz machine.

The Economic Fallout

In February 2011 a small miracle happened. The Harvard Graduate School of Education, once the epicenter of the silenced- and shortchanged-girl movement, published a major study that acknowledged the plight of males. It recognized the real problem that has no name. The study, *Pathways to Prosperity*, points out that a high school diploma was once the passport to the American dream; in 1973, 72 percent of the American workforce had earned only a high school diploma—or less. Nearly two-thirds of them made it into the middle class. "In an economy in which manufacturing was still dominant, it was possible for those with less education but a strong work ethic to earn a middle-class wage."[72] *Not any longer.* As the report makes clear, since the 1970s, "all of the net job growth in America has been generated by positions that require at least some post-secondary education."[73] The new passport to the American Dream is "education beyond high school." And today, far more women than men have that passport. As *Pathways to Prosperity* reports:

> Our system . . . clearly does not work well for many, especially young
> men. In recent years, a yawning gender gap has opened up in American
> higher education. Men now account for just 43 percent of enrollment
> in our nation's colleges, and earn only 43 percent of bachelor's degrees.
> Not surprisingly, women also account for 60 percent of the nation's
> graduate students.

This dramatic chart accompanied the report:

Figure 5: The Growing Gender Gap in Our Nation's Colleges: What Are the Implications?

Women now account for **57%** of college students

Women earn **57%** of college degrees   Men earn just **43%** of college degrees

Women now account for **60%** of graduate students

Source: *Pathways to Prosperity*,
Harvard Graduate School of Education, 2011.

A few months later, in the summer of 2011, the Brookings Institution published a study that reinforced the message of the Harvard study. Michael Greenstone, a professor of economics at MIT and senior fellow at Brookings, along with Adam Looney, another Brookings senior fellow, released a report on the fate of marginally educated men in today's workplace. It confirmed Mortenson's predictions—and more. To give one dramatic example, for men ages twenty-five to sixty-four with no high school diploma, median annual earnings have declined 66 percent since 1969. Say the authors, "Men with just a high school diploma did only marginally better. Their wages declined by 47 percent" (Figure 6). Not only have men with minimal educational credentials suffered severe setbacks in wages—a large number have vanished from the full-time workforce.

Figure 6: Change in Male Earnings, 1969–2009

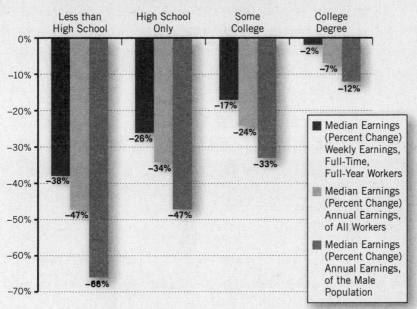

Source: "Trends: Reduced Earnings for Men in America,"
The Milken Institute Review.

Why have men suffered this decline? As jobs in manufacturing, construction, farming, and mining have disappeared and the United States has moved toward a knowledge-based economy, men have failed to adapt. At the same time, the education establishment, as well as the federal government, looked the other way. Male workers with only a high school degree, say Greenstone and Looney, have been "unhitched from the engine of growth."[74] According to these two economists, "Male college completion rates peaked in 1977 . . . and then barely changed over the next 30 years. This slowdown in educational attainment for men is puzzling because attainment among women has continued to rise, and higher education is richly rewarded in the labor market."[75]

These rewards are already in evidence. In major cities across the United States, single women ages twenty-two to thirty with no children now earn 8 percent more than their male counterparts (Figure 7). According to the latest Census Data, since 2007, the number of young men (ages twenty-five to thirty-four) living with their parents shot up from 14.2 percent to 18.6 percent. For young women the rates have remained steady—around 10 percent (Figure 8). The Population Reference Bureau notes, "The share of young men living at home has reached its highest level since the Census Bureau first started tracking the measure in 1960."[76]

Figure 7: Top Towns for Women

Percentage in which median full-time wages for single, childless women ages 22–30 exceeds those of single, childless men in the same age group.

Metro Areas	Wage Advantage
Atlanta, GA	21%
Memphis/Ark./Mo.	19%
New York City–Northeastern NJ	17%
Sacramento	16%
San Diego	15%
Miami–Hialeah, FL	14%
Charlotte–Gastonia–Rock Hill, NC/SC	14%
Raleigh–Durham, NC	14%

Source: Reach Advisory, New York, New York.

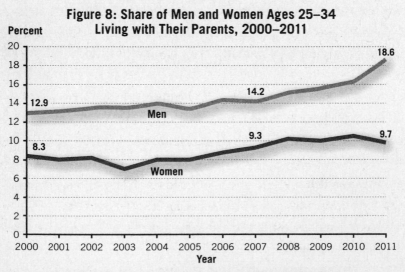

Figure 8: Share of Men and Women Ages 25–34 Living with Their Parents, 2000–2011

Source: US Census Bureau, Current Population Survey.
Graph from Population Reference Bureau, September 2011.

At the conclusion of their report, the Brookings authors offer suggestions on "the long road back." One of their top recommendations: more career academies for high school students that blend academic instruction with workplace experience. In other words, more schools like Aviation High School. Given the current climate, how likely is it that will happen?

The Women's Lobby Again

In June 2012, the National Coalition for Women and Girls in Education (NCWGE) published a new, 66-page report on the plight of girls in education, *Title IX at 40: Working to Ensure Gender Equity in Education*.[77] While acknowledging that women have made progress, and mentioning that men may face bias in nursing and child care programs, they once again present girls as the shortchanged gender. "Girls and women," they say, "are discouraged from pursuing traditionally male training programs."[78] Aviation High is not singled out by name, as it was at the White House equity seminar in 2010, but it is clearly in their sights. The report calls for aggressive Title IX compliance reviews and demands that Congress "hold states and municipalities accountable for increasing women's completion of career and technical education programs."[79] As we shall see in chapter 7, the effort to harass and subjugate one of the few styles of education that is working for boys is already bearing bitter fruit in law and regulation. The buzz machine never stops.

Soon after the AAUW published its 2008 report dismissing the boys' crisis, Linda Hallman boasted in her monthly newsletter about how its release was publicized by the major news organizations—NPR, the *New York Times*, and the *Washington Post*. She said, "[The] AAUW's ability to capture media attention demonstrates the power and credibility of our message."[80] Not so. Capturing media attention and being credible are distinct phenomena. What it demonstrates is these women's groups' preternatural ability to lobby, to network, and to spin.

Within living memory, the American feminist movement has been a valiant, broad-based vehicle for social equality. It achieved historic victories and enjoys continuing, well-deserved prestige for its contributions to social equality. But it has now harnessed that prestige to the ethos and methods of a conventional interest group. For leaders like Linda Hallman and Marcia Greenberger, men and women are two opposing camps engaged in a zero-sum struggle. Their job is to make sure women win. Few women, including feminist women, share their worldview. The AAUW and the National Women's Law Center represent a tiny ideological constituency. But, at the moment, the education establishment, the White House, and many in the media treat them as the authoritative voice of American women.

Male underachievement is more than an American problem. While men still outnumber women in higher education in China, Japan, and India, there is a growing college gap favoring women in countries as diverse as France, Brazil, Albania, Malaysia, and Australia. And the international dimension gives the problem special urgency, as education writer Richard Whitmire and literacy expert William Brozo remind us: "The global economic race we read so much about—the marathon to produce the most educated workforce and therefore the most prosperous nation—really comes down to a calculation: Whichever nation solves these 'boy troubles' wins the race."[81]

That is surely an overstatement, but we do know that the entry of large numbers of women into the workforce in recent decades has paid large economic dividends. There is no principle that says gender parity in education guarantees national economic success, but finding ways to get boys and men more engaged in school will certainly yield social and economic benefits that go beyond the welfare of the men themselves.

As we shall see, for countries such as Australia, England, and Canada, closing the boy gap has become a national priority. But the United States has an extra handicap. We are coping not only with millions of poorly educated boys and young men, but with a tenacious women's lobby that thwarts all efforts to help them. And today, that lobby appears to be setting the agenda for the US government.

In June 2012, the Department of Education's Office for Civil Rights published a report entitled *Gender Equity in Education*.[82] This new equity study might have been an occasion for federal officials to finally acknowledge the boy gap and alert the public to its social and economic hazards. After the department's 2000 *Trends in Educational Equity* study and alarming reports on male academic disaffection by the California Post-Secondary Education Commission, the Massachusetts Rennie Center, the Harvard Graduate School of Education, and the Brookings Institution, it would seem impossible for federal officials to ignore boys any longer. But *Gender Equity in Education* reads as if it were crafted by spin-mistresses at the AAUW and the National Women's Law Center. The reading, writing, and school engagement chasms favoring young women are never mentioned; the college gap is noted without comment. In contrast, the few areas where girls are behind boys are highlighted as examples of inequitable "disparities" and described as "underrepresentation."

The report's treatment of the gender gap in the elite Advanced Placement (AP) program is typical of the entire study. In 1985, boys and girls took AP courses at nearly the same rate. Around 1990, the girls moved ahead of boys and never looked back. By 2012, AP enrollment was 56 percent female. How do you turn that into bad news for girls? The authors of *Gender Equity in Education* found a way. They mention without elaboration that "girls outnumber boys in enrollment in AP science, AP foreign languages, and several other AP subjects"—and then they get down to business. Bullet point: "In AP mathematics, however, boys have consistently outnumbered girls by up to 10,000." A longitudinal graph emphasizes the point. But there are no bullet points or graphs showing that girls have consistently outnumbered boys by up to 32,000 in biology, 56,000 in history, and 206,000 in English.[83] Why don't the lower male numbers count as disparity and underrepresentation? Because they do not fit the shortchanged-girl narrative promoted by the women's lobby. Unfortunately for boys, that narrative has been adopted by the federal government and other influential quarters of the American education establishment.

A Smoking Gun on How Our Schools Fail Boys

What, finally, explains boys' plight in education? Why should they be so far behind girls in honors courses and college attendance? Boys score slightly better than girls on national math and science tests—yet their grades in those subjects are lower. They perform worse than girls on literacy tests—but their classroom grades are even lower than these test scores predict. How does that happen? Don't expect answers from the Department of Education.

In February 2013, three economists from the University of Georgia (UGA) and Columbia University may have inadvertently solved the mystery behind the boy gap. In "Non-cognitive Skills and the Gender Disparities in Test Scores and Teacher Assessments: Evidence from Primary School" (published in the *Journal of Human Resources*), they confirmed that boys across racial lines and in all major subject areas earn lower grades in elementary school than their test scores predict.[84] But then these economists did something no education official had thought to do: they looked for an explanation. And they appear to have found it. Teachers *as early as kindergarten* factor good behavior into grades—and girls, as a rule, comport themselves far better and are more amenable to classroom routines than boys. As the authors say, "We trace the misalignment of grades and test scores to differences between boys and girls in their non-cognitive development." Non-cognitive skills include self-control, attentiveness, organization, and the ability to sit still for long periods of time. As most parents know, girls tend to develop these skills earlier and more naturally than boys do. It is not unheard of for some males never to develop them at all.

The economists looked at data from 5,800 children in kindergarten through fifth grade. They examined students' performance on standardized tests in reading, math, and science. They then compared the test scores to the teachers' evaluations of student progress, both academically and socially. At all stages studied, teachers' assessments strongly favored the girls. Girls reap large academic benefits from good behavior and accommodation to the school environment. So do some boys, by the way. The researchers found that boys who possess social skills more commonly found in girls—those who are well-organized, well-behaved, and can sit still—are graded as well or better than girls. But such boys are rare. According to the authors "the seeds of a gender gap in educational attainment may be sown at an early age."

Figure 9: Male-Female Gender Gaps on Kindergarten Test Scores and Grades

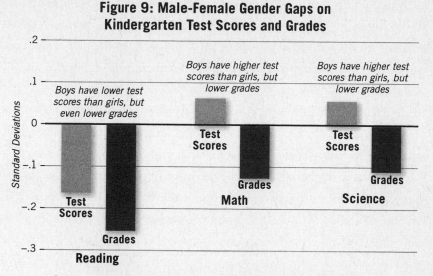

Source: "Non-cognitive Skills and the Gender Disparities in Test Scores and Teacher Assessments: Evidence from Primary School," Tables 4A, B and C (for Whites). All gender gaps are significant at the 5% level or higher.

Graph by Mark Perry (University of Michigan and American Enterprise Institute). Data from Department of Education, ECLS-K (Early Childhood Longitudinal Study—Kindergarten, 1998–1999 cohort).

Some will say: too bad for the boys. If young boys are inattentive, obstreperous, and upsetting to their teachers, that's their problem. After all, the ability to regulate one's impulses, delay gratification, sit still, and pay close attention to the teacher are building blocks of success in school and later life. As one critic told me, the classroom is no more rigged against boys than workplaces are rigged against lazy and unfocused workers.

But unfocused workers are adults. We are talking here about children as young as five and six. If little boys are restive and unfocused, why not look for ways to help them improve? When we realized that girls, as a group, were languishing behind boys in math and science, we mounted a concerted national effort to give female students more support and encouragement, an effort that has met with significant success. Surely we should try to provide similar help to boys. Much is at stake.

Grades, more than ever before, are crucially important to a child's future.

According to the lead author, UGA's Christopher Cornwell, "The trajectory at which kids move through school is often influenced by a teacher's assessment of their performance, their grades."[85] Grades determine a student's entry into enrichment programs and AP classes, as well as whether or not a student receives honors. Most of all, they open and close doors to higher education. So, says Cornwell, "If grade disparities emerge this early on, it's not surprising that by the time these children are ready to go to college, girls will be better positioned."

Boys, on average, lack the social maturity of girls—and for that, many are paying a high price that continues after they have become more purposive young adults. What is the answer? More boy-friendly curricula? More male teachers? More single-sex classrooms? Special preschool classes to improve boys' social skills? Extra recess where boys are allowed to engage in their characteristic rough-and-tumble play? More boy-engaging schools like Aviation High? As we will see in chapters to come, these are all promising solutions—and all are strenuously opposed by the women's lobby.

Teachers know their male students are struggling, and most would welcome new ideas on how to help them. But they get little help or support from official circles. The 2012 *Gender Equity in Education* report is striking proof that boys are nowhere on the agenda.

The sad truth is that the educational deficits of boys may be one of the least-studied phenomena in American education. If Professor Cornwell and his colleagues are right, our educational system may be punishing boys for the circumstance of being boys. And it is a punishment that can last a lifetime.

2

No Country for Young Men

Boys make adults nervous. As a group, they are noisy, rowdy, and hard to manage. Many are messy, disorganized, and won't sit still. Boys tend to like action, risk, and competition. When researchers asked a sample of boys why they did not spend a lot of time talking about their problems, most of them said it was "weird" and a waste of time.[1]

When my son David was a high school senior in 2003, his graduating class went on a camping trip in the desert. A creative writing educator visited the camp and led the group through an exercise designed to develop their sensitivity and imaginations. Each student was given a pen, a notebook, a candle, and matches. They were told to walk a short distance into the desert, sit down alone, and "discover themselves." The girls followed instructions. The boys, baffled by the assignment, gathered together, threw the notebooks into a pile, lit them with the matches, and made a little bonfire.

The creative writing teacher was horrified at the thought that she was teaching a pack of insipient arsonists—or *Lord of the Flies* sociopaths. In fact, they were just boys. But, increasingly, in our schools and in our homes, everyday boyishness is seen as aberrational, toxic—a pathology in need of a cure.

Boys today bear the burden of several powerful cultural trends: a thera-

peutic approach to education that valorizes feelings and denigrates competition and risk, zero-tolerance policies that punish normal antics of young
males, and a gender equity movement that views masculinity as predatory.
Natural male exuberance is no longer tolerated.

The Risk-Free Schoolyard

Many games much loved by boys have vanished from school playgrounds. At
some elementary schools, tug-of-war is being replaced with "tug-of-peace."[2]
Tag is under a cloud—schools across the country have either banned it or
found ways to repress it. When asked by a reporter why the game of tag was
discouraged in the Los Angeles Unified School District 4, the superintendent, Richard Alonzo, explained, "Why would we want to encourage a game
that may lead to more injuries and confrontation among students?"[3] But
safety is just one concern. Protecting children's self-esteem is another.

In May 2002, the principal of Franklin Elementary School in Santa
Monica, California, sent a newsletter to parents informing them that children could no longer play tag during the lunch recess. As she explained,
"The running part of this activity is healthy and encouraged; however, in
this game there is a 'victim' or 'it,' which creates a self-esteem issue."[4] School
districts in Texas, Maryland, New York, and Virginia "have banned, limited,
or discouraged" dodgeball.[5] "Any time you throw an object at somebody,"
said an elementary school coach in Cambridge, Massachusetts, "it creates an
environment of retaliation and resentment."[6] Coaches who permit children
to play dodgeball "should be fired immediately," according to the physical
education chairman at Central High School in Naperville, Illinois.[7]

The movement against competitive games gained momentum after the
publication of an article by Neil Williams, chair of the department of health
and physical education at Eastern Connecticut State University, in a journal
sponsored by the National Association for Sport and Physical Education,
which represents fifteen thousand gym teachers and physical education professors. In the article, Williams consigned games such as Red Rover, relay
races, and musical chairs to "the Hall of Shame."[8] Why? Because the games

are based on removing the weakest links. Presumably, this undercuts children's emotional development and erodes their self-esteem. The new therapeutic sensibility rejects almost all forms of competition in favor of a gentle and nurturing climate of cooperation. It is also a surefire way to bore and alienate boys.

From the earliest age, boys show a distinct preference for active outdoor play, with a strong predilection for games with body contact, conflict, and clearly defined winners and losers.[9] Girls, too, enjoy raucous outdoor play, but they engage in it less.[10] Deborah Tannen, professor of linguistics at Georgetown University and author of *You Just Don't Understand: Women and Men in Conversation*, sums up the research on male/female play differences:

> Boys tend to play outside, in large groups that are hierarchically structured. . . . Girls, on the other hand, play in small groups or in pairs: the center of a girl's social life is a best friend. Within the group intimacy is the key.[11]

Anthony Pellegrini, a professor of early childhood education at the University of Minnesota, defines rough-and-tumble play (R&T) as a behavior that includes "laughing, running, smiling, jumping, open-hand beating, wrestling, play fighting, chasing and fleeing."[12] This kind of play is often mistakenly regarded as aggression, but according to Pellegrini, R&T is the very opposite. In cases of schoolyard aggression, the participants are unhappy, they part as enemies, and there are often tears and injuries. Rough-and-tumble play brings boys together, makes them happy, and is a critical part of their socialization.

"Children who engaged in R&T, typically boys, also tended to be liked and to be good social problem solvers,"[13] says Pellegrini. Aggressive children, on the other hand, tend not to be liked by their peers and are not good at solving problems. He urges parents and teachers to be aware of the differences between R&T and aggression. The former is educationally and developmentally important and should be permitted and encouraged; the latter is destructive and should not be allowed. Increasingly, however, those in charge of little boys, including parents, teachers, and school officials, are blurring the distinction and interpreting R&T as aggression. This confusion threatens boys' welfare and normal development.[14]

Today, many educators regard the normal play of little boys with disapproval, and some ban it outright. Preschool boys, much to the consternation of teachers, are drawn to a style of rough-and-tumble play that involves action narratives. Typically, there are superheroes, "bad guys," rescues, and shoot-ups. As the boys play, the plots become more elaborate and the boys more transfixed. When researchers ask boys why they do it, "Because it's fun" is the standard reply.[15] According to at least one study, such play rarely escalates into real aggression—only about 1 percent of the time.[16] But when two researchers, Mary Ellin Logue and Hattie Harvey, studied the classroom practices of 98 teachers of four-year-olds, they found that this style of play was the least tolerated. Nearly half (48 percent) of teachers stopped or redirected boys' dramatic play *daily* or *several times* a week, whereas less than a third (29 percent) reported stopping or redirecting girls' dramatic play weekly.[17] Here are some sample quotes from teachers reported by the two authors:

- "My idea of dramatic play is experience created by an adult with a specific purpose in mind. In our learning environment, we perceive dramatic play as a homemaker in the kitchen [or a] postal worker sorting mail. Rough-and-tumble play is not an acceptable social interaction at our school."
- "We ban superhero toys at school."
- "Rough play is too dangerous. . . . playing house, going fishing, doctors, office work and grocery store keeps dramatic play positive."
- "Rough-and-tumble play typically leads to someone getting hurt, so I redirect. When a child talks about jail, using karate, etc. I'll ask questions and redirect."[18]

Such attitudes may help explain why boys are 4.5 times more likely to be expelled from preschool than girls.[19] Fortunately, there were champions of R&T among the teachers in the study. As one said,

Rough-and-tumble play is inevitable, particularly with boys. It seems
to satisfy innate physical and cultural drives. As long as all participants
are enjoying the play and are safe, I don't intervene. Play is the basis of
learning in all domains.[20]

Play is, indeed, the basis of learning. And the boy's superhero play is no
exception. Researchers have found that by allowing "bad guy" play, the children's conversation and imaginative writing skills improved.[21] Such play also
builds their moral imagination. It is through such play, say the authors, "that
children learn about justice . . . and their personal limits and the impact of
their behavior on others." Logue and Harvey ask an important question, "If
boys, due to their choices of dramatic play themes, are discouraged from
dramatic play, how will this affect their early language and literacy development and their engagement in school?"[22]

Carol Kennedy, a longtime teacher and now principal of a school in
Missouri, told the Washington Post, "We do take away a lot of the opportunity to do things boys like to do. That is to be rowdy, run and jump and roll
around. We don't allow that."[23] One Boston teacher, Barbara Wilder-Smith,
spent a year observing elementary school classrooms. She reports that an increasing number of mothers and teachers "believe that the key to producing
a nonviolent adult is to remove all conflict—toy weapons, wrestling, shoving
and imaginary explosions and crashes—from a boy's life."[24] She sees a chasm
between the "culture of women and the culture of boys."[25] That chasm is
growing, and it is harmful to boys.

The Decline of Recess

Recess itself is now under siege and may soon be a thing of the past. According to a summary of research by Science Daily, "Since the 1970s, children
have lost about 12 hours per week in free time, including a 25 percent decrease in play and a 50 percent decrease in unstructured outdoor activities,
according to another study."[26] In 1998, Atlanta eliminated recess in all its
public elementary schools. In Philadelphia, school officials have replaced

traditional recess with "socialized recesses," in which the children are assigned structured activities and carefully monitored.[27] "Recess," reported the
New York Times, "has become so anachronistic in Atlanta that the Cleveland
Avenue Grammar School, a handsome brick building, was built two years
ago without a playground."[28]

The move to eliminate recess has aroused some opposition, but almost
no one has noticed its impact on boys. It is surely not a deliberate effort to
thwart the desires of schoolboys. Just the same, it betrays a shocking indif-
ference to their natural proclivities, play preferences, and elemental needs.
Girls benefit from recess—but boys require it.[29] Ignoring differences between boys and girls can be just as damaging as creating differences where
none exist. Were schools to adopt policies harmful to girls, there would be a
storm of justified protests from well-organized women advocates. Boys have
no such protectors.

Boys playing tag, tug-of-war, dodgeball, or kickball together in the
schoolyard are not only having a great deal of fun, they are forging friendships with other males in ways that are critical to their healthy socialization.
Similarly, little girls who spend hours exchanging confidences with other
girls or playing theatrical games are happily and actively honing their social
skills. What these children are doing is developmentally sound. What justifi-
able reason can there be to interfere?

Of course, if it could be shown that sex segregation on the playground or
rambunctious competitive games were having harmful social consequences,
efforts to curb them would be justified. But that has never been shown. Nor
is there reason to believe it will ever be shown. In the absence of any evidence
that rough-and-tumble play is socially harmful, initiatives to suppress it are
unwarranted and a presumptuous attack on boys' natures.

Such bans are also compromising their health. Obesity has become a
serious problem for both boys and girls, but rather more so for boys. According to a study prepared for the US Department of Health and Human Services, "The obesity prevalence for male children quadrupled from 5.5% in
1976–1980 to 21.6% in 2007–2008. For female children, the obesity prevalence tripled from 5.8% in 1976–1980 to 17.7% in 2007–2008."[30] Diet is

a big part of the problem, but lack of exercise is as well. Strenuous rough-and-tumble play is part of the solution. And it is something most boys will happily do on their own—if their elders were not so busy discouraging it.

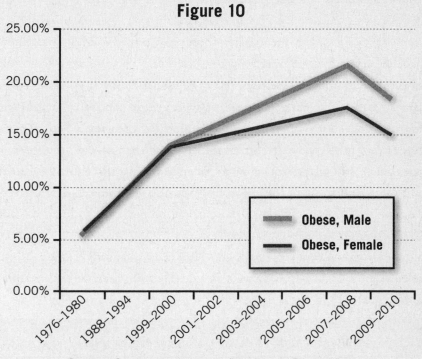

Figure 10

Source: Centers for Disease Control and Prevention.

Zero Tolerance for Boys

On February 2, 2010, nine-year-old Patrick Timoney was marched to the principal's office and threatened with suspension when he was caught in the cafeteria with a weapon. More precisely, he was found playing with a tiny LEGO soldier armed with a two-inch rifle. It was his favorite toy and he had brought it to school to show his friends. As he sat in the office, frightened and in tears, the principal, Evelyn Matroianni, called security administrators in the New York Department of Education for guidance. She confiscated the toy and summoned his parents to school for a conference. Patrick avoided suspension by signing an official statement and promising never again to bring a weapon to school. A spokesman for the Department of Education explained to reporters that the principal was just following the "no tolerance policy" that proscribes weapons at school.[31]

Zero-tolerance policies became popular in the 1990s as youth crime seemed to be surging and schools were coping with a rash of shootings. These policies mandate severe punishments—often suspension or expulsion—for any student who brings weapons or drugs to school, or who threatens others. Sanctions apply to all violations—regardless of the student's motives, the seriousness of the offense, or extenuating circumstances. School officials embraced zero tolerance because it seemed like the best way to make schools safe, plus it had the advantage of consistency. Inform students of the rules and subject everyone to the same punishments regardless of particular circumstances. Yes, the occasional student will be punished too harshly, but why not err on the side of caution?

But in many schools the policy has been taken to absurd extremes. More often than not, it is boys who are suffering. Here are a few recent examples of zero tolerance at work.

- 2011: Ten-year-old Nicholas Taylor, a fifth grader at the David Youree Elementary School in Smyrna, Tennessee, was sentenced to sit alone at lunch for six days. His crime? Waving around a slice of pizza that had been chewed to resemble a gun.

- 2010: David Morales, an eight-year-old in Providence, Rhode Island, ran afoul of zero tolerance when, for a special class project, he brought in a camouflage hat with little plastic army men glued on the flap.

- 2009: Zachary Christie, six, of Newark, Delaware, excited to be a new Cub Scout, packed his camping utensil in his lunch box. The gadget, which can be used as a knife, fork, or spoon, prompted school officials to charge him with possession of a weapon. Zachary faced forty-five days in the district's reform school but was later granted a reprieve by the school board and suspended for five days.[32]

It is tempting to dismiss these cases as aberrational. They are not. Punishing minor cases is not an unfortunate lapse: it is the heart of the policy. In defense of the schools, Jennifer Jankowski, a special education director at the school where Cub Scout Zachary Christie was suspended, explained to a reporter that "if Zachary or another student had been hurt by the knife, the district would have taken the blame. . . . There's more to the school's side than just us being mean and not taking this child's interests into account."[33] She is right of course, but it is still hard to see why common sense cannot be factored into the mix. School officials should be permitted to consider the student's motives, past behavior, and seriousness of the offense. But, of course, such discretion violates the take-no-prisoners logic behind zero tolerance.

Under the zero-tolerance regime, suspension rates have increased dramatically. In 1974, 1.7 million children in grades K–12 were suspended from the nation's schools. By 2007, when the K–12 population had increased by 5 percent, the number of suspensions had nearly doubled to 3.3 million— nearly 70 percent of them boys.[34] In 2007, according to the National Center for Education Statistics, 32 percent of boys in grades 9 through 12 had been suspended compared with 17 percent of girls.[35]

School suspensions, more than other punishments like detention, alternative classrooms, or community service, appear to accelerate a student's disengagement from school. Not only do students fall further behind in their studies, many of them enjoy what is often an unsupervised vacation from school. Also, if students perceive a punishment to be excessive, capricious, and unjust, this weakens the bond between them and the adults who are supposed to be their mentors. According to psychologists James Comer and Alvin Poussaint, suspensions can make it "more difficult for you to work with the child in school—he or she no longer trusts you."[36]

There is not a lot of research documenting a *direct* correlation between suspension and school failure, but one recent study by two economists, Marianne Bertrand (University of Chicago) and Jessica Pan (National University of Singapore) should give anyone pause. After controlling for reading and math scores, race, gender, and birth year, Bertrand and Pan quantified the damage: "We observe a negative relationship between school suspension and future educational outcomes."[37] For example, a single suspension lowers a student's chances of graduating from high school by 17 percent and the likelihood of attending college by 16 percent.[38] With so many boys at risk of academic failure, it would seem that suspensions should be reserved for the most egregious cases.

Zero tolerance was originally conceived as a means of ridding schools of violent predators and drug users. Who could object to that? But careful reviews of the policy show that most students are suspended for minor acts of insubordination and defiance.[39] No one is suggesting that such misconduct go unpunished. But there are many other ways to correct bad behavior besides suspension—ways shown to be much more effective.[40] Preventive programs appear to work best. In 2009, 2,740 at-risk Chicago boys in grades seven through ten took part in a life skills/ethics program called Becoming a Man: Sports Edition. Most of them had low grade point averages, had missed many weeks of school, and more than one third had been arrested. A carefully designed two-year University of Chicago study found that by the end of the program, their grades and school engagement had improved, prospects for graduation brightened (by as much as 10 percent to 23 percent). Compared to a control group, arrests diminished by 44 percent.[41]

In 2008, a task force for the American Psychological Association (APA) published a thorough review of literature on the efficacy of zero-tolerance policies. "Despite a 20-year history of implementation," the report concluded, "there are surprisingly few data that could directly test the assumptions of a zero-tolerance approach to school discipline, and the data that are available tend to contradict those assumptions."[42] Put another way, they found no evidence that it worked. But the evidence that it harmed boys was unequivocal. Not only are young boys being shamed and treated as deviants for bringing the wrong toys to school, but suspension may be correlated with school disengagement, poor achievement, and dropping out.[43]

The APA authors also noted that fears of school violence have been greatly exaggerated. While all violence is unacceptable, "the evidence does not support an assumption that violence in our schools is out of control or increasing."[44] But might it be that zero-tolerance policies had themselves suppressed school violence? The APA found no evidence for that. After controlling for socioeconomic factors, the task force found that schools with zero-tolerance policies had more behavior problems than those using other methods. School climate was worse, not better, under zero tolerance. Furthermore, far from making punishment more predictable and fair, the policy was applied unevenly—with African American boys most severely affected. The authors also found a negative correlation between the use of suspensions and academic achievement.[45] These uniformly negative findings raised a question: what had prompted schools to adopt such a draconian policy in the first place?

The Superpredators

To understand the evolution of zero tolerance, and the increasingly harsh treatment of even minor behavioral infractions among young boys, we need to recall the widespread fear of youth violence that prevailed in the mid-1990s. On January 15, 1996, *Time* magazine ran a cover story about a "teenage time bomb." Said *Time*, "They are just four, five, and six years old right now, but already they are making criminologists nervous."[46] The "they" were little boys who would soon grow into cold-blooded killers capable of "remorseless brutality." The story was based on alarming findings by several eminent criminologists, including James Q. Wilson (then at UCLA). Wilson had extrapolated from a famous 1972 study of the juvenile delinquency rate among young people born in Philadelphia in 1945 and estimated that within five years—by 2010—the nation would be plagued by "30,000 more muggers, killers and thieves."[47] John J. DiIulio Jr., then a professor in Princeton's Department of Politics, invoked Wilson's findings and coined a chilling cognomen for the rising violent horde: *superpredators*.[48] DiIulio believed that deteriorating social conditions were making matters much worse: Refining Wilson's definitions and extrapolations, he forecasted that "by the year 2010, there will be approximately 270,000 more juvenile superpredators on the streets than there were in 1990."[49] In a 1996 book, DiIulio and two coauthors, William J. Bennett and John P. Walters, proclaimed: "America is now home to thickening ranks of juvenile 'superpredators'—radically impulsive, brutally remorseless youngsters, including ever more preteenage boys . . . the youngest, biggest, and baddest generation any society has ever known."[50]

The fear of rising youth violence translated easily into fear of rising school violence, with support from additional research. Dewey Cornell, a forensic psychologist and professor of education at the University of Virginia, reports in his 2006 book, *School Violence: Fears Versus Facts*, "The perception that schools were dangerous seemed to be confirmed by a widely publicized report on school problems."[51] According to the report, when teachers in 1940 had been asked about "top problems in school," they had listed chewing gum, running in halls, and not putting paper in the wastebasket. Asked the same question in the 1990s, teachers listed rape, robbery, and assault. The story of the contrasting lists and the contemporary school jungle culture entered the media echo chamber and was repeated thousands of times.

Then, in the late 1990s, the fears were horribly realized. In 1997, teenage boys murdered schoolmates in Bethel, Alaska; West Paducah, Kentucky; Pearl, Mississippi; and Stamps, Arkansas. The bloody crescendo came in 1999, in the Columbine High School massacre in Littleton, Colorado. Seniors Eric Harris and Dylan Klebold murdered twelve classmates and a teacher before turning their guns on themselves. They had planned the assault for more than a year, hoping to kill at least five hundred schoolmates and teachers with bombs they had placed around the school (which failed to detonate).

Suspicion of the masculine gender quickly went generic, extending to all boys. "The carnage committed by two boys in Littleton, Colorado," said the *Congressional Quarterly Researcher*, "has forced the nation to reexamine the nature of boyhood in America."[52] Michael Kimmel, professor of sociology at Stony Brook University, explained that the Littleton shooters were "not deviants at all," but "over-conformists . . . to traditional notions of masculinity."[53]

The public was ready for tough defensive measures, and zero-tolerance policies fit the bill. But there was a problem with the picture of escalating school violence and the approaching superpredators: it was not true. At the very moment that DiIulio, Wilson, and other crime experts were predicting a superpredator surge, youth crime was beginning to plummet to historic lows. Criminologists are still at a loss to explain it. Between 1994 and 2009, the juvenile crime rate fell by 50 percent. A 2009 bulletin of the US Department of Justice noted that, "Contrary to the popular perception that juvenile crime is on the rise, the data reported in this bulletin tell a different story."[54] Here are a few highlights of the DOJ report:

- Compared with the prior twenty years, the juvenile murder arrest rate between 2000 and 2009 has been historically low and relatively stable.

- The 2009 rape arrest rate was at its lowest level in three decades.

- The 2009 juvenile arrest rate for aggravated assault was at its lowest since the mid-1980s.[55]

Could it be that youth violence diminished because fear of the superpredators led to harsher policies and more arrests? The best evidence we have says no. Rates of juvenile crimes in states with high arrests were not significantly different from those with low arrests.[56] What about school violence? The American Psychological Association task force study found no evidence that zero-tolerance policies had made schools more peaceable. More generally, rates of violent crime in school were low before zero tolerance and are even lower today[57] (see Figure 11).

Figure 11: Percentage of Students ages 12–18 Who Reported Serious Violent Victimization at School During the Previous Six Months

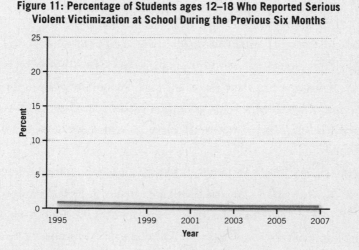

Source: Indicators of School Crime and Safety, US Department of Justice, Bureau of Justice Statistics, 2009.

The Bureau of Justice Statistics reports that in 2010, "One percent [of students] reported violent victimization, and less than half of a percent reported a serious violent victimization."[58] School shootings are ghastly, mortifying events and extremely rare. Dewey Cornell, in his study of school violence cited earlier, considered the number of school murders between 1994 and 2004 and did the math: "The average school can expect a student-perpetrated homicide about once every 13,870 years."[59] Rates of serious school violence were even lower between 2004 and 2010.[60]

Following the December 2012 slaughter of twenty first graders and six adults at Sandy Hook Elementary in Newtown, Connecticut, a Gallup poll found that 60 percent of women and 43 percent of men thought it "very likely" or "somewhat likely" that a similar shooting could happen in their own community.[61] The reactions were no doubt shaped by the particularly demented and horrifying nature of shooter Adam Lanza's deed, the national soul searching that ensued, and the fear of copy-cat incidents. It does no disrespect to the victims to note that homicidal school violence was a rare aberration in the 1990s when criminologists predicted the arrival of a horde of superpredators—and it is even rarer today.

Retreat and Reinforcements

The superpredator hypothesis was aggressively disputed by academics and child advocates almost as soon as it appeared in print. University of California, Berkeley, law professor and crime expert Franklin Zimring summed up the opposition in 1998: "His [DiIulio's] prediction wasn't just wrong, it was exactly the opposite. His theories of the superpredators were utter madness."[62]

To their credit, both Wilson and DiIulio quickly recanted. As early as 1999, Wilson conceded that he was wrong about a juvenile crime wave— "So far, it clearly hasn't happened. That is a good indication of what little all of us know about criminology."[63] DiIulio apologized for the mistakes and their "unintended consequences" and became a committed advocate of preventive measures rather than harsh punishment.[64]

And what about those widely reported surveys contrasting gum-chewing problems in 1940 with today's hyperviolent schools? It turned out to be an urban legend. When Yale professor Barry O'Neill tried to find a reliable source, he found that not a single one existed. It had been concocted by a Texas businessman, T. Cullen Davis, in the 1980s. What was his source? As he told O'Neill, "I read the newspaper." [65]

But the damage was done. The public would remain anxious about the specter of youth violence. Although Wilson and DiIulio renounced their theory about young male superpredators, a large group of activist gender scholars immediately took their place. Their theories were even more extravagant and far less empirically grounded. But the outraged criminologists, law professors, and child welfare activists who stood up to the superpredator myth left the new mythmakers alone.

Reimagining Boys

On July 28, 2005, the University of California, San Francisco (UCSF), hosted Take Our Daughters and Sons to Work Day. Parents were surprised to discover that the Center for Gender Equity, the UCSF group in charge of organizing the day, had planned distinctly different days for boys and girls. Girls were scheduled to participate in exciting hands-on activities: playing surgeon, wielding a microscope, and firing lasers. Boys would be spending most of the day learning about "violence prevention and how to be allies to the girls and women in their lives." When a reporter from the *San Francisco Chronicle* questioned the logic behind this plan, the director, Amy Levine, explained, "It's about dealing with effects of sexism on both boys and girls and how it can damage them." [66]

As Levine sees it, boys are potential predators in need of remedial socialization. Her view is the norm among gender activists. Consider how the Ms. Foundation explained its mission in a 2007 report, *Youth, Gender and Violence: Building a Movement for Gender Justice*: "At the center of this work must be a reimagining of what it means to be masculine, since violence appears to be built into the very core of what it is to be a man in US society." [67]

From its beginnings in the 1990s, the gender equity movement has been leery of boys and has looked for ways to reimagine their masculinity. By 1996, the Ms. Foundation, the creator of Take Our Daughters to Work Day, found itself on the defensive. Parents and employers were insisting that boys be included. To preserve the feminist purity of the girls-only holiday, Ms. went to work designing a special day for boys. The first Son's Day was planned for Sunday, October 20, 1996. October was especially desirable because, as the Ms. planners pointed out, "October is Domestic Violence Awareness Month, so there will be lots of activities scheduled."[68] Here are some of the ways Son's Day was to be celebrated:

- Take your son—or "son for a day"—to an event that focuses on . . . ending men's violence against women. Call the Family Violence Prevention Fund at 800 END-ABUSE for information.

- Plan a game or sport in which the contest specifically does not keep score or declare a winner. Invite the community to watch and celebrate boys playing on teams for the sheer joy of playing.

- Since Son's Day is on SUNDAY, make sure your son is involved in preparing the family for the work and school week ahead. This means: helping lay out clothes for siblings and making lunches.[69]

And for boys not exhausted by all the fun and excitement of the day's activities, the Ms. planners had a suggestion for the evening:

- Take your son grocery shopping, then help him plan and prepare the family's evening meal on Son's Day.[70]

Ms. made the mistake of sending their planning documents to a large number of child advocates. A few of them protested this little "holiday in Hell for Junior," and Son's Day was canceled. But Ms.'s attempt to inaugurate a boys' holiday is illuminating. It shows how female advocates think when they imagine what would be good for boys. And Ms. was hardly alone.

Sue Sattel, a "gender equity specialist" with the Minnesota Department of Education and coauthor of an antiharassment guide for children aged five to seven, said, "Serial killers say they started harassing at age ten. . . . They got away with it and went on from there."[71] Nan Stein, a senior research scientist at the Wellesley Centers for Women and a major figure in the movement to get antiharassment programs into the nation's elementary schools, has referred to little boys who chase girls in the playground and flip their skirts as "perpetrators" committing acts of "gendered terrorism."[72] Classroom curricula produced by the gender equity activists reflect their worldview.

Consider *Quit It!* This is a still-popular 1998 K–3 antiharassment and antiviolence teacher's guide and curriculum, produced by the Wellesley Center, the National Education Association, and other like-minded groups. (The guide was first published when the initial Harry Potter novels were gaining a passionate following among young people—its title seemed to be a critical pun on the novels' hyper-raucous, hyper-demanding, hyper-popular game of Quidditch.) The authors explain why boys as young as five need special training: "We view teasing and bullying as the precursors to adolescent sexual harassment, and believe that the roots of this behavior are to be found in early childhood socialization practices."[73]

Quit It! includes many activities designed to render little boys less volatile, less competitive, and less aggressive. It is not that "boys are bad," the authors assure us, "but rather that we must all do a much better job of addressing aggressive behavior of young boys to counteract the prevailing messages they receive from the media and society in general."[74]

The curriculum promises to develop children's cooperative skills through "wonderful noncompetitive activities."[75] The traditional game of tag, for example, includes elements that the authors consider socially undesirable. *Quit It!* shows teachers how to counteract the subtle influences of tag that encourage aggressiveness: "Before going outside to play, talk about how students feel when playing a game of tag. Do they like to be chased? Do they like to do the chasing? How does it feel to be tagged out? Get their ideas about other ways the game might be played." After students share their fears and apprehensions about tag, the teacher is advised to announce that there is a new, nonthreatening version of the game called Circle of Friends—where nobody is ever "out."

In reading *Quit It!*, you have to remind yourself that its suggestions are intended not for disturbed children but for normal five- to seven-year-olds in our nation's schools. These are mainstream materials. *Quit It!* was funded by the US Department of Education. According to the National Education Association's website, it is a "bestseller" among teachers. What motivates the girl partisans to sow their bitter seeds? The views of a prominent equity specialist shed some light on this question.

The Heart and Mind of a Gender Equity Activist

Katherine Hanson was the principal investigator for five National Science Foundation grants on gender equity. She was also director of the Women's Educational Equity Act (WEEA) Resource Center from 1988 to 2000. For twenty-five years, the WEEA Center served as a national clearinghouse for and publisher of "gender-fair materials." It was also the primary vehicle by which the US Department of Education promoted gender equity. As director, Hanson worked with schools and community organizations to "infuse equity" into all education policies, practices, and materials.[76]

In February 1998, an exultant Hanson announced that the WEEA Center had been awarded a new five-year contract with the Department of Education that offered "exciting new opportunities to become a more comprehensive national resource center for gender equity."[77] These included "developing a national report on the status of education for women and girls . . . an exciting opportunity for the education field, the Department, Congress and the nation to explore the successes, challenges, and complexity of gender equitable education."[78]

Who is Katherine Hanson, and what are her credentials for educating Congress and the nation on gender equity? Judging from her writings, she shares the view of Nan Stein, Sue Sattel, and the Ms. Foundation's would-be creators of "Son's Day": early intervention in the male "socialization process" is critical if we are to stem the tide of male violence.[79] Underscoring the need for radical changes in how we raise young males, Hanson offers some horrifying statistics on male violence in the United States. To wit:

- Every year nearly four million women are beaten to death by men.[80]

- Violence is the leading cause of death among women.[81]

- The leading cause of injury among women is being beaten by a man at home.[82]

- There was a 59 percent increase in rapes between 1990 and 1991.[83]

This "culture of violence," says Hanson, "stem[s] from cultural norms that socialize males to be aggressive, powerful, unemotional, and controlling."[84] She urges us to "honestly and lovingly" reexamine what it means to be a male or a female in our society. "And just as honestly and lovingly, we must help our young people develop new and more healthful models."[85] One old and unhealthful model of maleness that needs to be "reexamined" is found in Little League baseball. Writes Hanson, "One of the most overlooked arenas of violence training within schools may be the environment that surrounds athletics and sports. Beginning with Little League games where parents and friends sit on the sidelines and encourage aggressive, violent behavior."[86]

History is one long lesson in the dangers of combining moral fervor with misinformation. So the first question we should ask is: Does Hanson have her facts right? Her organization, under the auspices of the Department of Education, sent out more than 350 publications on gender equity and distributed materials to more than 200 education conferences for more almost thirty years. In my book *Who Stole Feminism?*, I write at length about the tide of feminist "Ms/information." Katherine Hanson's "facts" are the most distorted I have yet come across.

If Hanson were right, the United States would be the site of an atrocity unparalleled in the twentieth century. *Four million women beaten to death by men! Every year!* In fact, the total number of annual female deaths from all causes is approximately one million.[87] Only a minuscule fraction are caused by violence, and an even tinier fraction are caused by battery. According to the FBI, the total number of women who died by murder in 1996 was 3,631.[88] In contrast, Director Hanson calculates that 11,000 American women are beaten to death *every day.*

I spoke to Hanson in June 1999 to ask about her sources. Where did she get the statistic about four million American women being fatally beaten each year? Or the information that violence is the leading cause of death for women? She explained that "those were pulled from the research." What research? "They are from the Justice Department." I inquired about her academic background. She told me she had been "trained as a journalist" and had done many things in the past, including "studies in theology."[89]

For the record, the leading cause of death among women is heart disease (c. 370,000 deaths per year), followed by cancer (c. 250,000). Female deaths from homicide (c. 3,600) are far down the list, after suicide (c. 6,000).[90]

Male violence is also far down the list of causes of injury to women. Two studies of emergency room admissions, one by the US Bureau of Justice Statistics and one by the Centers for Disease Control and Prevention, suggest that fewer than 1 percent of women's injuries are caused by male partners.[91] Hanson's other factoids are no less fanciful: between 1990 and 1991, rapes increased by 4 percent, not 59 percent, and the number has gone down steadily since.[92]

Hanson is convinced that "our educational system is a primary carrier of the dominant culture's assumptions,"[93] and that that "dominant culture"—Western, patriarchal, sexist, and violent—is sick. Since the best cure is prevention, reeducating boys is a moral imperative. She gratefully quotes the words of male feminist Haki Madhubuti: "The liberation of the male psyche from preoccupation with domination, power hunger, control, and absolute rightness requires . . . a willingness for painful, uncomfortable and often shocking change."[94]

It would be comforting, but wrong, to assume that such male-averse rhetoric is a relic of the 1990s and no longer with us. The WEEA Center closed in 2003 and, according to Hanson's biography, she is "currently a writer and artist in New York."[95] But the Ms. Foundation is still going strong and has not softened its tone. If anything, it has become more extreme. Here, for example, is a typical pronouncement from its 2007 report *Youth, Gender & Violence*: "The roots of gendered violence lie in the efforts of the privileged and powerful—mainly white, middle-class men—to maintain their own status."[96] Misandry is very much alive and boys everywhere pay the price.

Imagine being a male student of Jessie Klein, assistant professor of sociology and criminal justice at Adelphi University. Professor Klein has been immersed in the gender equity culture for two decades. Before going to Adelphi, she worked in the New York City Schools as a conflict resolution coordinator, social worker, teacher, and administrator. In her 2012 book, *The Bully Society*, she says, "Boys learn from an early age that they assert manhood not only by being popular with girls but also by wielding power over them—physically, emotionally, and sexually."[97] And she has a ready explanation for the school shootings:

> The school shooters picked up guns to conform to the expected ethos dictating that boys dominate girls and take revenge against other boys who threatened their relationships with particular girls: their actions were incubated in a culture of violence that is largely accepted and allowed to fester every day. Transforming these hyper-masculine school cultures [is] essential to preventing . . . school shootings.[98]

Like Hanson, Klein has statistics to support her apocalyptic vision. She says, for example, that "in 1998, the FBI declared violent attacks by men to be the number one threat to the health of American women."[99] According to the Mayo Clinic, in reality the most serious threats are heart disease, cancer, stroke, chronic lower respiratory disease, and Alzheimer's disease.[100] Where did Professor Klein get her facts? Her source is an article in the *American Jurist* by a law professor from the University of Denver, Kyle Velte. But Velte gives no source. When my research assistant asked for the source, Velte explained that she no longer had it. There is no such FBI declaration. But what matters is that Professor Klein and Velte believe it and disseminate it.

If you think that "violent attacks by men pose the number one health threat to women," then it stands to reason that boys must be radically resocialized.

Klein also reports in her book, "Dating violence is another step on an escalating continuum of behaviors by which boys, schooled in traditional masculinity, demonstrate their power over girls." [101] But in the CDC's 2009 study on youth risk behavior in grades 9–12, it found that 9 percent of girls and *10 percent of boys* report being "hit, slapped, or physically hurt on purpose by a boyfriend or girlfriend." [102]

How much does it matter that equity experts in the federal government, WEEA, AAUW, Ms., Wellesley Center, Adelphi University, and the University of Denver believe a lot of nonsense about male brutality and think of little boys as insipient batterers and worse? None of these things would matter much if the activists promoting these views did not play a major role in American education. Title IX of the Education Amendments of 1972 prohibits sex discrimination in any educational institution that receives public funds. The WEEA Center's mission was to "provide financial assistance to enable educational agencies to meet the requirement of Title IX." [103] Eager to avoid charges of discrimination that trigger the punitive provisions of Title IX, many schools and school districts have "equity coordinators." These experts were trained on materials that reflect the mind-set of Hanson.

The Fallout

The fear of ruinous lawsuits is forcing schools to treat normal boys as sexist culprits. The climate of anxiety helps explain why, in 2004, Stephen Fogelman from Branson, Missouri, was suspended for sexual harassment for kissing a classmate on the cheek. He was eight at the time. The stunned parents explained that the boy had no idea what sexual harassment was and did not know he was doing anything wrong. [104]

Stories about little boys running afoul of sexual harassment codes are everywhere. In January 2011, Levina Subrata was astonished to receive a note informing her that her son was being suspended from his school in a San Francisco suburb for having "committed or attempted to commit a sexual assault or sexual battery." During a game of tag he allegedly touched another student on the groin. Her son was six years old at the time.[105]

In Gaston, North Carolina, a nine-year-old was suspended for remarking, to another student in a private conversation, that the teacher was "cute." In this case, charges were dropped once the case gained publicity. The distraught mother was gratified by all the supportive attention. "This is something that everyone needed to see," she told a local television station. "Just to see what's happening within our school systems."[106]

Sharon Lamb, a committed feminist and a professor of psychology, was shocked to hear that her ten-year-old son and his friend had been charged with sexual harassment. A girl had overheard them comment that her dangling belt looked like a penis. "It's against the law," the teacher informed the mother. This moved Lamb to ask, "If the message to boys is that their sex and sexuality is potentially harmful to girls, how will we ever raise them to be full partners in healthy relationships?"[107]

In early October 1998, Jerry, a seventeen-year-old at a progressive private school in Washington, DC, received the customary greeting card from the school director on his birthday. It was affectionately inscribed, "To Jerry—You are a wonderful person—a gift to all of us." Two weeks later, this same director would expel Jerry when he was accused of harassing a classmate, and school officials would urgently advise his parents to "get him professional attention."[108]

A female classmate accused Jerry of verbally harassing her. On one occasion, the girl claims, he said to her, "Why don't you give so-and-so a blow job?" She also alleged that he licked his lips in a suggestive way. He denied these allegations. Finally (and this may have been the last straw), someone overheard him ask another boy on the bus, referring to the other boy's girlfriend, "Did you get into her pants yet?"

When these allegations came to the attention of the school authorities, Jerry was ordered off school property. Following a hasty investigation, he was thrown out of the school. All of this transpired in little more than twenty-four hours. Jerry's parents agree that he deserved some kind of reprimand or punishment. But expulsion?

Why did the school react with such a severe punishment? Schools rightly fear lawsuits, and many feel they can no longer afford to tolerate the usual antics of teenage boys. "He's being punished for being an adolescent boy," said Jerry's mother. And she is right.

Pathological versus Healthy Masculinity

Sex differences in physical aggression are real.[109] Cross-cultural studies confirm the obvious: boys are universally more combative. In a classic 1973 study of the research on male-female differences, Eleanor Maccoby and Carol Jacklin conclude that, compared to girls, boys engage in more mock fighting and more aggressive fantasies. They insult and hit one another and retaliate more quickly when attacked: "The sex difference [in aggression] is found as early as social play begins—at 2 or 2½."[110] The equity specialists look at these insulting, hitting, chasing, competitive creatures and see proto-criminals. And that is where they go egregiously wrong.

There is an all-important difference between healthy and aberrational masculinity. Criminologists distinguish between "hypermasculinity" (or "protest masculinity") and the normal masculinity of healthy young males. Hypermasculine young men do indeed express their maleness through anti-social behavior—mostly against other males, but also through violent aggression toward and exploitation of women. Healthy young men express their manhood in competitive endeavors that are often physical. As they mature, they take on responsibility, strive for excellence, and achieve and "win." They assert their masculinity in ways that require physical and intellectual skills and self-discipline. In American society, the overwhelming majority of healthy, normal young men don't batter, rape, or terrorize women; they respect them and treat them as friends.

Unfortunately, many educators have become persuaded that there is truth in the relentlessly repeated proposition that masculinity per se is the cause of violence. Beginning with the premise that most violence is perpetrated by men, they move hastily, and fallaciously, to the proposition that maleness is the leading cause of violence. By this logic, every boy is a proto-predator.

Of course, when boys are violent or otherwise antisocially injurious to others, they must be disciplined, both for their own betterment and for the sake of society. But most boys' physicality and masculinity are not expressed in violent ways. A small percentage of boys are destined to become batterers and rapists: boys with severe conduct disorders are at high risk of becoming criminal predators. Such boys do need strong intervention, the earlier the better. But their numbers are small. There is no justification for a gender-bias industry that looks upon millions of normal male children as pathologically dangerous.

My message is not to "let boys be boys." Boys should not be left to their boyishness but should rather be guided and civilized. It has been said that every year civilization is invaded by millions of tiny barbarians; they're called children. All societies confront the problem of civilizing children—both boys and girls, but particularly boys. History teaches us that masculinity without morality is lethal. But masculinity constrained by morality is powerful and constructive, and a gift to women.

Boys need to be shown how to grow into respectful human beings. They must be shown, in ways that leave them in no doubt, that they cannot get away with bullying or harassing other students. Schools must enforce firm codes of discipline and clear, unequivocal rules against incivility and malicious behavior. Teachers and administrators have to establish school environments that do not tolerate egregious meanness, sexual or nonsexual.

These are demanding tasks, but they are not mysterious. We have a set of proven social practices for raising young men. The traditional approach is through character education: to develop a boy's sense of honor and to help him become considerate, conscientious, and gentlemanly. This approach respects boys' masculinity and does not require that they sit in sedate circles playing tug-of-peace or run around aimlessly playing tag where no one is ever out. And it does not include making seven-year-old boys feel ashamed for playing with toy soldiers. Boys do need discipline, but in today's educational environment they also need protection—from self-esteem promoters, roughhouse prohibitionists, zero-tolerance enforcers, and gender equity activists who are at war with their very natures.

3

Guys and Dolls

In the summer of 1997, I took part in a television debate with feminist lawyer Gloria Allred. Allred was representing a fourteen-year-old girl who was suing the Boy Scouts of America for excluding girls. Girls fifteen and older can join the Explorer Scouts, which is coed, but Allred was outraged that girls younger than fifteen are not allowed in. She referred to same-sex scouting as a form of "gender apartheid." [1]

I pointed out that younger boys and girls have markedly different preferences and behaviors, citing the following homespun example: Hasbro Toys, a major toy manufacturing company, tested a playhouse the company was considering marketing to both boys and girls. But it soon emerged that girls and boys did not interact with the structure in the same way. The girls dressed the dolls, kissed them, and played house. The boys catapulted the toy baby carriage from the roof. A Hasbro general manager came up with a novel explanation: "Boys and girls are different." [2]

Allred flatly denied there were innate differences. She seemed shocked by the boys' catapulting behavior. Apparently, she took it as a sign of a propensity for violence. She said, "If there are some boys who catapult baby carriages off the roofs of dollhouses, that is just an argument why we need to socialize boys at an earlier age, perhaps, to be playing with dollhouses."

Allred has powerful allies. Resocializing boys to play more like girls has been a part of the gender equity agenda for several decades. Notably active on this front throughout the 1990s and early 2000s were the Wellesley Center for Research on Women, US Department of Education, and Harvard School of Education.

A Wellesley College Equity Seminar

In 1998, the Wellesley College Center for Research on Women sponsored a daylong teacher-training seminar entitled Gender Equity for Girls and Boys: A Conference for K–12 Teachers and Administrators. It attracted two hundred teachers and administrators from the Northeast (teachers received state recertification credits for attending). One session, "Dolls, Gender and Make-Believe in the Early Childhood Classroom," was concerned with sex stereotypes and how to defeat them. It was led by Dr. Nancy Marshall, a senior research scientist and associate director of the Wellesley Center, and two of her associates.

According to Marshall, a child's sexual identity is learned by observing others. As she noted, "When babies are born they do not know about gender." Since newborn babies know very little about anything, Marshall's comment was puzzling. They don't know their blood type either, after all, but they still have one. Marshall explained that gender, indeterminate at birth, is formed and fixed later by a process of socialization that guides the child in adopting a male or female identity. According to Marshall and her colleagues, a child learns what it means to be a boy or a girl between the ages of two and seven. In those early years the child develops a "gender schema"—a set of ideas about appropriate roles, attitudes, and preferences for males and females. The best prospects for influencing the child's gender schema are in these early malleable years: these years are the opportunity zone.

Marshall and her associates presented a slide show, explaining, "A young mind is like Jell-O: you learn to fill it up with all the good stuff before it sets." What counts as "good stuff" for the Wellesley pedagogues is making children as comfortable as possible participating in activities traditionally "associated with the other gender." One favorite slide—to which they re-peatedly referred—showed a preschool boy dressed up in high heels and a dress. "It's perfectly natural for a little boy to try on a skirt," they said.

The group leaders suggested that teachers "use water and bathing" to encourage boys to play with dolls. Acknowledging that preschoolers tend to prefer same-sex play, which reinforces "gender stereotypes," they advised teachers in the audience to "force boy/girl mixed pairs." In a follow-up discussion, one of the participating teachers boasted of her success in persuading her kindergarten-aged boys to dress up in skirts. Another proudly reported that she makes a point of informing boys that their action figures are really dolls.

At no time during this eight-hour conference did any of the two hundred participating teachers and administrators challenge the assumption that gender identity is a learned ("socially constructed") characteristic. Nor did anyone mention the immense body of scientific literature from biologists and developmental psychologists showing that many male/female differences are natural, healthy, and, by implication, best left alone.[3] On the contrary, everyone simply assumed that preschool children were mal-leable enough to adopt either gender identity to suit the ends of equity and social justice. The possibility that they were tampering with the chil-dren's individuality or intruding on their privacy was never broached.

Early Interventions

Throughout the 1990s, equity activists in the Department of Education pro-moted a national effort to liberate children from the constraints of gender. The Women's Educational Equity Act Resource Center (a national center for "gender-fair materials" maintained by the Department of Education) distributed pamphlets that confidently asserted the social origins of femin-ity and masculinity. Here, for example, is a passage from the center's guide, entitled *Gender Equity for Educators, Parents, and Community*:

We know that biological, psychological, and intellectual differences between males and females are minimal during early childhood. Nevertheless, in our society we tend to socialize children in ways that serve to emphasize gender-based differences.[4]

In fact, we know no such thing. Play preferences of chimps, rhesus monkeys, and other primates parallel those of children.[5] A special issue of *Scientific American* in the spring of 1999 reviewed the evidence that these play preferences are, in large part, hormonally driven. Doreen Kimura, a psychologist at Vancouver's Simon Fraser University, wrote, "We know, for instance, from observations of both humans and nonhumans, that males are more aggressive than females, that young males engage in more rough-and-tumble play, and that females are more nurturing. . . . How do these and other sex differences come about?"[6] Kimura points to animal studies that show how hormonal manipulation can reverse sex-typed behavior. (When researchers exposed female rhesus monkeys to male hormones prenatally, these females later displayed malelike levels of rough-and-tumble play.) Similar results are found in human beings. Congenital adrenal hyperplasia (CAH) is a genetic defect that results when the female fetus is subjected to abnormally large quantities of male hormones—adrenal androgens. Girls with CAH consistently prefer trucks, cars, and construction sets over dolls and play tea sets. "It appears," says Kimura, "that perhaps the most important factor in the differential of males and females . . . is the level of exposure to various sex hormones early in life."[7] These sorts of findings undermine the simplistic view that gender-specific play is primarily shaped by socialization.

The Department of Education equity educators promoted materials in the schools that ignored the scientific research. They assumed, along with Gloria Allred and the Wellesley Center experts, that typical male and female play preferences were the result of imposed cultural stereotypes. *Creating Sex-Fair Family Day Care* is a model curriculum guide for day-care teachers developed by the department's Office of Educational Research and Improvement. It offers concrete suggestions on how to change children's gender schemas.[8]

The central thesis of the guide is that the only way to win the battle over gender stereotypes is to stage interventions as early as possible, preferably in infancy. Masculine stereotypes receive the lion's share of attention. Getting little boys to play with dolls is a principal goal. The 130-page guide includes ten photographs: two show a little boy with a baby girl doll; in one, he is feeding her, in the other, kissing her. The guide urges day-care teachers to reinforce the boys' nurturing side: "It is important for boys and girls to learn nurturing and sensitivity, as well as general parenting skills. Have as many boy dolls as girl dolls (preferably anatomically correct). Boys and girls should be encouraged to play with them."[9]

Ever vigilant for gender stereotypes, the guide warns child care workers to "be wary of charming Mommy Bears . . . wearing little aprons and holding a broom in one hand."[10] And it offers a new second verse for "Jack and Jill," now with Jill leading a safety-conscious, rough-and-tumble-free adventure:

> *Jill and Jack went up the track*
> *To fetch the pail again.*
> *They climbed with care,*
> *Got safely there*
> *And finished the job they began.*[11]

This government-sponsored day-care guide also urges teachers to carefully monitor children's fantasy play: "Watch your children at play. Are stereotypes present in the fantasies and situations they act out? Intervene to set the record straight. 'Why don't you be the doctor, Amy, and you the nurse, Billy?'"[12] The purpose of these interventions is described expansively: "Unless we practice nonsexist child-rearing, we cannot fulfill our dreams of equality for all people."[13]

William's Doll

Boys do not always cooperate with efforts to rescue them from their masculinity. Sometimes they openly rebel. In their 1994 book *Failing at Fairness*, education scholars Myra and David Sadker describe a fourth-grade class in

Maryland in which the teacher worked with the boys to help them "push the borders of the male stereotype."[14] She asked them to imagine themselves as authors of an advice column in their local newspaper. One day they received the following letter:

Dear Adviser:

My seven-year-old son wants me to buy him a doll. I don't know what to do. Should I go ahead and get it for him? Is it normal, or is my son sick? Please help!

The nine-year-old "advisers" were unsympathetic to the boy. The teacher then read aloud from a popular feminist book, *William's Doll*. It is a story about a boy who wants a doll "to hug it and cradle it in his arms."[15] His father refused and tried instead to interest him in a basketball or in an electric train. But William persisted in wanting the doll. When the grandmother arrived, she gently scolded the father for thwarting William's wish. She took William to the store and bought him "a baby doll with curly eyelashes, and a long white dress with a bonnet." William "loved it right away."

The story did little to change the fourth graders' minds. According to the Sadkers, "Their reaction was so hostile that the teacher had trouble keeping order."[16] A few reluctantly agreed that the boy could have a doll—but only if it were a G.I. Joe. The Sadkers were surprised that boys so young could be so inflexibly traditional. "As we observed her lesson, we were struck by how much effort it took to stretch outmoded attitudes."

William's Doll has been made into a play. Boston University professor Glenn Loury tells about sitting through a production at his son's elementary school in Brookline, Massachusetts, in 1998. Loury, the father of two boys—one starring in the play—was not impressed: "First of all, what is wrong with wanting your boy not to play with a doll but to play ball? There is nothing that needs to be fixed there."[17] Loury was speaking for many fathers and mothers. However, his voice and sensibility seemed to count for naught with the resocializers.

Shaping the gender identities of schoolchildren was a heady enterprise.

And it was inspired and informed by the scholars in some of our leading universities. Preeminent among them was Carol Gilligan. Gilligan and her colleagues at the Harvard School of Education saw themselves leading a profound revolution that would change the way society constructs young males and females. Once children were freed of oppressive gender roles, Gilligan predicted a change in their play preferences. She and her associate Elizabeth Debold firmly believed that so-called male behaviors—roughhousing and aggressive competition—are not natural but are artifacts of culture. Superheroes and macho toys, they said, "cause boys to be angry and aggressive." Debold reported on their studies of three- and four-year-old boys who "are comfortable playing house or dress-up with girls, and in assuming nurturing roles in play." Unfortunately, as they saw it, boys' interest in playing dress-up with the girls is rarely encouraged or sustained. "By kindergarten, peer socialization and media images kick in."[18]

The gender reformers at Wellesley, the Department of Education, and Harvard helped shape attitudes and policy in schools throughout the country. They were convinced that breaking down male stereotypes, starting in preschool, was good for society. Whether it was good for the boys never came up. In classrooms across the country little boys got the message that there was something wrong with them—something the teacher was trying to change.

It is doubtful that these efforts at resocialization were ever successful. But they surely succeeded in making lots of little boys confused and unhappy. Questions abound. What sort of credentials do the critics of masculinity bring to their project of reconstructing the nation's schoolboys? How well do they understand and like boys? Who has authorized their mission? To better understand the logic and motives of the resocializers, it is helpful to consider the arguments of a contemporary gender theorist.

The World According to Virginia Valian

Virginia Valian, a professor of psychology at Hunter College, is one of the most frequently cited authorities on gender schemas and how to change them.[19] She is also a leading light in the National Science Foundation's gender equity campaign ADVANCE.[20] With the help of a $3.9 million National Science Foundation grant, she and her colleagues established the Hunter College Gender Equity Project, where they have developed tutorials on gender role transformation.[21] Her 1998 book, *Why So Slow? The Advancement of Women* explains the urgency of that mission:

> In white, Western middle-class society, the gender schema for men includes being capable of independent, autonomous action . . . [and being] assertive, instrumental, and task-oriented. Men act. The gender schema for women is different; it includes being nurturant, expressive, communal, and concerned about others.[22]

Our society, says Valian, pressures women to indulge their nurturing propensities while it encourages men to develop "a strong commitment to earning and prestige, great dedication to the job, and an intense desire for achievement."[23] Such gender role socialization, she says, exacts a high toll on women and confers an unfair advantage on men.

To achieve a gender-fair society, Valian advocates a concerted attack on conventional schemas. Changing how parents interact with children is at the top of her list. For example, says Valian, there is a widespread assumption that women are better with babies than men. Where did that come from? The commonsense answer is that women's special affinity for babies is a powerful, universal, time-immemorial biological instinct. But Valian dismisses such explanations and cites a large body of research showing how parents and other adults aid and abet children's preferences and propensities.

Valian describes a study in which fathers are placed in rooms with their one-year-old sons or daughters. "On the shelf, within the babies' sight but out of reach were two dolls, two trucks, a toy vacuum cleaner and a shovel." What does the father do? Over and over again, fathers were observed giving their sons a truck twice as often as they gave them a doll.[24] (They gave daughters dolls and trucks at similar rates.) She mentions another study in which parents appear to reward children for choosing sex-appropriate toys. Valian concludes, "It appears that [parents] want their children . . . to conform to gender norms." And, according to Valian, those norms inhibit a child's potential to flourish later in life.

> As things stand, children learn to enjoy only half of what is potentially open to them, the half adults give them access to. Girls learn to take pleasure in being nurturant, boys learn to take pleasure in physical skills. Girls' increasing interest in sports shows how quickly some of them acquire a taste for physical activity. We have yet to provide boys with a parallel opportunity for nurturance.[25]

In the closing sentences of *Why So Slow?*, Valian says, "Egalitarian parents can bring up their children so that both boys and girls play with dolls and trucks. . . . From the standpoint of equality, nothing is more important."[26]

From the standpoint of reality, nothing seems more unlikely. Most little girls don't want to play with trucks, as almost any parent can attest. Including me: when my son gave his daughter Eliza a toy train, she placed it in a baby carriage and covered it with a blanket so it could get some sleep.

Valian has heard this sort of objection many times, and she has an answer. She does not deny that sex differences have some foundation in biology, but she insists that culture can intensify or diminish their power and effect. Even if Eliza is prompted by nature to interact with the train in a stereotypical female way, that is no reason for her father not to energetically correct her behavior. "We don't," says Valian, "accept biology as destiny. . . . We vaccinate, we inoculate, we medicate. . . . I propose we adopt the same attitude toward biological sex differences."[27]

Few would deny that parents and teachers should expose children to a wide range of toys and play activities. And Valian is right when she says that culture can intensify or diminish our natural inclinations. But gender identity is notoriously difficult to change. As one neuroscientist, Lise Eliot, observes, "[I]t is a potent, irreversible piece of self-knowledge that crystalizes children's perceptions and choice about much in their world, creating pink and blue barriers that parents find difficult to maneuver around."[28] In the hands of little boys, toy baby carriages will be catapulted from the roofs of dollhouses. In the hands of little girls, toy trains will be nurtured. Nothing short of radical and sustained behavior modification could change these elemental play preferences. Is it worth it? Is it even ethical?

We vaccinate, inoculate, and medicate children against *disease*. Being a typical little boy or girl is not a pathology in need of a cure. Failure to protect children from smallpox, diphtheria, or measles places them in harm's way. There is no such harm in allowing male/female differences to flourish in early childhood. The resocializers talk of "gender apartheid," of the schoolyard as a training ground for incipient batterers, of conventional masculinity as toxic. For Valian, the gender system is a source of massive social injustice. But these are all extravagant exaggerations. These would-be reformers completely ignore or discount all the good achieved by a tolerant policy that allows the sexes to freely pursue their different styles of play. More than that, this movement to change children's concept of themselves is invasive and authoritarian.

Gender-variant children (once called "tomboy girls" and "sissy boys" in the medical literature) are a lesson to us all. These children are powerfully drawn to the toys of the opposite sex. They will often persist in playing with the "wrong" toys despite relentless pressure from parents, peers, and doctors. There was a time when a boy who behaved like William in *William's Doll* would have been considered mentally ill and subject to behavior modification therapy. Today, we have developed more enlightened and compassionate attitudes. Most experts encourage tolerance, understanding, and acceptance.[29] But surely the same tolerance and understanding should extend to the gender identity and preferences of the vast majority of children.

What If Mother Nature Is Not a Feminist?

On March 21, 2005, the Radcliffe Institute for Advanced Study at Harvard University hosted a conference entitled Impediments to Change: Revisiting the Women in Science Question. The auditorium in Agassiz Theatre in Radcliffe Yard was packed. Dedicated in 1904, the theater has been the site

of many a spirited intellectual exchange. But this conference was a forum
not for debate but for indignation over (then) Harvard president Lawrence
Summers's speculation that innate differences between the sexes might be
one reason there are fewer women than men at the highest echelons of math
and science.

The six panelists—four from Harvard, two from MIT—did not challenge one another in the fashion of typical academic seminars, but rather
repeated and reinforced a common conviction that there is only one possible explanation for why fewer women than men teach math and physics at
Harvard and MIT: sexist bias. Why were no dissenters invited? Because from
the point of view of the assembled, that would be like inviting a flat-earther
or a Holocaust denier. One panelist, Harvard psychologist Elizabeth Spelke,
flatly declared that the case against significant inborn cognitive differences
"is as conclusive as any finding I know of in science."[30]

For any scholar, especially a Harvard University social scientist, to sweep
aside all the evidence for innate differences defies belief. In 2010, David
Geary, a University of Missouri psychologist, published *Male, Female: The
Evolution of Human Sex Differences.* This thorough, fair-minded, and comprehensive survey of the literature includes more than fifty pages of footnotes
citing studies by neuroscientists, endocrinologists, geneticists, anthropolo-
gists, and psychologists showing a strong biological basis for many gender
differences.[31] While these particular studies may not be the final word, they
cannot be dismissed or ignored.

Nor can human reality be tossed aside. In all known societies, wom-
en have better verbal skills, and men excel at spatial reasoning.[32] Women
tend to be the nurturers and men the warriors. Harvard psychologist Steven Pinker points to the absurdity of ascribing these universal differences
to socialization: "It would be an amazing coincidence that in every society
the coin flip that assigns each sex to one set of roles would land the same
way."[33] A recent study on sex differences by researchers from the University
of Turin and the University of Manchester confirms what most of us see
with our eyes: despite some exceptions, women tend to be more sensitive,
esthetic, sentimental, intuitive, and tender-minded; while men tend to be

more utilitarian, objective, unsentimental, and tough-minded.[34] It is true that we do not yet fully understand the precise biological underpinnings of these universal tendencies, but that is no reason to deny they exist. And there are many tantalizing theories.

Consider, for example, Cambridge University's Simon Baron-Cohen. He is one of the world's leading experts on autism, a disorder that affects far more males than females. Individuals with autism tend to be socially disconnected and unaware of the emotional states of others. But they often exhibit obsessive fixation on objects and machines. Baron-Cohen suggests that autism may be the far end of the male norm, or the "extreme male brain." He believes that men are, "on average," wired to be better "systematizers" and women to be better "empathizers."[35] It is a daring claim—but he has data to back it up, presenting a wide range of correlations between the level of fetal testosterone and behaviors in both girls and boys from infancy into grade school.

It is hard not to be attracted to theories like Simon Baron-Cohen's when one looks at the way children play and how men and women are distributed in the workplace. After two major waves of feminism, women still predominate—sometimes overwhelmingly—in empathy-centered fields such as early-childhood education,[36] social work,[37] nursing,[38] and psychology[39]; while men are overrepresented in the "systematizing" vocations such as car repair,[40] oil drilling,[41] and electrical engineering.[42] And there are no signs that boys are going to surrender their trucks, rockets, and weapons for glittery lavender ponies anytime soon.

Harvard psychologist Marc Hauser has what seems to be the appropriate attitude about the research on sex differences: respectful, intrigued but also cautious. When asked about Baron-Cohen's work, Hauser said, "I am sympathetic . . . and find it odd that anyone would consider the work controversial."[43] Hauser referred to research that shows, for example, that if asked to make a drawing, little girls almost always create scenes with at least one person, while males nearly always draw things—cars, rockets, or trucks. And he mentioned that among primates—including our closest relations, the chimpanzees—males are more technologically innovative, while females are more involved in details of family life. Still, Hauser warns that a lot of seemingly exciting and promising research on sex differences has not panned out and urges us to treat the biological theories with caution.[44]

Clearly, gender differences are driven by some yet-to-be understood interaction between culture and biology. And we must always bear in mind that no one is claiming that *all* men and women embody the tendencies of their sexes: some girls have superb spatial reasoning skills and little interest in nurturing, while some males reject rough-and-tumble play and prefer calm, imaginative games. When we speak of gender differences, we are referring to statistical differences between groups, not the rigid determination of individuals. If we say, for example, that women tend to enjoy romance novels more than men do, we are not saying that *all* women enjoy them. Hauser is right that we need to proceed with care.

But where is that care where the social constructionists are concerned? Though their research appears to be going nowhere, they are still marching ahead with their workshops, curriculum guides, and tutorials. Confident in their theories, they have taken on the task of resocializing the American child.

Ms. Logan's Classroom

There is much to be learned from classrooms where teachers are actively attacking the schemas of their pupils. Peggy Orenstein's *SchoolGirls: Young Women, Self-Esteem, and the Confidence Gap* was written in association with the American Association of University Women.[45] Just after the AAUW had alerted the country to the plight of its shortchanged adolescent girls, Orenstein visited several middle schools to see firsthand how they were coping with the "confidence gap." As a trusted insider, Orenstein was given full access to classrooms that were "raising the gender consciousness" of students. From her detailed report, we get a good understanding of how the new gender-fair activists view boys and what they have in mind for them.

The climatic section of *SchoolGirls* is entitled "Anita Hill Is a Boy: Tales from a Gender-Fair Classroom." Orenstein describes the classroom of Ms.

Judy Logan, an award-winning English and social studies teacher at the Everett Middle School, a public school in San Francisco. Logan has gone as far as anyone in transforming her classroom into a woman-centered community of learners. Indeed, Logan is something of a pedagogical legend among girl-partisan activists. Jackie DeFazio, former president of the AAUW, says that a teacher like Logan, "who puts equity at the center of her classroom," fills her with hope.[46] Mary Pipher, author of *Reviving Ophelia,* praises Logan for offering "a new vision of what our schools can give to our children."[47]

When Orenstein stepped into Logan's classroom for the first time she found it "somewhat of a shock." There are images of women everywhere:

> The faces of Abigail Adams, Rachel Carson, Faye Wattleton, and even a fanciful "Future Woman" smile out from three student-made quilts that are draped on the walls. . . . Reading racks overflow with biographies of Lucretia Mott, Ida B. Wells, Emma Goldman, Sally Ride, and Rigoberta Menchú. . . . There is a section on Pele, the Hawaiian goddess of volcanoes. . . . A giant computer-paper banner spans the width of another wall proclaiming, "Women are one-half of the world's people, they do two-thirds of the world's work, they earn one-tenth of the world's income; they own one hundredth of the world's property."[48]

At first, Orenstein found herself wondering "Where are the men?" But then in one of those characteristic "click" moments that feminists often report, the light dawned and all was clear: "In Ms. Logan's class, girls may be dazzled by the reflection of the women that surround them. And, perhaps for the first time, the boys are the ones looking through the window."[49]

Logan's classes are unusual and fun. She is popular with her students. But, according to Orenstein, many students complain that she is unfair to boys. One sixth grader, Holly, says, "Sometimes, I worry about the boys, that they kind of get ignored." Another says that her brother had taken one of Ms. Logan's classes, and "all she ever talked about was women, women, women. And he did not like it." Even the girls get tired of all the "women-centeredness." Orenstein reports one as complaining, "Ms. Logan, I feel like I am not learning anything about men, and I do not think that is right." Orenstein attributes the girls' objections to their low self-esteem; because of the "hidden curriculum," girls "have already become used to taking up less space, to feeling less worthy of attention than boys." By contrast, one older student, Mindy, who spent three years with Logan (Orenstein describes her as "a model of grunge chic"), has clearly learned the lessons that Logan strives to impart. Here is how this student explains the boys' resentment:

> I think it's the resentment of losing their place. In our other classes, the teachers just focus on men, but the boys don't complain that that's sexist. They say, "It's different in those classes because we focus on the important people in history, who just happen to be men."[50]

As Orenstein describes her, Mindy rolls her eyes to indicate the incredible cluelessness of the boys. Mindy's reference to those other classes shows she has, indeed, learned her lesson well. The new pedagogy justifies its intense focus on women by reminding us that allegedly gender-neutral classes on such subjects as the Age of Discovery or the Rise of Science are "all about men" like Columbus and Isaac Newton. Now it is time to put women in their rightful place at the center of attention.

In one history class, the girls take over the discussion and go after the boys for being sexual predators. As the girls get angrier, Logan gets more animated. The girls' anger is the sign that her pedagogy is working. "This is a very important, scary, and profound conversation you are having."[51] What do the boys have to say for themselves?

One boy tries to placate the girls: "It's true that some guys are ass-holes in school. But there are nice people too." During a subsequent male-bashing session, a girl points out that though sexual harassment happens to girls more often, the girls are doing it to boys as well. "We go up and feel on guys too."[52]

"That's a good point," says Logan. But not one she chooses to pursue. She soon stops the discussion, "We've gotten a lot done on this, but the class isn't about sexual harassment. It's American Women Making History." But later, she will return to the topic of sexual harassment and explain to her students how it is a part of a "hidden curriculum" that teaches girls to be second-class citizens. "They learn to become silent, careful, not active or assertive in life." [53]

Logan's pedagogy turns out to have its own hidden curriculum, which she teaches in every class, regardless of the subject. It is unflattering to males, and they learn the lesson. Luis, a seventh grader, later confessed to Orenstein, "I couldn't really defend myself, because it's true. Men are pigs, you know?" [54]

As a final "unifying project," Logan's sixth-grade social studies class made a quilt to celebrate "women we admire." Logan was alarmed by one student's muslin square. A boy named Jimmy had chosen to honor the tennis player Monica Seles, who, in 1993, was stabbed on the court by a deranged man. He had drawn a bloody dagger on a tennis racket. It's not the sort of thing a girl would think of. Jimmy's square may be unique in the history of quilting, but Ms. Logan did not appreciate its originality. In his own defense, he said, "I thought it was kind of important, a tennis player stabbed just so she wouldn't win." The teacher insisted he start again and make an acceptable contribution to the class quilt.

I can see why Logan did not want Jimmy's square on the class quilt. But perhaps Jimmy was looking for some way—within the confines of a feminist quilting environment—to assert his young maleness, which was under direct assault by his teacher. Logan, clearly exasperated, did not see it that way. She confided to Orenstein: "When boys feel like they're being forced to admire women, they try to pick one that they think behaves sort of like a man." [55] Jimmy is left looking "despondently" at his rejected square.

Jeremy, another boy in the class, showed more progress. His muslin quilting square celebrating Rosa Parks had been done to Logan's specifications. When he handed it in, Logan turned to Orenstein, saying, "This is how you teach about gender. You do it one stitch at a time." [56] Much taken by that remark, Orenstein used it to end her book.

Interdicted Research

A female colleague of Steven Pinker, the Harvard psychologist, once told him, "Look, I know that males and females are not identical. I see it in my kids. I see it in myself. I know about the research. I can't explain it, but when I read claims about sex difference, steam comes out of my ears."[57] Feminist Gloria Steinem has called research on sex differences "anti-American." She says, "It is what is keeping us down."[58] According to Gloria Allred, such research simply should not be done. "This is harmful and dangerous to our daughters' lives, to our mothers' lives, and I am very angry about it."[59] Feminist critics have a term for neurologists who study sex differences: "neurosexists."[60]

From a historical perspective, apprehension over research on sex differences is understandable. The idea of natural difference was once the thinking man's justification for keeping women in their place, socially, legally, and politically. Before the women's movement took root in the nineteenth century, patriarchal thinking was the norm. It was then taken for granted that women were not just innately different but naturally inferior to men. Even an enlightened moral philosopher such as Immanuel Kant comfortably held the view that women were by nature ethically substandard. Kant believed that women have little respect for concepts like right and obligation, which are at the very foundation of ethical living: "Women will avoid the wicked not because it is unright, but because it is ugly; and virtuous actions mean to them such as are morally beautiful. Nothing of duty, nothing of compulsion, nothing of obligation! Woman is intolerant of all commands and all morose constraint. They do something only because it pleases them. . . . I hardly believe that the fair sex is capable of principles."[61]

It was also widely believed that women are less intelligent than men. Stereotypes that demeaned women were commonly accepted, and women everywhere paid the price. Soon eminent scientists were weighing in to confirm women's inferiority. In the mid-nineteenth century, when anatomy and physiology were gaining scientific respectability, Paul Broca, a French professor of clinical surgery and pioneer in brain anatomy, concluded that "the relatively small size of the female brain depends in part upon her physical inferiority and in part upon her intellectual inferiority." [62] A contemporary of Broca, French psychologist Gustave Le Bon, went further: "In most intelligent races, as among the Parisians, there are a large number of women whose brains are closer in size to those of gorillas than to the most developed male brains. This inferiority is so obvious that one cannot contest it for a moment." [63]

Given the history of interpreting natural differences between men and women as proof of male superiority, it is understandable that women like Allred and Steinem and Lawrence Summers's tormentors react with suspicion to the suggestion that men and women are innately different in any way. But the proper corrective to bad science and rancorous philosophy is not more of the same but rather good science and clear thinking. For the moment, bad science and rancor are ubiquitous.

The ACLU Goes to War Against Single-Sex Schools

When students, especially boys, were falling behind academically at the Van Devender Middle School in Parkersburg, West Virginia, school officials decided to experiment with single-sex classes for sixth and seventh graders. Leonard Sax, a physician and prominent advocate of single-sex education, had visited the school and offered teachers suggestions for classroom activities. Many boys think of reading as "feminine," but following Sax's advice, teacher Mackenzie Lackey found a way around their resistance. For the past two years, she has divided her all-male sixth-grade classes into two teams and organized a Battle of the Books competition. Her students read a series of books and then competed to see which team could answer the most questions about the readings. The boys started reading like mad. The exercise was so successful that in both 2010 and 2011, in a schoolwide Battle of the Books, Lackey's sixth-grade boy teams beat the entire school, including coed teams from traditional seventh- and eigth-grade classes. To her delight, her pupils asked for more books to read over the summer. "Imagine," says Sax, "boys from a low-income neighborhood who demanded more books to read." [64]

But on May 21, 2012, the American Civil Liberties Union sent the school authorities a ten-page cease-and-desist letter demanding that they terminate their "gender-specific" programs post haste. "Our analysis demonstrates that this program is unlawful because it is premised upon and likely promotes harmful stereotypes about the different learning styles and development of boys and girls."[65] Failure to terminate the programs, warned the ACLU, could result in a lawsuit and/or a formal complaint with the pertinent federal agency. "We expect your response no later than June 4, 2012."[66] Similar letters were sent to school districts with single-sex programs in Florida, Mississippi, Maine, Virginia, and Alabama.

Wealthy families have always had the option of sending their children to all-male or all-female academies, but parents of lesser means have rarely had the choice. That changed in 2002, when the No Child Left Behind Act sanctioned innovative programs—including single-sex classes and academies—in public schools.[67] Then-senator Hillary Clinton, a coauthor of the provision, urged that the single-sex option be broadly expanded and not limited to a fortunate few: "There should not be any obstacle to providing single-sex choice within the public school system. . . . We have to look at the achievements of [single-sex] schools that are springing up around the country. We know this has energized students and parents. We could use more schools such as this."[68]

There are now nearly 400 public schools that offer single-sex classes and about 116 public all-girl and all-boy academies.[69] Single-sex programs are especially popular in low-income neighborhoods where parents are worried about their daughters and panicked about their sons. The Claremont Academy in Chicago, for example, offers a single-sex academic program for seventh- and eighth-grade, mostly poor, African American students. "It helps us to focus more," said one eighth grader. According to a profile of the school in *Phi Delta Kappan* magazine, students' test scores have improved dramatically since the program began in 2007.[70]

The Irma Lerma Rangel Young Women's Leadership School in Dallas opened in 2004 and enrolls 4,525 girls in grades six through twelve. Its success has been dazzling. The school has scored at or near the top of all Dallas public schools on state tests for the past five years.[71] Dallas has now opened a comparable academy for young men—the Barack Obama Male Leadership Academy. Madeline Hayes, a mother of a young man attending the school, said she'd always dreamed "that there would be a boys' school that doesn't charge $25,000 a year, but would give the same academics, the same level of interaction and leadership."[72]

Galen Sherwin, an attorney for the ACLU's Women's Rights Project, explained why she and her organization want such programs eliminated: "Over and over we find that these programs are based on stereotypes that limit opportunities by reinforcing outdated ideas about how boys and girls behave."[73]

It is hard to see how the classes limit anyone's opportunities. In West Virginia, boys are behind girls about one year in reading and two and a half years in writing. And West Virginia places close to last in national reading tests.[74] Put another way, boys in West Virginia are among the worst readers in the nation. The reading classes seem to be improving their abilities and opportunities. The seventh and eighth graders at the Claremont Academy are scoring higher on standardized tests. Children at the Irma Lerma Rangel School and Barack Obama Male Leadership Academy appear to be thriving. What is wrong with a voluntary program that seems to be helping? Plenty, says the ACLU—and they claim to have the research to prove it: a 2011 critique of single-sex education published in the prestigious journal *Science*.[75]

Eight Professors and a "Study"

Teachers visiting the website of the American Council for CoEducational Schooling (ACCES) are invited to take a quiz that measures their gender inclusiveness.[76] The quiz asks how often they do the following:

A. I say "Good morning, boys and girls";
B. I call students "boys" and "girls";
C. I refer to my students as "ladies" and "gentlemen."

Any teacher guilty of using such gendered language receives low marks on "gender mixing." The executive director of the ACCES, Rebecca Bigler, a psychology professor at the University of Texas, explained her organization's logic in *Education Week*. "If you compare it to race, if you said to your first-grade classrooms, 'Good morning, whites and Latinos; let's have the Latinos get your pencils,' what would happen is you would go to federal prison. . . . Labeling children routinely by race in your classroom is a violation of federal law, and, of course, you can do this routinely with gender."[77]

Bigler's mention of federal prison is hyperbolic, but it highlights her passion and moral certainty. Success stories from schools like the Claremont Academy do not impress her. As she told the *Phi Delta Kappan*, "African American males should be schooled right next to white girls because they would benefit from it. And those white girls need to know and understand the views of other people." She and her fellow ACCES officers, all professors, view "male" and "female" as arbitrary and invidious distinctions that should be left behind. They are now waging a major campaign against single-sex schools.[78]

Bigler and seven ACCES colleagues are the authors of the article cited by the ACLU, "The Pseudoscience of Single-Sex Schooling." Because it appeared in *Science*, it has proved to be a potent weapon against programs like those in West Virginia and Chicago.[79] What does the article say?

The *Science* article is a two-page summary of the state of the literature on single-sex education. That could be useful, were the authors not so blatantly biased. It is little more than a compendium of their opinions, supported by cherry-picked findings. They try to persuade the reader of two propositions: (1) There is no well-designed research that proves that single-sex education improves academic achievement, and (2) there is good evidence that sex segregation increases gender stereotyping and "legitimizes institutional sexism."[80]

On the first point, it is certainly true that the research connecting single-sex schools to improved performance is inconclusive. Historically, students have flourished in such schools; throughout the world, wealthy parents have sought them out for their children (think of England's Eton and Harrow).

But critics reply that the purported success of single-sex institutions is due to the social standing of the parents, the schools' resources, the quality of faculty—some feature other than it being single-sex. What was needed was a study that controlled for such factors. That came in 2012, when three University of Pennsylvania researchers looked at single-sex education in Seoul, Korea.[81] In Seoul, until 2009, students were randomly assigned to single-sex and coeducational schools; parents had little choice on which schools their children attended. After controlling for other variables such as teacher quality, student-teacher ratio, and the proportion of students receiving lunch support, the study found *significant* advantages in single-sex education. The students earned higher scores on their college entrance exams and were more likely to attend four-year colleges. The authors describe the positive effects as "substantial."

They note that their study is inconclusive. For example, the proportion of male teachers is much higher in Seoul's all-boys schools than in coeducational schools. The sex of the faculty could be importantly connected to student achievement. Further research is in order. But these findings are more than suggestive and may point the way to one solution to the boy gap—with positive outcomes for girls as well.

When the Department of Education carried out a research review on single-sex education in 2005, it found a tangle of contradictory results. Like much education research—large schools versus small, charter versus traditional public schools—advocates on either side can find vindication if they look hard enough. The Department of Education rightly deemed the research "equivocal" and called for more studies. But it drew no strong conclusions and advised that the question of single-sex schooling might never be resolved by quantitative investigation because it involves issues "of philosophy and worldview."[82] If that is so, then the matter would seem to be ideally suited to practical experience, individual circumstance, and voluntary choice.

But the *Science* article goes further, claiming that such schools actually harm students by promoting sexism. And this is where the eight professors discard any pretense to objectivity. As proof of harm, they cite a 2007 British study that showed an increase in divorce rates for men (but not women) who had attended single-sex schools, and another study finding that "boys who spend more time with other boys become increasingly aggressive."[83] The latter study, coauthored by two ACCES board members, consisted of observations of preschoolers and kindergarteners in coed classes; its relevance to single-sex classes for older children is never explained.[84]

That 2007 British study compared life outcomes for thousands of middle-age graduates of single-sex and coed schools. On most measures, the two groups looked about the same: Both had similar levels of marital satisfaction and similar views on gender roles. It did conclude that the males who attended single-sex schools were "somewhat" more likely to have divorced, but the report carried a lot of good news about single-sex education as well. To wit: "For girls . . . single-sex schooling was linked to higher wages." It was also linked to boys focusing their studies on languages and literature and girls on math and science. Did the British study address the central argument of the *Science* authors, that single-sex schooling promotes "sexism and gender stereotyping"? Yes, it did—finding that "gender stereotypes are exacerbated" in *coed schools* and "moderated" in single-sex schools![85] All of these glaring contradictions go unmentioned by the eight authors.[86]

In a subsequent issue of *Science*, several academic critics faulted the authors for failing to cite any serious research showing that single-sex schools foster sexism. The authors' reply conceded the point: "We agree with [critics] that systematic reviews have yet to address the potential harm of single-sex schools in increasing stereotyping and sexism."[87] But, to bolster their original claim, they cited a 2001 study of a single-sex experiment in California in which "increased gender stereotypes was a prominent finding."[88]

They better hope no one looks up the study. Its three feminist authors do not use a conventional methodology. As they explain, "Drawing upon feminist theory, we provide a critique that illuminates how power which is 'both the medium and the expression of wider structural relations and social forms, positions subjects within ideological matrixes of constraint and possibility.'"[89] True to this murky goal, they devote most of the study to critiquing parents, teachers, and students for their "gendered perceptions" and evaluating how effectively they challenge "oppressive power relations inherent in traditional education."[90] One unwitting instructor explained why the all-male class voted to read *All Quiet on the Western Front* and why the all-female class chose *Pride and Prejudice*: "The girls tend to choose the romantic spiel . . . and guys tend to go for the action." This sensible and innocent remark is grist for the authors' mill. "Significantly," they say, "teachers did little to change student choices by suggesting alternative book choices or topics that might potentially challenge gendered dispositions."[91] These authors warn how "gender ideologies" can shape an instructor's classroom practices. But they have their own ideology—and it shaped every word of their bizarre study.

What explains the determination of the *Science* authors? For them—as for Gloria Allred in the case of Boy Scouts and Girl Scouts—organizing children by girls and boys is analogous to racial segregation. As the lead author, Claremont McKenna's Diane Halpern, explains, "Advocates for single-sex education don't like the parallel with racial segregation, but the parallels are there."[92] No, they are not. Mandatory racial separatism demeans human beings and forecloses on their life prospects. Single-sex education is freely chosen, and millions of pupils have thrived intellectually and socially within it. Boys and girls, taken as groups, have different interests, propensities, and needs. And they, and their parents and teachers, know it: The teacher who begins the day with "Good morning, boys and girls," is being friendly and conventional, not invidious and oppressive.

But the ACLU is not circulating the letters from critics of the *Science* article, nor highlighting the outré worldview of the authors or their misuse of the research of others. The article is presented as settled science. So far, the ACLU campaign is working. As it boasts on its website:

> Many school districts in the nation have responded to our letters pointing out Title IX violations by shutting down their single-sex education programs in states such as Maine, Pennsylvania, and Alabama. To spread the message further, we've launched a nationwide campaign called Teach Kids, Not Stereotypes, to combat the harmful gender stereotypes at the root of the new wave of single-sex programs.[93]

Schools with successful single-sex programs are responding to the ACLU threats because they cannot afford costly court battles. School board members in West Virginia, for example, estimate that it could cost as much as $10,000 to defend the Van Devender program in court.[94] But on July 3, 2012, they voted to continue the single-sex classes. The ACLU immediately filed a suit, and a judge has issued a temporary injunction against the program. The Van Devender principal was dismayed that the ACLU refused to meet with teachers and parents. "If [the ACLU] would sit down with us . . . we could all be on the same page." He is certain they would see the merits of the program.[95]

Unfortunately, the ACLU's success in other school districts, its sense of momentum, and its determination to expand its campaign suggest otherwise. In September 2012, the ACLU successfully pressured the school officials in Cranston, Rhode Island, to ban the traditional father-daughter dance and mother-son baseball game. According to the ACLU, "Public schools have no business fostering the notion that girls prefer to go to formal dances while boys prefer baseball games. This type of gender stereotyping only perpetuates outdated notions of 'girl' and 'boy' activities and is contrary to federal law."[96]

Girls will be hurt where the ACLU and ACCES succeed in their campaign to shut down single-sex classrooms. But boys will lose the most. The activist professors and lawyers may believe that "male" and "female" are superficial distinctions best ignored. But here is one glaring gender distinction we ignore at our peril: boys are seriously behind girls in school. We do a far better job educating girls than boys, and we must find out why. All-male schools and classrooms may not be panaceas and are certainly not for everyone, but they have produced many promising results. They seem to be especially effective in poor districts, where boys are the most vulnerable. These boys' schools and programs are experimenting with male-friendly pedagogy, and they may offer the best hope for discovering classroom practices that work for boys everywhere. Turning a blind eye to real differences and dogmatically insisting that masculinity and femininity are irrelevant distinctions poses serious dangers of its own.

Respect for Difference

In 1984, Vivian Gussin Paley, a beloved kindergarten teacher at the University of Chicago Laboratory Schools, published a highly acclaimed book about a children's play entitled *Boys & Girls: Superheroes in the Doll Corner.* The book would not be well received in today's boy-averse environment. Her observations are worth dwelling on, if only to remind ourselves how teachers used to talk about children before the gender police appeared. Paley felt free to express her fondness for boys as they are, warts and all. She also accepted and enjoyed the clear differences between the sexes and had no illusions about the prospects of success for any efforts to do away with these differences: "Kindergarten is a triumph of sexual self-stereotyping. No amount of adult subterfuge or propaganda deflects the five-year-old's passion for segregation by sex."[97]

In one passage, she describes the distinctive behavior of some nursery school boys and girls in the "tumbling room," a room full of climbing structures, ladders, and mats: "The boys run and climb the entire time they are in the room, resting momentarily when they 'fall down dead.' The girls, after several minutes of arranging one another's shoes, concentrate on somersaults. . . . After a few somersaults, they stretch out on the mats and watch the boys."[98]

When the girls are left alone in the room without the boys, they run, climb, and become much more active—but then, after a few minutes, they suddenly lose interest and move on to other, quieter activities, saying, "Let's paint" or "Let's play in the doll corner." Boys, on the other hand, never lose interest in the tumbling room. They leave only when forced to. "No boy," says Paley, "exits on his own." The "raw energy" of boys delights this teacher: "They run because they prefer to run, and their tempo appears to increase in direct proportion to crowded conditions, noise levels, and time spent running, all of which have the opposite effect on the girls."[99]

At the time Paley wrote her book, Luke Skywalker and Darth Vader were all the rage with the boys in her kindergarten class and all across America. The more she studied and analyzed the boys' play, the more she grew to understand and accept it; she also learned to be less sentimental about what the girls were doing in the doll corner, and to accept that as well. Not all in the doll corner was preparation for nurturing and caring. She learned that girls were interested in their own kind of domination: "Mothers and princesses are as powerful as any superheroes the boys can devise." [100]

Boys' imaginative play involves a lot of conflict and violence; that of girls seems to be much gentler and more peaceful. But as Paley looked more carefully, she noticed that the girls' fantasies were just as exciting and intense as the boys'. The doll corner was in fact a center of conflict, pesky characters, and imaginary power struggles. [101]

Refreshingly, Paley does not have the urge to reform the kindergarten to some accepted specification of social justice or gender equality. In particular, she doesn't need to step in to guide boys to more caring ways of playing. "Let the boys be robbers, then, or tough guys in space. It is the natural, universal, and essential play of little boys. Everything is make-believe except the obvious feelings of well-being that emerge from fantasy play." [102]

Many teachers, perhaps most, share the tolerant and generous views of Paley. But they are proving to be no match for the army of change agents at the ACLU, ACCES, US Department of Education, Wellesley, Harvard, Hunter College, and numerous other schools and activist organizations across the country. Today, these determined reformers are rarely challenged; their influence is growing and can be expected to grow. Few teachers will risk opposing the cause of gender justice backed up by science and lawsuits. Few parents have much of an idea of what their children are facing. As for the children themselves, they are usually in no position to complain—and, when they are asked and do complain, their answers are taken as further proof of their need for resocialization.

4

Carol Gilligan and the Incredible Shrinking Girl

Confident at 11, Confused at 16" read the title of a 1990 *New York Times Magazine* story reporting an alarming discovery about the psychological development of girls.[1] Research by Professor Carol Gilligan, Harvard University's first professor of gender studies, had demonstrated that as girls move into adolescence they are "silenced" and their native confident spirit is forced "underground." The piece, by novelist Francine Prose, was laudatory and urgent; it mentioned in passing that Gilligan's research faced intense opposition from academics but provided few details.

Prose's nearly 4,000-word panegyric gave *Times* readers the heady feeling of being at the center of world-changing science. Gilligan and two colleagues had just published *Making Connections: The Relational Worlds of Adolescent Girls at Emma Willard School.*[2] Prose described the book as "a major phase" in Gilligan's Harvard research project on adolescent girls, extending the findings of her famous 1982 work, *In a Different Voice.* In the preface to *Making Connections,* Gilligan states her latest discovery dramatically: "As the river of a girl's life flows into the sea of Western culture, she is in danger of drowning or disappearing."[3] The stakes are enormous, she says: helping girls negotiate this adolescent maelstrom may be the "key to girls' development and to Western Civilization."[4]

Had Prose interviewed experts in adolescent development, she might have alerted her readers to anomalies in Gilligan's methods, and contrasted Gilligan's findings with those of a substantial academic literature that describes adolescent girls far more optimistically. But no such skeptics were consulted.

The *Times Magazine* article generated a panicky concern for girls that would profoundly affect education policy throughout the 1990s and 2000s. Just when—as we now know—an educational gender gap was opening up with girls well in the lead, boys became objects of neglect while the education establishment focused on rescuing the afflicted girls. A brief review of Gilligan's research methods, and of the findings of empirically minded developmental psychologists, will show why the *Times* should have engaged a science writer rather than a novelist to present Gilligan's discovery to the world.

Unfairness and Not Listening

For *Making Connections*, sixteen authors, including Gilligan, interviewed Emma Willard students about how they felt growing into adolescence. The school, located in Troy, New York, takes both boarding and day students and is one of the oldest private girls' academies in the country. These interviews at Emma Willard seemed to confirm their darkest suspicions about the precarious mental state of teenage girls.

Preteen girls, Gilligan writes, are confident, forthright, and clear-sighted. But, as they enter adolescence, they become frightened by their own insights into our male-dominated culture. It is a culture, says Gilligan, that tells them, "Keep quiet and notice the absence of women, and say nothing." Girls no longer see themselves as what the culture is about. This realization is "seditious" and places girls in psychological danger. So girls learn to hide what they know—not only from others, but even from themselves. In her *Times* article, Prose cited what became oft-quoted words of Gilligan's: "By 15 or 16 . . . [girls] start saying, 'I don't know, I don't know, I don't know.' They start not knowing what they had known."[5]

To protect themselves, girls begin to hide the vast well of knowledge they possess about human relations and injustice. Many bury it so deep inside themselves that they lose touch with it. Says Gilligan: "Interviewing girls in adolescence . . . I felt at times that I was entering an underground world that I was led in by girls to caverns of knowledge, which then suddenly were covered over, as if nothing was known and nothing was happening."[6] According to Gilligan, girls possess an uncanny understanding of the "human social world . . . compelling in its explanatory power and intricate in its psychological logic."[7] The sophisticated understanding of human relations that girls have but do not show, she says, rivals that of trained professional adults: "Much of what psychologists know about relationships is also known by adolescent girls."

What sort of experiments did Gilligan and her colleagues carry out at the Emma Willard School that led to the discovery of girls' acute insights into human relations? A chapter called "Unfairness and Not Listening: Converging Themes in Emma Willard Girls' Development" gives a fair idea of Gilligan's methods and style of research. Gilligan and her coinvestigator, Elizabeth Bernstein, asked thirty-four girls to describe an occasion of someone "not being fair" and an occasion when someone "didn't listen."[8] Here are some sample replies of the Emma Willard girls:

Barbara, twelfth grader

Unfairness: "We had three final assignments . . . knowing the students were feeling very burdened, it was unfair of her [the teacher] to contribute to that."

Not listening: "She did not seem terribly moved by how the class was feeling."

Susan, eleventh grader

Unfairness: "A friend of mine was kicked out because . . . she had a friend of hers who got 600s on the SATs go in and take them [for her] . . . I understand punishing her, but I don't think her life should be ruined. It makes me angry. I think they should have had her come back here. . . . I don't think they cared."

Not listening: "We were going to spend a weekend at a boys' school and [the dean] said I understand you are going to do some drinking. I was just so mad. . . . I said, 'I will follow the rules.' But she didn't listen. I didn't like her getting involved in my plans, because I didn't think that was fair."[9]

To the untrained observer, these teenage girls don't sound exceptionally insightful. Susan seems to be immature and ethically clueless. She seems not to understand the seriousness of the SAT deception; she is indignant that the dean of her boarding school, concerned about underage girls drinking, is so "involved" in her plans. But Gilligan and her colleague Bernstein seem never to notice the moral shortcomings of their subjects. Instead they tell us that girls such as Susan and Barbara are "unsettling" conventional modes of thinking about morality. They credit their callow subjects with exceptional moral insight: "The convergence of concerns with fairness and listening in older girls, for the most part, gives rise to a moral stance of depth and power."[10] Normally, say Gilligan and Bernstein, we disassociate the concepts of fairness and listening, but "remarkably, for these girls fairness and listening appear to be intimately related concepts."[11]

But how remarkable is it that the girls, asked by an interviewer to say something about (a) unfairness and (b) not listening, got the idea that they were expected to describe instances in which they had felt that they were unfairly treated and their views were ignored?

Gilligan's sentimental, valorizing descriptions of adolescent girls are frankly absurd. Her study of "unfairness and not listening"—despite its charts, graphs, and tables—is a caricature of research. Most of the girls' comments are entirely ordinary. Gilligan inflates their significance by reading profound meanings into them.

What About Boys?

Gilligan would have us believe that preteen girls are cognitively special. But what about boys? Do boys of eleven also make "outrageously wonderful statements"? Are they also spontaneous and incorruptibly frank? Or does Gilligan believe that, unlike girls, eleven-year-old boys *are* "for sale"? As boys move into adolescence, do they, too, suffer a loss of openness and frankness? Are they also diminished in their teen years? Could it be that girls' specialness consists of their sophistication when compared with relatively clueless boys?

To establish her thesis that our culture silences adolescent girls, Gilligan would need to identify some clear notions of candor and measures of outspokenness, then embark on a carefully designed study of thousands of American boys and girls. Anecdotal methods—especially anecdotal methods applied to one sex—cannot begin to make the case. Moreover, Gilligan does not offer even anecdotal evidence that preteen boys and girls differ in natural wisdom and forthrightness.

It might actually be, then, that preteen boys are just as astute and alive as preteen girls. That would have several possible implications for Gilligan's theory. Perhaps, like girls, adolescent boys are silenced and "forced underground." But if that is the case, sex is not a decisive factor; instead we are dealing with the familiar problem of adolescent insecurity that afflicts both girls and boys, and Gilligan's sensational claim that girls are at special risk would turn out to be false.

Alternatively, it may be that *only* girls "sell out" and become inarticulate and conformist; that adolescent boys remain independent, honest, and open interpreters of social reality. This, too, doesn't seem right; certainly Gilligan would reject any alternative that valorized boys as more candid and articulate than girls.

Unlike Gilligan, the rest of us enjoy the option of avoiding gender politics and returning to the conventional view that normal girls and boys do not differ significantly in respect to astuteness and candor. Both pass from childhood to adolescence by becoming less narcissistic, more reflective, and less sure about their grasp of the complex world that is opening up to them. Leaving junior high school, both boys and girls emerge from a "know-it-all" stage into a more mature stage in which they begin to appreciate that there is a vast amount they do not know. If so, it is not true that "girls start not knowing what they had known," but rather that most older children of both sexes quite sensibly go through a period of realizing that what they thought they knew may not be true at all—and that there is a lot out there to be learned.

When the *Times* article appeared, Gilligan had not yet studied boys. The article gave the impression that boys, beneficiaries of the male-voiced culture, were doing comparatively well. A few years later, Gilligan would announce that boys, too, were victims of the dominant culture, forced in early childhood to adopt masculine stereotypes that cause a host of ills, including their own loss of "voice." But in the early nineties, her focus was exclusively girls.

Prose did not deem Gilligan's neglect of boys a failing. On the contrary, she treated it as a virtue: "By concentrating on girls, the project's new studies avoid the muddle of gender comparisons and the issue of whether boys experience a similar 'moment of resistance.' Gilligan and her colleagues are simply telling us how girls sound at two proximate but radically dissimilar stages of growing up."[12] What Prose considered a muddle to be avoided is, however, clearly a crucial part of any research on adolescent development. For how, in the absence of comparative studies, can we possibly know whether what Gilligan described is specific to girls?

Gilligan might at least have warned Prose of the limitations of her findings. Quite apart from Gilligan's scholarly obligation to give us a comprehensive picture of adolescence as a backdrop for her assertions about girls, she should have taken care that the public was not misled. Instead, her inattention to boys invited the conclusion that girls were in distress because the system was biased in favor of boys. And indeed, many of her readers (including some who are in charge of important women's organizations) did take Gilligan's research as surefire proof that our society favors boys and shortchanges girls.

The Girl Crisis

Popular writers, electrified by Gilligan's discovery, began to see evidence of the crisis everywhere. Anna Quindlen, who was then a *New York Times* columnist, recounted in a 1990 column how Gilligan's research had cast an ominous shadow on the celebration of her daughter's second birthday: "My daughter is ready to leap into the world, as though life were chicken soup and she a delighted noodle. The work of Professor Carol Gilligan of Harvard suggests that some time after the age of 11 this will change, that even this lively little girl will pull back [and] shrink." [13]

The country's adolescent girls were both pitied and exalted. The novelist Carolyn See wrote in the *Washington Post Book World* in 1994, "The most heroic, fearless, graceful, tortured human beings in this land must be girls from the ages of 12 to 15." [14] In the same vein, American University professors Myra and David Sadker in *Failing at Fairness* predicted the fate of a lively six-year-old on top of a playground slide: "There she stood on her sturdy legs, with her head thrown back and her arms flung wide. As ruler of the playground, she was at the very zenith of her world." But all would soon change: "If the camera had photographed the girl . . . at twelve instead of six . . . she would have been looking at the ground instead of the sky; her sense of self-worth would have been an accelerating downward spiral." [15] In Mary Pipher's 1994 *Reviving Ophelia*, by far the most successful of the girl-crisis books, girls undergo a fiery demise. "Just as planes and ships disappear mysteriously into the Bermuda Triangle, so do the selves of girls go down in droves. They crash and burn." [16]

The description of America's teenage girls as silenced, tortured, and otherwise personally diminished was (and is) indeed dismaying. But no real evidence has ever been offered to support it. Scholars who abide by the conventional protocols of social science research describe adolescent girls in far more positive terms. Anne Petersen, a former professor of adolescent development and pediatrics at the University of Minnesota (now at the University of Michigan), reports the consensus of researchers working in adolescent psychology: "It is now known that the majority of adolescents of both genders successfully negotiate this developmental period without any major psychological or emotional disorder, develop a positive sense of personal identity, and manage to forge adaptive peer relationships with their families." [17] Daniel Offer, a (now retired) professor of psychiatry at Northwestern, concurs. He refers to a "new generation of studies" that find 80 percent of adolescents to be normal and well adjusted. [18]

Gilligan offered little in the way of conventional evidence to support her alarming findings. Indeed, it is hard to imagine what sort of empirical research could establish large such claims. But, after the *Times* article, she quickly attracted powerful allies. None would prove more important than the Ms. Foundation and the American Association of University Women. With their help, the allegedly fragile and demoralized state of American adolescent girls would achieve the status of a national emergency.

Seven Women and a Fax Machine

Marie Wilson, then president of the Ms. Foundation, has described the impact of Gilligan's findings on her staff: "The research on girls struck a chord (perhaps a nerve) with the women at the Ms. organization. It resonated deeply and profoundly." [19] Gilligan would soon come down from her ivory tower to discuss her research with Wilson. Wilson recalls their first meeting: "The two of us met soon after the [*New York Times Magazine*] article appeared. The more we talked, the more we became determined to get this information out to the world."

So Gilligan, who had herself described her findings as "new and fragile," nevertheless joined Ms. staffers in their mission to alert the world to the plight of girls. Together they searched for solutions. Marie Wilson writes, "The more we read and learned, and the more we collaborated with the Harvard researchers, the more often we said: Yes, that was me— confident at 11, confused at 16. . . . What if this confidence could be tapped—and maintained? What if girls didn't have to lose self-esteem? Our blood quickened." [20]

The mood at Ms. was tense but excited. What should be done to help stem the terrible drain of girls' self-confidence? It was in pondering this question that Wilson, Gilligan, and Nell Merlino, a public relations specialist, hit on the idea of a school holiday exclusively for girls. What became Take Our Daughters to Work Day was designed to achieve two purposes. First, an unprecedented girls-only holiday (the boys would stay in school) would raise public awareness about the precarious state of girls' self-esteem. Second, it would address that problem by taking a dramatic step to alleviate the drain of confidence girls suffer. As Ms. explained: for one day, at least, girls would feel "visible, valued and heard."[21]

Looking back to the beginnings of a school holiday now observed by millions, Wilson and Gilligan are understandably self-congratulatory: "Miracle of miracles, seven women and a fax machine at the Ms. Foundation for Women pulled off the largest public education campaign in the history of the women's movement. In a nutshell, that's how Take Our Daughters to Work Day was born."[22]

Gilligan's description of the grim fate of American girls' self-esteem is central to the rationale for Daughters' Day. Here is the sort of information the Ms. sponsors included in the information packet: "Talk to an eight-, nine-, or ten-year-old girl. Chances are she'll be BURSTING WITH ENERGY. . . . Young girls are confident, lively, ENTERPRISING, straightforward—and bent on doing great things in the world."[23] But, the guide points out, this does not last: "Harvard Project members found that by age 12 or 13 many girls start censoring vital parts of themselves—their honesty, insights, and anger—to conform to cultural norms for women. What has happened? Gilligan described girls coming up against a 'wall'—the wall of culture that values women less than men."[24]

An American Tragedy

Gilligan's ideas also had special resonance with leaders of the venerable and politically influential American Association of University Women (AAUW). Officers at the AAUW were reported to be "intrigued and alarmed" by Gilligan's findings.[25] "Wanting to know more," they quickly commissioned a study from the polling firm Greenberg-Lake. With help from Gilligan, the pollsters asked 3,000 children (2,400 girls and 600 boys in grades four through ten) about their self-perceptions. In 1991 the AAUW announced the disturbing results in a report titled *Shortchanging Girls, Shortchanging America*: "Girls aged eight and nine are confident, assertive, and feel authoritative about themselves. Yet most emerge from adolescence with a poor self-image, constrained views of their future and their place in society, and much less confidence about themselves and their abilities." [26]

Anne Bryant, then executive director of the AAUW and an expert in public relations, organized a media campaign to spread the word: "What happens to girls during their school years is an unacknowledged American tragedy. . . . By the time girls finish high school, their doubts have crowded out their dreams." [27] Newspapers and magazines around the country carried reports that girls were being adversely affected by gender bias that eroded their self-esteem. Sharon Schuster, at the time the president of the AAUW, candidly explained to the *New York Times* why the association had undertaken the research in the first place: "We wanted to put some factual data behind our belief that girls are getting shortchanged in the classroom." [28]

As the AAUW's self-esteem study was making headlines, *Science News,* which has been supplying information on scientific and technical developments to newspapers since 1922, reported the skeptical reaction of leading specialists on adolescent development. [29] The late Roberta Simmons, a professor of sociology at the University of Pittsburgh (described by *Science News* as "director of the most ambitious longitudinal study of adolescent self-esteem to date"), said that her research showed nothing like the substantial gender gap described by the AAUW. According to Simmons, "Most kids come through the years from 10 to 20 without major problems and with an increasing sense of self-esteem." [30] But the doubts of Simmons and several other prominent experts were not reported in the hundreds of news stories that the Greenberg-Lake study generated. [31]

Ironically, Gilligan's portrait of adolescent girls "losing their voice" did not agree with the findings of the AAUW self-esteem research—research she herself helped design. In that survey of children aged nine to fifteen, 57 percent of students said teachers call on girls more and 59 percent said that teachers pay more attention to girls. [32] One question in the AAUW survey specifically tested Gilligan's hypothesis: "Do you think of yourself as someone who keeps quiet or someone who speaks out?" [33] Among elementary school girls, 41 percent said they speak out; for high school girls the number went up to 56 percent. For boys, the reverse was true: 59 percent of elementary school boys said they speak out, but by high school they were 1 point behind girls, at 55 percent. These differences are small and well within the margin of error for this survey of 2,942 students (2,350 girls and 592 boys), but the results should have prompted Gilligan to ask herself whether her claim that girls increasingly lose confidence as they move into adolescence was tenable.

The AAUW quickly commissioned a second study, *How Schools Shortchange Girls.* This one, conducted by the Wellesley College Center for Research on Women and released in 1992, asserted a direct causal relationship between girls' alleged second-class status in the nations' schools and deficiencies in their self-esteem. Carol Gilligan's girl crisis was thus transformed into a civil rights issue: girls were the victims of widespread discrimination. "The implications are clear," the AAUW said. "The system must change."[34]

Education Week reported that the AAUW spent $100,000 for the second study and $150,000 promoting it.[35] With great fanfare, *How Schools Shortchange Girls* was released to the remarkably credulous media. A 1992 page-one article for the *New York Times* by Susan Chira was typical of coverage throughout the country. The headline read "Bias Against Girls Is Found Rife in Schools, with Lasting Damage."[36] The piece was later reproduced by the AAUW and sent out as part of a fund-raising package. Chira had not interviewed a single critic of the study.

A few years later, when the academic plight of boys was making itself known, I called Chira and asked about the way she had handled the AAUW study. Would she write her article the same way today? No, she said, pointing out that we have since learned much more about boys' problems in school. Why had she not canvassed dissenting opinions? She explained that she had been traveling when the AAUW study came out, and was on a short deadline. Yes, perhaps she had relied too much on the AAUW's report. She had tried to reach Diane Ravitch, a former US Assistant Secretary of Education and a known critic of women's-advocacy findings, but without success.

Six years after the release of *How Schools Shortchange Girls,* the *New York Times* ran a story that raised questions about its validity. This time the reporter, Tamar Lewin, did reach Diane Ravitch, who told her, "That [1992]

AAUW report was just completely wrong. What was so bizarre is that it came out right at the time that girls had just overtaken boys in almost every area. It might have been the right story twenty years earlier, but coming out when it did, it was like calling a wedding a funeral. . . . There were all these special programs put in place for girls, and no one paid any attention to boys."[37]

One of the many things about which the report was wrong was the famous "call-out" gap. According to the AAUW, "In a study conducted by the Sadkers, boys in elementary and middle school called out answers eight times more often than girls. When boys called out, teachers listened. But when girls called out, they were told 'raise your hand if you want to speak.'"[38]

But the Sadker data is missing—and meaningless, to boot. In 1994 Amy Saltzman, of *U.S. News & World Report,* asked David Sadker for a copy of the research backing up the eight-to-one call-out claim. Sadker said that he had presented the findings in an unpublished paper at a symposium sponsored by the American Educational Research Association; neither he nor the AERA had a copy.[39] Sadker conceded to Saltzman that the ratio may have been inaccurate. Indeed, Saltzman cited an independent study by Gail Jones, an associate professor of education at the University of North Carolina at Chapel Hill, which found that boys called out only twice as often as girls. Whatever the accurate number is, no one has shown that permitting a student to call out answers in the classroom confers any kind of academic advantage. What does confer advantage is a student's *attentiveness.* Boys are less attentive—which could explain why some teachers might call on them more or be more tolerant of call-outs.[40]

Despite the errors, the campaign to persuade the public that girls were being diminished personally and academically was a spectacular success. The Sadkers described an exultant Anne Bryant, of the AAUW, telling her friends, "I remember going to bed the night our report was issued, totally exhilarated. When I woke up the next morning, the first thought in my mind was, 'Oh, my God, what do we do next?'"[41] Political action came next, and here, too, girls' advocates were successful.

The National Council for Research on Women reported on the next major victory in its 1993 newsletter:

Last year a report by the American Association of University Women (AAUW) documented serious inequities in education for girls and women. As a result of that work, an omnibus package of legislation, The Gender Equity in Education Act (HR 1793), was recently introduced in the House of Representatives. . . . The introduction of HR 1793 is a milestone for demonstrating valuable linkages between feminist research and policy in investigating gender discrimination in education.[42]

The Gender Equity Act enjoyed strong bipartisan support and became law in 1994. According to the act, "Excellence in education . . . cannot be achieved without educational equity for women and girls." It provided millions of dollars for equity workshops, training materials, and girl-enhancing curriculum development. The AAUW lobbied vigorously for the legislation. But, as the *New York Times* would report in a 2002, "Ms. Gilligan is often cited as an impetus behind the 1994 Gender Equity in Education Act."[43]

The Myth Unraveling

By the late 1990s the myth of the downtrodden girl was showing some signs of unraveling, and concern over boys was growing. In November 1997, the Public Education Network (PEN), a council of organizations that support public schools, sponsored a conference entitled Gender, Race and Student Achievement. The conference's honored celebrities were Carol Gilligan and Cornel West, who at the time was a professor of Afro-American studies and philosophy of religion at Harvard University. Gilligan talked about how girls and women "lose their voice," how they "go underground" in adolescence, and how women teachers are "absent," having been "silenced" within the "patriarchal structure" that governs our schools. Cornel West spoke of having had to overcome his own feelings of "male supremacy."

Even at this most politically correct of gatherings, the serious deficits of boys kept surfacing. On the first day of the conference, during a special three-hour session, the PEN staff announced the results of a new teacher/ student survey entitled *The Metropolitan Life Survey of the American Teacher 1997: Examining Gender Issues in Public Schools.* The survey was funded by Metropolitan Life Insurance Company as part of its American Teacher series and conducted by Louis Harris and Associates.[44]

During a three-month period in 1997 various questions about gender equity were asked of 1,306 students and 1,035 teachers in grades seven through twelve. The MetLife study had no doctrinal ax to grind. What it found contradicted most of the findings of Gilligan, the AAUW, the Sadkers, and the Wellesley College Center for Research on Women: "Contrary to the commonly held view that boys are at an advantage over girls in school, girls appear to have an advantage over boys in terms of their future plans, teachers' expectations, everyday experiences at school and interactions in the classroom."[45]

The MetLife study also asked students to respond to the statement "I feel that teachers do not listen to what I have to say." Thirty-one percent of boys but only 19 percent of girls said the statement was "mostly true."[46] If Gilligan is right, we should expect more than 19 percent of girls to feel ignored, and certainly more girls than boys. Some other conclusions from the MetLife study: Girls are more likely than boys to see themselves as college-bound and more likely to want a good education.

At the PEN conference, Nancy Leffert, a child psychologist then at the Search Institute in Minneapolis, reported the results of a survey that she and colleagues had recently completed of more than 99,000 children in grades six through twelve.[47] The children were asked about what the researchers call "developmental assets." The Search Institute identified forty critical assets— "building blocks for healthy development." Half of these are external, such as a supportive family and adult role models, and half are internal, such as motivation to achieve, a sense of purpose in life, and interpersonal confidence. Leffert explained, somewhat apologetically, that girls were ahead of boys with respect to thirty-seven out of forty assets. By almost every significant measure of well-being, girls had the better of boys: they felt closer to their families and had higher aspirations, stronger connections to school, and even superior assertiveness skills. Leffert concluded her talk by saying that in the past she had referred to girls as fragile or vulnerable, but that the survey "tells me that girls have very powerful assets."

The Horatio Alger Association of Distinguished Americans, founded in 1947 and devoted to promoting and affirming individual initiative and "the American dream," releases annual back-to-school surveys.[48] Its survey for 1998 contrasted two groups of students: the "highly successful" (approximately 18 percent of American students) and the "disillusioned" (approximately 15 percent). The successful students work hard, choose challenging classes, make schoolwork a top priority, get good grades, participate in extracurricular activities, and feel that teachers and administrators care about them and listen to them. According to the association, the successful group in the 1998 survey is 63 percent female and 37 percent male. The disillusioned students are pessimistic about their future, get low grades, and have little contact with teachers. The disillusioned group could accurately be characterized as demoralized. According to the Alger Association, "Nearly seven out of ten are male."[49]

Finally, in 2000, the Department of Education published its comprehensive analysis of gender and education, *Trends in Educational Equity of Girls and Women*. According to the report, "There is evidence that the female advantage in school performance is real and persistent."[50] Not only did girls earn better grades, take more rigorous courses, have far better reading and writing abilities, and hold higher academic aspirations, they were also somewhat more willing to speak out. When thousands of students were asked if they would be willing to "make a public statement at a meeting," more girls than boys at every grade level answered "yes" (83 percent of boys and 87 percent of girls among twelfth graders).[51] Contrary to Carol Gilligan's claims, girls appear to become more confident about speaking out as they move from early to late adolescence.

Gilligan's theory would suffer another devastating blow from Susan Harter, a psychologist at the University of Denver. Using the common notion of voice as "having a say," "speaking one's mind," and "feeling listened to" and applying relatively objective measures, Harter and her colleagues tested the claims that adolescent girls have a lower "level of voice" than boys and that girls' level of voice drops sometime between the ages of eleven and seventeen.

In one study, "Level of Voice Among Female and Male High School Students," Harter and her colleagues distributed a questionnaire to 307 middle-class students in a high school in Aurora, Colorado (165 females, 142 males). The students were asked whether they felt they were able to "express their opinions," "say what is on their minds," and "express their point of view." Harter concludes, "Findings revealed no gender differences nor any evidence that voice declines in female adolescents."[52]

In a second study, "Lack of Voice as a Manifestation of False Self-Behavior Among Adolescents,"[53] Harter and her associates looked at responses of approximately nine hundred male and female students from grades six to twelve to see if they could find evidence of a decline in female expressiveness. Their conclusion: "Gilligan's argument is that girls in our society are particularly vulnerable to loss of voice. . . . Our cross-sectional data revealed no significant mean differences associated with grade level for either gender, nor are there even any trends, in either the co-educational or all-girl schools."[54]

Harter admires Gilligan and is careful to say that these studies are inconclusive and that Gilligan's predictions about loss of voice may be true in certain domains for a certain subset of girls. She also suggests that more in-depth interviews might lend support to Gilligan's claims that girls struggle more with conflicts over authenticity and voice. But for the time being, Harter cautions "against making generalizations about gender differences in voice."[55]

Gilligan is the matron saint of the girl-crisis movement. Without her, there would have been no Daughters' Day, no AAUW self-esteem study, and no Gender Equity in Education Act. Yet her thesis about a nation of silenced and diminished girls was a chimera. Why was her research taken so seriously? Why were the women's groups moved to "get this information out to the world"?

For one thing, her message was music to orthodox feminist ears: not only women but *girls* were being silenced in our male culture. More important, Gilligan was not just another activist deploring patriarchal oppression. She was a Harvard professor who had authored a classic book on women's psychology—*In a Different Voice*. She offered the women's groups something powerful and new—the cachet of university science. Here was a high-powered scholar telling us that girls were being crushed. And she had "data" to prove it.

For a better understanding of the manufactured crisis, and for a ringside view of the phenomenon of faux social science, it is worth carefully considering Gilligan's brilliant early career.

"Landmark Research"

In 1984 Carol Gilligan published her book on women's distinctive moral psychology—*In a Different Voice*. Its success was dazzling. It sold more than seven hundred thousand copies and has been translated into sixteen languages. A reviewer at *Vogue* explained its appeal: "[Gilligan] flips old prejudices against women on their ears. She reframes qualities regarded as women's weaknesses and shows them to be human strengths. It is impossible to consider [her] ideas without having your estimation of women rise." [56]

Journalists routinely used words like "groundbreaking" or "landmark research" to describe *In a Different Voice*. Because of that book, Gilligan was *Ms.* magazine's Woman of the Year in 1984, and *Time* put her on its short list of most influential Americans in 1996. In 1997 she received the $250,000 Heinz Award for "transform[ing] the paradigm for what it means to be human." In 2000, Jane Fonda was moved to donate $12.5 million to Harvard for a new Center on Gender and Education—devoted to advancing the research of Carol Gilligan. For Fonda, *In a Different Voice* was life-changing. As she said in a speech at the Harvard Graduate School of Education, "I know what Professor Gilligan writes about. I know it in my skin, in my gut, as well as in my voice." [57]

Francine Prose noted in her 1990 *New York Times Magazine* story that *In a Different Voice* had made Gilligan "the object of almost cult-like veneration" with readers, journalists, and activists. By contrast, said Prose, it "provoked intense hostility" on the part of academics. Why the hostility? For one thing, most of Gilligan's research on women's loss of voice consists of anecdotes based on a small number of interviews. Her data are otherwise unavailable for review, giving rise to some reasonable doubts about their merits and persuasiveness. Transforming the paradigm for what it means to be human would certainly be an admirable feat—but scholars want to see the supporting evidence.

In a Different Voice offered the provocative thesis that men and women have distinctly different ways of reasoning about moral quandaries. Relying on data from three studies she had conducted, Gilligan found that women tend to make moral decisions based on an "ethic of care." When reasoning about right and wrong, they focus on their responsibilities and connections to others. For women, according to Gilligan, morality tends to be contextual, personal, and motivated by concern rather than duty. Men, by contrast, are more likely to deploy an "ethic of justice," with a focus on individual rights and abstract principles. Male moral reasoning is impersonal, separate-from-others, and focused on noninterference, rights, and duties. Gilligan argued further that women's moral style (their "different voice") had been denigrated by professional psychologists. She complained that the entire fields of psychology and moral philosophy had been built on studies that excluded or depreciated women's moral orientation. According to Gilligan, women's culture of nurture and care and their habits of peaceful accommodation could be the salvation of a world governed by hypercompetitive males and their habits of abstract moral reasoning.

The book received a mixed reaction from feminists. Some—such as the philosophers Virginia Held and Sara Ruddick, and those in various fields who would come to be known as "difference feminists"—were excited by the idea that women were different from, and quite probably better than, men. But other academic feminists attacked Gilligan for reinforcing stereotypes about women as nurturers and caretakers.

Many academic psychologists, feminist and nonfeminist alike, found Gilligan's specific claims about distinct male and female moral orientations unpersuasive and without empirical support. Lawrence Walker, of the University of British Columbia, has reviewed 108 studies of sex differences in solving moral problems. He concluded in a 1984 review article in *Child Development* that "sex differences in moral reasoning in late adolescence and youth are rare."[58] In 1987 three psychologists at Oberlin College attempted to test Gilligan's hypothesis: they administered a moral-reasoning test to 101 students (males and females) and concluded, "There were no reliable sex differences . . . in the directions predicted by Gilligan."[59] Concurring with Walker, the Oberlin researchers pointed out that "Gilligan failed to provide acceptable empirical support for her model."

The thesis of *In a Different Voice* is based on three studies Gilligan conducted: the "college student study," the "abortion decision study," and the "rights and responsibilities study." Here is how Gilligan described the last:

> This study involved a sample of males and females matched for age, intelligence, education, occupation, and social class at nine points across the life cycle: ages 6–9, 11, 15, 19, 22, 25–27, 35, 45, and 60. From a total sample of 144 (8 males and 8 females at each age), including a more intensively interviewed subsample of 36 (2 males and 2 females at each age), data were collected on conceptions of self and morality, experiences of moral conflicts and choice, and judgments of hypothetical moral dilemmas.

This description is all we ever learn about the mechanics of the study, which seems to have no proper name; it was never published, never peer-reviewed. It was, in any case, very small in scope and in number of subjects. And the data are tantalizingly inaccessible. In September 1998, my research assistant, Elizabeth Bowen, called Gilligan's office and asked where she could find copies of the three studies that were the basis for *In a Different Voice*. Gilligan's assistant, Tatiana Bertsch, told her that they were unavailable and not in the public domain; because of the sensitivity of the data (especially the abortion study), the information had been kept confidential. Asked where the studies were now kept, Bertsch explained that the original data were being prepared to be placed in a Harvard library: "They are physically in the office. We are in the process of sending them to the archives at the Murray Center."

In October 1998, Hugh Liebert, a sophomore at Harvard who had been my intern the previous summer, spoke to Bertsch. She told him that the data would not be available until the end of the academic year, adding, "They have been kept secret because the issues [raised in the study] are so sensitive." She suggested that he check back occasionally. He tried again in March. This time she informed him, "They will not be available anytime soon." Several months later he sent an email message directly to Gilligan, and received this reply from Bertsch:

> None of the *In a Different Voice* studies have been published. We are in the process of donating the college student study to the Murray Research Center at Radcliffe, but that will not be completed for another year, probably. At this point Professor Gilligan has no immediate plans of donating the abortion or the rights and responsibilities studies. Sorry that none of what you are interested in is available.

Brendan Maher is a professor emeritus at Harvard University and a former chairman of the psychology department. I told him about the inaccessibility of Gilligan's data and the explanation that their sensitive nature precluded public dissemination. He laughed and said, "It would be extraordinary to say [that one's data] are too sensitive for others to see." He pointed out that there are standard methods for handling confidential materials in research. Names are left out but raw scores are reported, "so others can see if they can replicate your study." You also must disclose such details as how you chose your subjects, how the interviews were recorded, and the method by which you derived meaning from them (your coding system). There is a real risk of bias and prejudice in coding, so it is critical to have two or three people code the same interview to see if you have "interrater reliability." Even with all these controls, there is no guarantee your research is significant or accurate. But, said, Maher, "without them, what do you have?"

What you have are unpublished, unexamined, uncriticized data that are nevertheless deemed to be of such historical importance to merit being donated to a prestigious Harvard research center for posterity. No doubt Gilligan will insist on continued confidentiality.[60]

Over the years, scholars have criticized Gilligan for her cavalier way with research data. In 1986, then Tufts University professor Zella Luria commented on the elusive character of Gilligan's "studies": "One is left with the knowledge that there were some studies involving women and sometimes men and that women were somehow sampled and somehow interviewed on some issues. . . . Somehow the data were sifted and somehow yielded a clear impression that women could be powerfully characterized as caring and interrelated. This is an exceedingly intriguing proposal, but it is not yet substantiated as a research conclusion."[61]

In 1991, Faye Crosby, a Smith College psychologist (now at the University of California, Santa Cruz), rebuked Gilligan for creating this "illusion of data": "Gilligan referred throughout her book to the information obtained in her studies, but did not present any tabulations. Indeed, she never quantified anything. The reader never learns anything about 136 of the 144 people from the third study, as only 8 are quoted in the book. One probably does not have to be a trained researcher to worry about this tactic."[62]

These are serious complaints of a type that, in disciplines that respect scholarly standards, have been known to lead to censure or worse. Why has so little notice been taken of the scarcity of Gilligan's evidence? I see at least two explanations. First of all, in the Harvard School of Education, where Gilligan held her professorship, the standards for acceptable research are very different from those in other Harvard departments. Second, Gilligan writes on "gender theory," which immediately confers ideological sensitivity on her findings. The political climate makes it very awkward for anyone (especially a man) to criticize her. Apart from the small group of feminist critics who bristled at her suggestion that men and women are different, few academics have dared to suggest that the empress had no clothes.

Gilligan's defenders will argue that to criticize her for her shortcomings as an empirical psychologist is to miss the point. The true power of *In a Dif-*

ferent Voice, they say, has little to do with proving this or that claim about male and female behavior. It is groundbreaking research because it advanced the idea that past psychological research was largely a male-centered discipline based on the experiences of only half the human race. Gilligan revolutionized modern psychology by introducing women's voices into a social science tradition that had systematically ignored them.

There is merit to this argument. Gilligan was not the first to urge that women be studied directly, rather than by way of male models, but she was more effective than anyone at getting that message through to both scholars and the wider public. For this she deserves credit. Moreover, at a time (in the early 1980s) when women's scholarship was blinkered by the dogma that men and women were cognitively interchangeable, Gilligan's "difference feminism" was refreshing. But her specific and much-celebrated claim about women's distinctive moral voice turns out to be nothing more than a seductive hypothesis, without evidential basis.

With the success of *In a Different Voice* and with the considerable resources available to her at Harvard, Gilligan might have gone on to answer her scholarly critics. She might have refined her thesis about male and female differences in moral reasoning and done the genuine research scholars expected of her. She might have tried to put her purported discoveries on a scientific footing. But that is not what she did. In the years following publication of *In a Different Voice,* Gilligan's methods remained anecdotal and impressionistic, with increasingly heavy doses of psychoanalytic theorizing and gender ideology.[63] Her research on adolescent girls in *Making Connections* is a case in point. The gloomy picture of adolescent girls that she presented to Ms., the AAUW, and a concerned public is every bit as distorted as any ever presented by social scientists using (in Gilligan's words) "androcentric and patriarchal norms."[64]

Gilligan is unruffled by scholarly criticism and shows few signs of changing her research methods. She boldly insists that to give in to the demand for conventional evidence would be to give in to the standards of the "dominant culture" she is criticizing. She justifies her lack of scientific proof for her large claims quoting the late poet Audre Lorde: "The master's tools will never dismantle the master's house."[65]

Lorde's remark is often used to fend off "masculinist" criticism of un-scientific feminist methods. One might well ask, especially if one's research is part of a larger antipatriarchal project aimed at "dismantling the master's house," what better way to accomplish that end than by using the master's own tools? More to the point, Gilligan's justification for deserting sound scientific method in establishing her claims is deeply anti-intellectual. She seems to be saying, I don't *have* to play by the rules; the men wrote them. That rejection of conventional scientific standards simply will not do: if Gilligan feels justified in abandoning the methods of social science, she has to critique them. She should tell us what's wrong with them and show us a better set of tools.

Conclusion

The *New York Times Magazine* profile that played so large a role in populariz-ing Gilligan's views described her as having a "Darwinian sense of mission to excavate the hidden chambers of a common buried past." [66] Gilligan herself is not averse to the comparison with Darwin. When *Education Week* asked me what I thought of Gilligan's work and claims, I said, "I'm not sure what she does has much status as social science." *Education Week* reported Gilli-gan's response to my remarks: "[I]f quantitative studies are the only kind that qualify as 'research,' then Charles Darwin, the father of evolutionary theory, would not be considered a researcher." [67]

Gilligan actually sees herself as pursuing a Darwinian method of in-quiry. She informs us that when she read Darwin's *Voyage of the* Beagle, she wondered if she "could find some place like the Galapagos Islands" to do her research in developmental psychology. [68] And she did: "I went to my own version of the Galapagos Islands with a group of colleagues. . . . We travelled to girls in search of the origins of women's development."

Even a casual look at Gilligan's contributions suggests that she should not be comparing herself to Darwin. Darwin openly presented masses of data and invited criticism. His main thesis has been confirmed by count-less observations of the fossil record. By contrast, no one has been able to replicate even the three secret studies that were the basis for Gilligan's central claims in her most influential work, *In a Different Voice*. In 2012, the *Boston Globe* reviewed the history of Gilligan's "feminist classic." Its verdict: "Today, *In a Different Voice* has been the subject of so many rebuttals that it is no longer taken seriously as an academic work." [69]

Gilligan's writings on silenced girls, the limits of "androcentric and patriarchal norms," and the hazards of Western culture are not science or scholarship. They are, at best, eccentric social criticism. Yet by borrowing the prestige of academic science, her theories persuaded parents, educators, political officials, and women's activists that girls are being diminished and led them to policies that have indeed diminished boys.

But that is only half the problem. In 1995, Gilligan and her colleagues at the Harvard School of Education inaugurated the Harvard Project on Women's Psychology, Boys' Development and the Culture of Manhood. Within a year, she announced the discovery of a crisis among boys even worse than the one afflicting girls. "Girls' psychological development in patriarchy involves a process of eclipse that is even more total for boys." [70] She and her colleagues would soon focus on liberating boys from the mask of masculinity. The war against boys was about to intensify.

5

Gilligan's Island

I n 1996, Carol Gilligan announced the need for a revolution in how we raise boys. The stakes are high, she said. She called for a new pedagogy to free boys from an errant masculinity that is endangering civilization: "After a century of unparalleled violence, at a time when violence has become appalling . . . [w]e understand better the critical importance of emotional intimacy and vulnerability." [1] Gilligan asked us to reflect on these vital questions: "What if the equation of civilization with patriarchy were broken? What if boys did not psychologically disconnect from women and dissociate themselves from vital parts of relationships?" [2]

But those who followed Gilligan's earlier claims and campaigns might pose different questions: What if her studies of boys are a travesty of scientific inquiry? What if the programs and policies she recommends do more harm than good? What can be done to protect boys from the trusting educators who faithfully accept Gilligan's theories?

"Masculinity in a Patriarchal Social Order"

Gilligan claimed to have discovered "a startling asymmetry"—girls undergo social trauma as they enter adolescence. For boys, she says, the period of crisis is early childhood. Boys aged three to seven are pressured to "take into themselves the structure or moral order of a patriarchal civilization: to internalize a patriarchal voice."[3] This masculinizing process, says Gilligan, is psychologically damaging and dehumanizing.

Gilligan's views on masculine identity built on earlier psychological theories of female and male development, in particular the theories of feminist psychoanalyst Nancy Chodorow, which Gilligan made use of in her 1982 book, *In a Different Voice*.[4] In Chodorow's 1978 *The Reproduction of Mothering*, she argued that traditional masculine and feminine roles are rooted not so much in biology as in a self-perpetuating sex/gender system that is universal to human societies: "Hitherto . . . all sex/gender systems have been male-dominated."[5] The sex/gender system, says Chodorow, is the way society has organized sexuality and reproduction to perpetuate the subordination of women. The system keeps women down by permanently assigning to them the primary care of infants and children, while men dominate the public sphere.

Because mothers do most of the nurturing, all children start out life more strongly identified with their mothers than their fathers. That identification and attachment, says Chodorow, have profoundly different consequences for boys and girls. A girl grows up with a "sense of continuity and similarity to the mother." Boys, on the other hand, learn that to be masculine is to be unlike their caregiver: "Women, as mothers, produce daughters with mothering capacities and the desire to mother. . . . By contrast, women as mothers produce sons whose nurturant capacities and needs have been systematically curtailed and repressed."[6]

According to Chodorow, both women and men perpetuate male supremacy by the way they socialize boys: "Women's mothering in the isolated nuclear family of contemporary capitalist society" shows boys that nurturing is women's work.[7] This "prepares men for participation in a male-dominant family, and society, for their lesser emotional participation in family life, and for their participation in the capitalist world of work."[8] In this way, the social organization of parental roles supports a capitalist/patriarchal system that Chodorow finds exploitative and unfair—especially to women: "It is politically and socially important to confront this organization of parenting. . . . It can be changed."[9]

In a Different Voice cites Chodorow's view that "boys, in defining them-selves as masculine, separate their mothers from themselves, thus curtailing their 'primary love and sense of empathetic tie.'" [10] Feeling no correspond-ing need to disconnect themselves from their mothers, "girls emerge with a stronger basis for experiencing another's needs or feelings as one's own." [11] These ideas on the different ways girls and boys develop—girls in "continu-ity" with their female nurturers, boys in forced "separation" from their nur-turers—helped Gilligan explain why women and men should have different moral styles, with women having an empathetic morality of care and men having an abstract morality of duty and justice.

Chodorow believed that males and females have the same capacity to nurture. In males this capacity is repressed, largely because male-dominated societies find it expedient to assign the primary nurturing role to girls and women. In Chodorow's view, this social ordering of parenting not only can but should be changed. Permanent reform will mean a radical change in gender identities; it will require "the conscious organization and activity of men and women who recognize that their interests lie in transforming the social organization of gender." [12]

Chodorow's call for the transformation of the patriarchal sex/gender sys-tem and her condemnation of the "capitalist world of work" do not resonate today as they did in the 1970s. Her theories of child development and the construction of gender are dated. [13] The female propensity for nurture ap-pears to be more than an artifice of culture. The more we learn about the power of hormones to shape behavior, the harder it becomes to think of sex differences the way Chodorow thought of them.

Hard, but not impossible. Having read Chodorow in the 1970s, Gil-ligan appears to have been convinced that her views on the harms inflicted on children by the culture were profoundly right. Gilligan would repack-age them, giving them the powerful support of her beguiling metaphorical prose. She was especially impressed with Chodorow's idea that patriarchy dictates styles of child rearing that are responsible for developmental defor-mations in both males and females.

Following Chodorow, Gilligan claims that boys get the message that in order to be "male"—to become "one of the boys"—they must suppress those parts of themselves that are most like their mothers. Gilligan speaks of a "relational crisis" that very young boys undergo as part of their initiation into the patriarchy. In effect, says Gilligan, boys are forced to "hide [their] humanity" and submerge their best qualit[y]—their sensitivity."[14] Though this diminishes boys psychologically and morally, it does offer them the advantage of feeling superior to girls. But the male culture that enthrones the boy is dangerously aggressive and competitive. Boys cannot opt out of it without paying a terrible price, writes Gilligan: "If boys in early childhood resist the break between the inner and outer worlds, they are resisting an initiation into masculinity or manhood as it is defined and established in cultures that value or valorize heroism, honor, war, competition—the culture of the warrior, the economy of capitalism."[15] At the same time, the process of masculine acculturation in the "patriarchal social order" is psychologically devastating: "To be a real boy or man in such a culture means to be able to hurt without feeling hurt, to separate without feeling sadness or loss, and then to inflict hurt and separation on others."[16]

In 1997, the *New York Times Magazine* ran another admiring piece on Gilligan, an interview entitled "From Carol Gilligan's Chair." "Can we talk about your new work—your research on boys?" asked the interviewer. Gilligan described a boy she had observed the day before: "His face was very still. It didn't register a lot of emotion. He was around 6, when boys want to become 'one of the boys.' They feel they have to separate from women. And they are not allowed to feel that separation as a real loss."[17] To this, her interviewer remarked, "Sounds as if you're trying to discover in boys the reasons men feel compelled to adopt certain models of what it means to be a man—models that many men feel to be enslaving."

"That's exactly it," Gilligan replied. She then explained that this must be changed: "We have to build a culture that does not reward that separation from the person who raised them." She said she hopes to develop a research method, in particular a way of relating to her boy subjects, that "will free boys' voices, to create conditions that allow boys to say what they know,"[18] and allow her to learn what the boys are suppressing. Through her earlier studies she claims to have learned how to liberate the repressed voices of adolescent girls; now she hopes to repeat that feat with boys. The aim is to devise a new kind of socialization for boys that will make their aggressiveness and need for dominance things of the past. Gilligan envisions a new era in which boys will not be forced into a stereotypical masculinity that separates them from their nurtures but will be allowed to remain "relationally connected" to those close to them. Once boys are freed of oppressive gender roles, far fewer will suffer the early trauma that leads to so many disorders: "We might be close to a time similar to the Reformation, where the fundamental structure of authority is about to change."

Gilligan's theory about boys' development includes three claims: (1) Boys are being psychically deformed and made sick by a traumatic, forced separation from their mothers. (2) Seemingly healthy boys are cut off from their own feelings and damaged in their capacity to develop healthy relationships. (3) The well-being of society may depend on freeing boys from the culture of warriors and capitalism. Let us consider each proposition in turn.

Boys and Their Mothers

According to Gilligan, boys are at special risk in early childhood: they suffer "more stuttering, more bedwetting, more learning problems . . . when cultural norms pressure them to separate from their mother." [19] (Sometimes she adds allergies, attention deficit disorder, and attempted suicide to the list.[20]) She does not cite any pediatric research that supports her theories about the origin of these early-childhood disorders. Is there a single study, for example, that shows that young males who remain intimately bonded with their mothers are less likely to develop allergies or wet their beds?

Gilligan's assertion that the "pressure of cultural norms" causes boys to separate from their mothers and thereby generates physical disorders has not been tested empirically. Nor does Gilligan suggest how it might be tested or even allow that empirical support might be called for. We are asked, in effect, to take it on her say-so that boys need to be protected from our warmongering, patriarchal, capitalistic culture that desensitizes them, submerges their humanity, undermines their mental health, and turns many into violent predators.

But are boys aggressive and violent because they are psychically separated from their mothers? Thirty years of research suggest that it is the absence of the *male* parent that is more often the problem. The boys who are most at risk for juvenile delinquency and violence are boys who are literally separated from their fathers. The US Bureau of Census reports that in 1960, 5.1 million children lived with only their mothers; by 1996, the number was more than 16 million.[21] (Today it is 24 million.[22]) As far back as 1965, Daniel Patrick Moynihan called attention to the social dangers of raising boys without the benefit of paternal presence. "A community that allows a large number of young men to grow up in broken families, dominated by women, never acquiring any stable relationship to male authority, never acquiring any rational expectations about the future—that community asks for and gets chaos."[23]

Elaine Kamarck of the Harvard Kennedy School, and William Galston of the University of Maryland and Brookings Institution, agree with Moynihan. Writing for the Progressive Policy Institute in 1990, they say, "The relationship [between crime and one-parent families, which are typically fatherless families] is so strong that controlling for family configuration erases the relationship between race and crime and between low income and crime. This conclusion shows up time and again in the literature."[24]

It showed up in 2004 when Cynthia Harper of the University of Pennsylvania and Sara McLanahan of Princeton University studied the incarceration rates of fatherless boys: "Young men who grow up in homes without fathers are twice as likely to end up in jail as those who come from traditional two-parent families. . . . Those boys whose fathers were absent from the household had double the odds of being incarcerated—even when other factors such as race, income, parent education and urban residence were held constant."[25]

Effective fathers need not be paragons of emotional sensitivity. In fact, they may possess qualities that would distress gender experts at the Harvard School of Education. As sociologist David Blankenhorn explains in *Fatherless America*, the typically masculine dad who plays roughly with his kids, who teaches his sons to be stoical and competitive, who is often glued to the television watching football games—is in fact unlikely to produce a violent son. Says Blankenhorn, "There are exceptions, of course. But here is the rule. Boys raised by traditionally masculine fathers generally do not commit crimes. Fatherless boys commit crimes." [26]

Given Gilligan's animus toward the "patriarchal social order," it is not surprising that her research appears to attach no importance to fathers. All the same, the more we learn about the reasons for juvenile aggression, the clearer it becomes that the progressive weakening of the family—in particular, the absence of fathers from the home—plays an important role.

Restoring fathers to the home is of course nowhere on Gilligan's to-do list. Instead, she and her Harvard associates concentrate on changing things like boys' play preferences. In an interview for *Education Week*, Gilligan spoke of a moment when each little boy stands at a crossroad: "You see this picture of a little boy with a stuffed bunny in one hand and a Lego gun in the other. You could almost freeze-frame that moment in development." [27] The interviewer reports Gilligan's comment on this crucial development period in boys' lives: "If becoming a boy means becoming tough, then boys may feel at an early age that they have to hide the part of themselves that is more caring or stereotypically feminine."

Recall the suggestion of Gilligan's colleague Elizabeth Debold (discussed in chapter 3) that it is superheroes and macho toys that "cause [boys] to be angry and act aggressive." The patriarchal pressures on boys to hide their feminine side create the problem. This is something the Harvard team hopes to change.

Describing the purpose of the Harvard Project on *Women's Psychology, Boys' Development and the Culture of Manhood,* Gilligan and her codirector, Barney Brawer, state the following "working theory":

- "that the relational crisis which men typically experience in early childhood occurs for women in adolescence,"
- "that this relational crisis in boys and girls involves disconnection from women which is essential to the perpetuation of patriarchal societies." [28]

A project that posits a crisis engulfing both boys and girls, caused by a patriarchal order that perpetuates itself by forcing children to disconnect from women, is not about to take a serious look at the problem of absent fathers. In his contribution to the statement describing the purpose of the Harvard Project, Brawer seeks to address this point by "adding two additional questions to Gilligan's analysis":

First: How do we include in our view of boyhood and manhood not only the problems of the traditional model but also potential strengths?

Second: What is the particular conundrum of boys living without fathers within a culture of patriarchy?

To the first of Brawer's questions, the answer is, how indeed? Having identified the "traditional model" of manhood as the cause of the boys' crisis, how can we now turn around to acknowledge that the traditional "manly" virtues (courage, honor, self-discipline, competitiveness) play a vital role in the healthy socialization of boys? The second question oddly hints that the problems being caused by fatherlessness are somehow due to the culture of patriarchy—the default villain of the piece. We can see why Brawer finds fatherlessness a conundrum. The puzzle is why, in a Gilliganesque world where the ills suffered by boys are caused by a male culture that forcibly separates boys from their mothers, the absence of fathers wouldn't be a blessing. In the real world, of course, fatherlessness is not a puzzle but a personal and social tragedy.

Boys Out of Touch with Their Feelings

Oblivious to all the factual evidence that points to paternal separation as a significant cause of aberrant behavior in boys, Gilligan bravely calls for a fundamental change in the rearing of boys. We must, she says, free young men from a destructive culture of manhood that "impedes their capacity to feel their own and other people's hurt, to know their own and other people's sadness."[29] Since, as she has diagnosed it, the purported disorder is universal, the cure must be radical. We must change the very nature of childhood: we must find ways to keep boys bonded to their mothers. We must undercut the system of socialization that is so "essential to the perpetuation of patriarchal societies."

Gilligan's views are attractive to many who believe that boys could profit by being more sensitive and empathetic. But before parents and educators enlist in Gilligan's project, they would do well to note that her central thesis—that boys are being imprisoned by their conventional masculinity—is not a scientific hypothesis. It is an extravagant piece of speculative psychology of the kind that sometimes finds acceptance in schools of education but is not creditable in most departments of psychology.

Gilligan talks about radically reforming "the fundamental structure of authority" by freeing boys from the masculine stereotypes that bind them. But in what sense are American boys unfree? Was the young Mark Twain or the young Teddy Roosevelt enslaved by conventional modes of boyhood? Is the average Little Leaguer or Cub Scout defective in the ways suggested by Gilligan? It is certainly true that a small subset of male children fit Gilligan's description of being desensitized and cut off from feelings of tenderness and care. However, these boys are not representative of the male sex. Gilligan speaks of boys "hiding their humanity" and showing a capacity to "hurt without feeling hurt." This, she maintains, is a general condition brought about because the vast majority of boys are forced into separation from their nurturers. But the idea that boys are abnormally insensitive flies in the face of everyday experience. Boys are competitive and often rowdy. But anyone in close contact with them—parents, grandparents, teachers, coaches, friends—gets daily proof of most boys' humanity, loyalty, and compassion.

Gilligan appears to be making the same mistake with boys that she made with girls. She observes a few children and interprets their problems as indicative of a deep and general malaise caused by the way our society imposes sex-role stereotypes on them. By adolescence, she concludes, the pressure to meet these stereotypes has impaired, distressed, and deformed both sexes. However, most boys are not violent. Most are not unfeeling or antisocial. Gilligan finds boys lacking in empathy, but does she empathize with them?

We have yet to see a single reasonable argument for radically reforming the identities of boys and girls. As I argued in chapter 3, there is no reason to believe that such reform is achievable, but even if it were, the attempt to obtrude on boys and girls at this level of their natures is ethically questionable.

A Good Word for the Martial Virtues

Consider, finally, Gilligan's criticism of how American boys are initiated into a patriarchal social order that valorizes heroism, honor, war, and competition. In Gilligan's world, the military man is one of the potent and deplorable stereotypes that "the culture of manhood" holds up to boys as a male ideal. But her criticism of military culture is flawed. First, the military ethos that Gilligan castigates as insensitive and uncaring is probably less influential in the lives of American boys today than at most periods in our history. At the same time, it needs to be pointed out, our military and its culture are nothing to be ashamed of. Indeed, if you want to cite an American institution that inculcates high levels of human concern, cooperation, and sacrifice, you could aptly choose the military.

Anyone who has firsthand knowledge of American military personnel knows that most are highly competent, self-disciplined, honorable, and moral men and women ready to risk their lives for their country. Gilligan and her followers are confused about military ethics. Yes, the military "valorizes" honor, competition, and winning. Offering no reasons for impugning these values, which in fact are necessary for an effective life, she contents herself with insinuating that they are dehumanizing by contrast with the values she admires: cooperation, caring, self-sacrifice. To suggest that the military ethic promotes callousness and heedlessness is deeply wrong. To accuse the military of being uncaring is to ignore the selflessness and camaraderie that make the martial ethos so attractive to those who intensely desire to live lives of high purpose and service.

The historian Stephen Ambrose, who spent half his career listening to the stories of soldiers, tells of a course on the Second World War he gave at the University of Wisconsin in 1996 to an overflow class of 350. Most students were unfamiliar with the salient events of that war. According to Ambrose, "They were dumbstruck by descriptions of what it was like to be on the front lines. They were even more amazed by the responsibilities carried by junior officers . . . who were as young as they . . . they wondered how anyone could have done it." [30]

Ambrose tried to explain to them what brought so many men and women to such feats of courage, such levels of excellence. He told them it hadn't been anything abstract. It had involved two things: "unit cohesion"—a concern for the safety and well-being of their soldier comrades that equaled and sometimes exceeded their concern for their own well-being—and an understanding of the moral dimensions of the fight: "At the core, the American citizen soldiers knew the difference between right and wrong, and they didn't want to live in a world in which wrong prevailed. So they fought, and won, and we all of us, living and yet to be born, must be forever profoundly grateful." [31]

What Ambrose understands and Gilligan does not is that the ethic of duty encompasses the ethic of care. The martial virtues of honor, duty, and self-sacrifice are caring virtues, and it is wrong to deride them as lesser virtues. Gilligan's depreciation of the military is standard among certain academics. Ambrose says that after he finished college in the late 1950s, he too shared the anti-military, anti-business snobbery that prevails in many universities today. He writes:

By the time I was a graduate student, I was full of scorn for [ex-GIs]. . . . But in fact these were the men who built modern America. They had learned to work together in the armed services in World War II. They had seen enough destruction: they wanted to construct. They built the Interstate Highway system, the St. Lawrence Seaway, the suburbs. . . . They had seen enough killing; they wanted to save lives. They licked polio and made other revolutionary advances in medicine. They had learned in the army the virtues of a solid organization and teamwork, and the value of individual initiative, inventiveness, and responsibility. [32]

Gilligan's Direction

What are we to make of Carol Gilligan's contribution and influence? Her earlier work on the different moral voices of males and females had some merit; her demand that psychologists and philosophers take into account the possibility that women and men have different styles of moral reasoning was original and interesting. As it turns out, the differences are less important than Gilligan predicted. All the same, her suggestive ideas on sex and moral psychology stimulated an important discussion. For that she deserves recognition.

Her later work on adolescent girls and their "silenced" voices shows us a different Gilligan. Her ideas were successful in the sense that they inspired activists in organizations like the AAUW and the Ms. Foundation to go on red alert in an effort to save the nation's "drowning and disappearing" daughters. But all their activism was based on a false premise: that girls were subdued, neglected, and diminished. In fact, the opposite was true: girls were moving ahead of boys in most of the ways that count. Gilligan's powerful myth of the incredible shrinking girl did more harm than good. It patronized girls, portraying them as victims of the culture. It diverted attention from the academic deficits of boys. It also gave urgency and credibility to a specious self-esteem movement that wasted everybody's time.

Gilligan's later work on boys is even more removed from reality. The myth of the emotionally repressed boy was taken seriously by many educators and lead to insipid, dispiriting school programs designed to get boys in touch with their feelings. More ominously, it lead to increasingly aggressive efforts to insist that boys behave more like girls—for their own sakes and for the supposed good of society. In this call for deliverance, Gilligan has been joined by some prominent male disciples—with their own research, extravagant claims, and proposals for rescuing a nation of stricken young Hamlets.

6

Save the Males

On June 4, 1998, McLean Hospital, the psychiatric teaching hospital of the Harvard Medical School, announced the results of a new study of boys.[1] The press release, headlined "Adolescence Is Time of Crisis for Even 'Healthy' Boys," reported that researchers at McLean and Harvard Medical had found that "psychologically 'healthy' middle-class boys" are anxious, alienated, lonely, and isolated—"despite appearing outwardly content."[2]

The study, "Listening to Boys' Voices," was conducted by Dr. William Pollack, codirector of the Center for Men at McLean Hospital and assistant clinical professor of psychiatry at Harvard Medical School. Pollack, a psychologist, had already come out with a book publicizing the report's dismaying findings, entitled *Real Boys: Rescuing Our Sons from the Myths of Boyhood.*[3]

Real Boys was moderately successful before the Columbine High School massacre in April 1999. But it really took off when a startled public, hungry for expert counsel on the rash of school shootings, saw in Pollack a confident authority. He appeared on *Oprah, CBS This Morning*, and *Dateline NBC* to explain his discovery that a silent crisis was engulfing American boys. He joined Vice President Al Gore on CNN's *Larry King Live* for a program dedicated to understanding school violence. Among Pollack's many speeches in the Columbine aftermath were a May 1999 keynote address to a convention of more than fourteen hundred Texas elementary school counselors and a June address to two thousand PTA leaders in Portland, Oregon.[4] Referring to boys as "Ophelia's brothers," Pollack tried to do for boys what Carol Gilligan and Mary Pipher had done for girls: bring news of their diminished and damaged young lives to a large public. *Real Boys* stayed on the *New York Times* bestseller list for more than six months. What sort of research findings did Pollack provide in support of his disturbing portrait? Let's go back to the McLean announcement of his discovery. The press release listed the study's major findings. Among them:

- "As boys mature, they feel increased pressure to conform to an aggressive dominant male stereotype, which leads to low self-esteem and high incidence of depression."
- "Boys feel significant anxiety and sadness about growing up to be men."
- "Despite appearing outwardly content, many boys feel deep feelings of loneliness and alienation."

We must bear in mind that Pollack is not talking about a small percentage of boys who are seriously disturbed and lethally dangerous. He is attributing pathology to normal boys, and his conclusions are expansive. "These findings," he said, "carry massive implications for what appears to be a larger national crisis, one that we are now seeing can occasion serious violence."[5] This national emergency called for a major social reform: "The time has come to change the way boys are raised—in our homes, in our schools and in society."[6]

It is unusual to find such sensational claims and recommendations issued from a staid research institution such as McLean. McLean is routinely ranked among the top three psychiatric hospitals in the United States, and its research program is the best endowed and largest of any private psychiatric hospital in the country. Any study bearing its imprimatur receives and deserves respectful attention. But this one strained credulity.

I requested a copy of "Listening to Boys' Voices" from McLean. A few days later, a thirty-page typed manuscript arrived. It had not been published, nor was it marked as about to be published. It had none of the usual properties of a professional research paper. Unlike most scientific papers, which alert readers to their limits, Pollack's was unabashedly extravagant, declaring that "these findings about boys are unprecedented in the literature of research psychology."[7]

Pollack said he had been moved to do his research on boys in great part because of the "startling findings" of Gilligan and others on girls, which had awakened "our nation . . . from its gender slumbers," alerting us to "the plight of adolescent girls lacking for voice and a coherent sense of self . . . many sinking into a depressive joyless existence." Except for Pollack's adulatory references to Carol Gilligan and Nancy Chodorow for their "profound insights," the manuscript contained not a single footnote referencing "the literature of research psychology" to which he was making an unprecedented addition, or any other prior research. And his own research, interpretations, and reporting were eerily similar to Gilligan's loose, impressionistic methods.

Pollack's discovery of a boy crisis with national implications was based on a battery of vaguely described tests administered to 150 boys. He gives no explanation of how the boys had been selected or whether they constituted anything like a representative sample. And even if we disregard the limitations of the database, the findings appeared on first impression to be anything but grim and unprecedented.

On several of the tests he and his group administered, most of the 150 boys showed themselves to be healthy and well-adjusted. A self-esteem test found them confident. The Beck Depression Inventory, a widely used psychological assessment tool, uncovered "little or no clinical depression."[8] In private interviews, the boys said they were close to their families and enjoyed strong friendships with both males and females. Something called the King & King's Sex-Role Egalitarianism Scale found the vast majority of them agreeing that "there should be equal pay for equal work," "men should share in the housework," and "men should express their feelings."[9]

Pollack, however, repeatedly warns readers not to be fooled by such seemingly encouraging results. By interviewing boys and giving them tests that measure "unconscious attitudes," he claims to have found a truer picture, one of forlorn, alienated, and unconfident boys: "The results of this study of 'normal' everyday boys were deeply disturbing. They showed that while boys on the surface pretend to be doing 'fine,' beneath the outward bravado—what I have called the 'mask of masculinity'—many of our sons are in crisis." [10]

In one probe of the boys' "deeper unconscious processes," Pollack used a "modified" Thematic Apperception Test (TAT). In TAT tests, subjects are shown ambiguous pictures of people and scenes and asked to describe them; it is assumed that subjects will project their own hopes and fears into the pictures. Pollack and his colleagues presented the boys with a series of drawings and asked them to write stories about them. One drawing depicts a young, blond-haired boy sitting by himself in the open doorway of an old, wooden house. The sun is shining on the boy, but a shadow eclipses the interior of the house. Pollack was alarmed by the boys' responses.

"What was shocking," he wrote, "was that *sixty percent* interpreted the picture as that of an *abandoned boy*, an *isolated child* or a *victim* of adult mistreatment" [11] (emphasis in the original). Pollack saw the children's stories as corroboration for the Gilligan/Chodorow thesis about early maternal abandonment: "The high percentage of stories featuring themes of abandonment, loneliness, and isolation, I believe, is suggestive of subconscious memories of premature traumatic separation." [12]

Pollack called his test a "modified" TAT. Modified how? He did not say. Even if it were accurate to say that the boys' reaction to the picture suggested feelings of loneliness and isolation, it is quite a leap to attribute their response to an early separation trauma. Before concluding that the boys' stories are the effect of premature independence from mothers, we would need to know whether other groups—say, a group of girls or of adult female psychologists—would have similarly "shocking" reactions to Pollack's modified TAT. Pollack makes no mention of control groups. In any case, before projecting his findings onto the entire population of American boys, he would need to establish that the boys he was testing were a representative sample.

It is worth mentioning that Pollack's claimed discovery of an early and devastating separation trauma for boys contradicts findings of the American Psychiatric Association. Its official diagnostic guidebook, *DSM-IV*, says that separation anxiety disorder afflicts no more than 4 percent of children and more girls than boys. Furthermore, the disorder does not appear to be related to a premature separation from one's mother. "Children with [this disorder]," says *DSM-IV*, "tend to come from families that are close knit."[13]

Pollack also expressed concern about the boys' apparent confusion about masculinity. A high percentage of his boys agreed with statements such as:

- "It is essential for a guy to get respect."
- "Men are always ready for sex."[14]

He pointed out that these are the very same boys who said they believed "men and women deserve equal pay" and "boys and girls should both be allowed to express feelings." Pollack took these responses as evidence that the boys are hostage to a "double standard of masculinity." He concluded, "These boys reveal a dangerous psychological fissure: a split in their sense of what it means to become a man."[15]

This is unpersuasive, to put it mildly. We might well find teenage girls telling us that "it is essential for a girl to get respect." As for "Men are always ready for sex," why should any psychologist find it startling that adolescent boys agree with that? There is massive evidence—anthropological, psychological, even endocrinological, abundantly corroborated by everyday experience—that males are, on the whole, primed for sex and more ready to casually engage in it than females are. And this begins in adolescence. One well-known experiment compared male and female college students' responses to invitations to have casual sex from an attractive stranger of the opposite sex. Seventy percent of males said, "Okay, let's do it," and almost all seemed comfortable with the request. Of the females, 100 percent said, "No," and a majority felt insulted by the proposal.[16]

To recognize that males tend to welcome sexual opportunities is not to say that boys endorse an exploitative promiscuity. Given the biological changes boys are undergoing, their eagerness is natural and not unhealthy. On the other hand, society correctly demands that they suppress what is natural in favor of what is moral. So most parents try to teach their sons to practice responsible restraint. Pollack regards the boys' positive response to "Men are always ready for sex" as an indication that something is deeply wrong with them. While this response may indicate some confusion among today's young men about right and wrong, nothing in it suggests any kind of psychological disorder. Pollack's reaction tells us more about his own limitations as a reliable guide to the nature of boys than it does about what boys are really like.

In sum, Pollack's paper does not present a single persuasive piece of evidence for a national boy crisis. I do not know whether "Listening to Boys' Voices" was ever submitted for publication in a professional journal. Its sparse data and its strident and implausible conclusions render it unpublishable as a scholarly article.

Why did a research institute such as McLean give what amounts to a seal of approval to such dubious research? The press release speaks of "findings" and "correlations" and gives readers the impression that "Listening to Boys' Voices" is a study that meets McLean/Harvard standards for responsible, data-backed research. McLean requires investigators to submit research projects to a twelve-member institutional review board for approval. According to Geena Murphy, a member of this board, approval is granted "on the basis of the study's scientific merit."

Pollack's study, with its outsized claims and lack of evidence, could hardly have been approved on the basis of scientific merit. How did it get past the board? In conversations with psychiatrists, I learned that because of managed care, hospitals, administrators, and staff are continuously looking for ways to generate revenue and publicity for their institutions. Members of the McLean Institutional Review Board might have decided that an attention-grabbing "boys-are-in-crisis study" produced by its own "Center for Men," would bring favorable attention to the hospital. If so, scientific merit, usually indispensable for a McLean study, may have been compromised.

I asked Dr. Bruce Cohen, chief psychiatrist at McLean, how Pollack's "research" had managed to receive McLean's endorsement and was told, "I prefer not to talk about this at this time." Had he read Pollack's study? I asked. "I don't read every study that comes out of McLean," he answered. I explained that this study was quite unusual. Pollack claims to have uncovered a national crisis; his findings are "unprecedented in the literature of research psychology." Surely that must have come to Dr. Cohen's notice. I asked how it was that, without having reviewed Pollack's evidence, McLean had issued a press release giving Pollack's work the cachet of genuine science. Cohen told me someone would get back to me. But before he hung up, I asked him for his opinion "as a clinician" of Pollack's description of the nation's boys as "young Hamlets who succumb to an inner state of Denmark." "That's in there?" he asked, in the worried tone of a high school principal inquiring about what seniors have put in the yearbook.

The next day, I received a call from Roberta Shaw, director of public relations at McLean. She explained that the decision to issue a press release had been based on the "news value" of the study. "We ask ourselves, 'Is it of public interest?'" She also assured me that Pollack "had several journals interested in publishing his study." She didn't know what they were. She suggested I call him directly. I did, but he never returned the call.

Universities such as Harvard are clearly uncomfortable with the use of their names to confer prestige on dubious work. In October 1998, Harvard announced a new policy barring faculty members from labeling their work as sponsored or endorsed by Harvard without the express permission of the dean or provost. As the Associated Press reported, "Many institutions in the Ivy League have found themselves . . . linked to disputed data or research."[17] Yale faced the same problem, and now anyone who wants to use the phrase "Yale University study" must get permission from the university's director of licensing. McLean might consider establishing a similar requirement for its researchers.

The Media Blitz

Even before the shootings in Littleton, Colorado, news organizations around the country were carrying stories about new research on the nation's anguished boys, citing Harvard and McLean scholars as authorities. In March

1998, the *Washington Post* ran a front-page story about the "plight of young males." It quoted Barney Brawer, Carol Gilligan's former partner at the Harvard Project on Women's Psychology, Boys' Development and the Culture of Manhood, who said, "An enormous crisis of men and boys is happening before our eyes without our seeing it . . . an extraordinary shift in the plate tectonics of gender."[18]

In a May 1998 *Newsweek* cover story on boys, Pollack warned readers, "Boys are in silent crisis. The only time we notice is when they pull the trigger."[19] ABC's *20/20* aired a segment on Pollack and his disturbing message, "Why Boys Hide Their Emotions."[20] *People* ran a profile of Pollack in which he explained how boys who massacre their schoolmates are the "tip of the iceberg, the extreme end of one large crisis."[21]

On July 15, 1998, Maria Shriver interviewed Pollack on the NBC *Today* show. He informed the program's mass audience of the results of his research:

Shriver: You say there is really a silent crisis going on with, quote, "normal boys." As a parent of a young boy, that concerns me, scares me a lot.

Pollack: Well, absolutely. In addition to the national crisis, the boys who pick up guns, the boys who are suicidal and homicidal, the boys next door or the boy living in the room next door is also, I have found in my research, isolated, feeling lonely, can't express his feelings. And that happens because of the way we bring boys up.

Pollack's easy slide from "boys who pick up guns" to "the boy next door"—who, he assures us, are not very different inside—scared a lot of parents. This slide from abnormal boys to normal ones is, of course, illegitimate. There is not a shred of evidence in Pollack's research that justifies his "tip of the iceberg," "boys-are-in-crisis" hypothesis. Yet Pollack tossed it into the media echo chamber.

In an earlier interview (March 28), Jack Ford, the cohost of NBC's *Saturday Today*, asked Pollack, "Should I sit down with my eleven-year-old son and say to him, 'Look at what happened here down in Arkansas. Let me tell you why. Part of it is your makeup, part of it is how we've been bringing you up. Now let's sort of work through this together,' or is it too late for that?"

Pollack did not tell Ford that it would be wrong to suggest to his son that he too is capable of killing people. Instead he replied: "I think we should do that with eleven-year-old boys. I think we should start with two- and three- and four- and five-year-old boys and not push them . . . from their mothers."[22]

This is a remarkable exchange—one that would be inconceivable if the children under discussion were girls. No one takes disturbed young women like Susan Smith (who made headlines in 1994 when she drowned her two sons by pushing her car into a lake) or Melissa Drexler (the New Jersey teenager who, in 1997, gave birth to a healthy baby at her senior prom, strangled him, and threw him in a trash bin) as tip-of-the-iceberg exemplars of American young women. Girl criminals are never taken to be representative of girls in general. But when the boy reformers generalize from school killers to "our sons," they're including your son and mine as well as Jack Ford's and Maria Shriver's. Would it ever occur to Jack Ford to ask a psychologist whether he should sit down with his daughter and say to her, "Look at what happened at that New Jersey prom . . . Part of it is your makeup, part of it is how we've been bringing you up. Now let's sort of work through this together"?

Pollack sees the killer boys at the extreme end of a continuum that includes "everyday boys." To the contrary, what is typically striking about killer boys is their extreme abnormality. Thirteen-year-old Mitchell Johnson, one of the two Jonesboro, Arkansas, shooters, practiced self-mutilation and was also undergoing court-ordered psychological counseling for molesting a two-year old girl.[23] Kip Kinkel, the fifteen-year-old boy who shot classmates in Springfield, Oregon, had been diagnosed with major depressive disorder. The night before the school shooting, he killed his parents and spent the night in his house with their dead bodies, playing opera music from *Romeo and Juliet* continuously. As for the Columbine High killers, they were sociopaths inspired by the example of Timothy McVeigh, the domestic terrorist who blew up the Oklahoma City Federal Building, killing 168 people and injuring 680.[24]

By putting all boys "pushed from their mothers" onto a continuum with the school shooters, Pollack does not adequately distinguish between healthy and unhealthy young men. Before we call for radical changes in the way we rear our male children, we ought to ask the boy reformers to tell us why there are so many seemingly healthy boys who, despite having been "pushed from their mothers," are nonviolent, morally responsible human beings. How do those who say boys are disturbed account for the fact that in any given year less than one half of 1 percent of males under eighteen are arrested for a violent crime?[25]

With the help of the media, Pollack's explanation for adolescent male violence in schools contributes to the national climate of prejudice against boys. That is surely not his intention. It is, however, an inevitable consequence of his sensationalizing approach to boys—treating healthy boys as if they were abnormal and abnormal, lethally violent boys as "the extreme end of one large pattern."[26]

A Nation of Hamlets and Ophelias

In regarding seemingly normal children as abnormally afflicted, Pollack was taking the well-trodden path pioneered by Carol Gilligan and Mary Pipher. Gilligan had described the nation's girls as drowning, disappearing, traumatized, and undergoing various kinds of "psychological foot-binding." Following Gilligan, Mary Pipher, in *Reviving Ophelia*, had written of the selves of girls going down in flames, "crashing and burning." Pollack's *Real Boys* continues in this vein: "Hamlet fared little better than Ophelia. . . . He grew increasingly isolated, desolate, and alone, and those who loved him were never able to get through to him. In the end he died a tragic and unnecessary death."[27]

By using Ophelia and Hamlet as symbols, Pipher and Pollack paint a picture of American children as disturbed and in need of rescue. But once one discounts the anecdotal, scientifically vacuous reports that have issued from the Harvard Graduate School of Education and the McLean Hospital's Center for Men, there remains no reason to believe that girls or boys are in crisis. Mainstream researchers see no evidence of it.[28] To be sure, adolescence is a time of some "inner turmoil"—for boys and girls, in America and everywhere else, from time immemorial. But American children, boys as well as girls, are on the whole psychologically sound. They are not isolated, full of despair, or "hiding parts of themselves from the world's gaze"—no more so, at least, than any other age group in the population.

One wonders why the irresponsible and baseless claims that girls and boys are psychologically fractured have been so uncritically received by the media and the public. One reason, perhaps, is that Americans seem all too ready to entertain almost any suggestion that a large group of outwardly normal people are suffering from some pathological affliction. By 1999, bestselling books had successively identified women, girls, and boys as being mentally anguished and in need of rescue. Then, in late 1999, Susan Faludi's *Stiffed: The Betrayal of the American Man* called our attention to yet another segment of the population that no one had previously realized was in serious psychological trouble: adult men.[29] Faludi claims to have unmasked a "masculinity crisis" so severe and pervasive, she finds it hard to understand why men do not rise up in rebellion.

Although Faludi seems to have arrived at her view of men without having read Pollack's analysis of boys, her conclusions about men are identical to his about boys. She claims that men are suffering because the culture imposes stultifying myths and ideals of manliness. *Stiffed* shows us the hapless baby-boomer males, burdened "with dangerous prescriptions of manhood,"[30] trying vainly to cope with a world in which they are bound to fail. Men have been taught that "to be a man means to be at the controls and at all times to feel yourself in control."[31] They cannot live up to this stoical ideal of manliness. At the same time, our "misogynist culture" now imposes its humiliating "ornamental" demands on men as well as women. "No wonder," says Faludi, "men are in such agony."[32]

What is Faludi's evidence of an "American masculinity crisis"? She talked to *dozens* of unhappy men, among them wife batterers in Long Beach, California, distressed male pornography stars, and teenage sex predators known as the Spur Posse. Most of Faludi's subjects have sad stories to tell about inadequate fathers, personal alienation, and feelings of helplessness. But she never tells us why the disconsolate men she selected for attention should be regarded as representative.

If men are experiencing the agonies Faludi speaks of, they are doing so with remarkable equanimity. The National Opinion Research Center at the University of Chicago, which has been tracking levels of general happiness and life satisfaction since 1957, consistently finds that approximately 90 percent of Americans describe themselves as happy with their lives, with no significant differences between men and women.[33] When I asked its survey director, Tom Smith, if there had been any unusual signs of distress among men in the last few decades—the years in which Faludi claims that a generation of men have seen "all their hopes and dreams burn up on the launch pad."[34] Smith replied, "There have been no trends in a negative direction during those years." But Faludi believes otherwise and joins Gilligan, Pollack, and the others in calling for a "new paradigm" of how to be men.

Faludi cites the work of Dr. Darrel Regier, director of the Division of Epidemiology at the National Institute of Mental Health, to support her thesis that men are increasingly unhappy.[35] I asked Dr. Regier what he thought of her men-are-in-distress claim. "I am not sure where she gets her evidence for any substantial rise in male distress." He was surprised that one of his own 1988 studies was cited by Faludi as evidence for an increase in "anxiety, depressive disorders, suicide." "Well," Dr. Regier said, "that is a fallacy. The article shows no such thing."[36] What does he think of these false mental health scares? I asked. "I guess they sell books," he said.

Apocalyptic alarms about looming mental health disasters do sell well. In a satirical article entitled "A Nation of Nuts," *New York Observer* editor Jim Windolf tallied the number of Americans allegedly suffering from some kind of mental disorder. He sent away for brochures and literature of dozens of advocacy agencies and mental health organizations. Then he did the math. "If you believe the statistics," Windolf reported, "77 percent of America's adult population is a mess. . . . And we haven't even thrown in alien abductees, road ragers, and internet addicts."[37] If you factor in Gilligan's and Pipher's hapless girls, Pollack's suffering and dangerous boys, and Faludi's agonized men, the figure must be very close to 100 percent.

Gilligan, Pipher, Pollack, and Faludi all find abnormality and inner anguish in an outwardly normal and happy population. Each traces the malaise to the "male culture," which forces harmful gender stereotypes, myths, or "masks" on the population in crisis—women, girls, boys, and men. Girls and women are constrained to be "nice and kind"; boys and men are constrained to be "in control" and emotionally disconnected. Each writer projects an air of sympathy, and of earnest desire to rescue the anguished casualties of our patriarchal culture. But the Gilligan-Pipher-Pollack-Faludi construct creates a serious problem. By taking a small, unhappy minority as representative of an entire group, the writers present the groups themselves as pitiable, incompetent, and unworthy of respect. Pollack, for example, wants to rescue boys from "the myths of boyhood," but unwittingly harms them by arousing public fear, dismay, and suspicion. In characterizing boys as "Hamlets," he stigmatizes an entire sex and age group. His seemingly benign project of reconnecting boys to their inner nurturers pressures boys to be more like girls. The effect is to put boys on the defensive—not an incidental effect, as we shall see.

Boys Out of Touch

I have inveighed against the large, extreme, and irresponsible claims of the crisis writers, pointing out that no credible evidence backs them up. What about their more moderate and seemingly reasonable assertions? Gilligan and Pollack speak of boys as hiding their humanity and submerging their sensitivity. They suggest that apparently healthy boys are emotionally repressed and out of touch with their feelings. Is that true?

When my son David was thirteen, he sometimes showed the kind of emotional disengagement that worries the boy reformers. He came to me one evening when he was in the seventh grade, utterly confused by his homework assignment. Like many contemporary English and social studies textbooks, his book, *Write Source 2000*, was chock-full of exercises designed to improve children's self-esteem and draw them out emotionally.[38] "Mom, what do they want?" David asked. He had read a short story in which one character always compared himself to another. Here are the questions David had to answer:

- Do you often compare yourself with someone?
- Do you compare to make yourself feel better?
- Does your comparison ever make you feel inferior?

Another set of questions asked about profanity in the story:

- How do you feel about [the main character's] choice of words?
- Do you curse? Why? When? Why not?
- Does cursing make you feel more powerful? Are you feeling a bit uneasy about discussing cursing? Why? Why not?

The *Write Source 2000 Teacher's Guide* suggests grading students on a scale from 1 to 10: 10 for a student who is "intensely engaged," down to a 1 for a student who "does not engage at all." My son did not engage at all. Here is how he answered:

Do you often compare yourself with someone?
"Sometimes."

Do you compare to make yourself feel better?
"No. I do not."

Does your comparison ever make you feel inferior?
"No."

I was amused by his terse replies. But in the spirit of Gilligan and Pollack, the authors of *Write Source 2000* might see them as signs of emotional shutdown. Toy manufacturers know about boys' reluctance to engage in social interactions. They have never been able to interest boys in the kinds of interactive social games that girls love. In the computer game Talk with Me Barbie, Barbie develops a personal relationship with the player: she learns her name and chats with her about dating, careers, and playing house. These Barbie games are among the all-time bestselling interactive games. But boys don't buy them.

Males, whether young or old, are on the whole, less interested than females in talking about feelings and personal relationships. In one experiment, researchers at Northeastern University analyzed college students' conversations at the cafeteria table. They found that young women were far more likely to discuss intimates: close friends, boyfriends, family members. "Specifically," say the authors, "56 percent of the women's targets but only 25 percent of the men's targets were friends and relatives."[39] This is just one study, but it is backed up by massive evidence of distinct male and female interests and preferences.

In another study, boys and girls differed in how they perceived objects and people.[40] Researchers simultaneously presented male and female college students with two images on a stereoscope: one of an object, the other of a person. Asked to say what they saw, the male subjects saw the object more often than they saw the person; the female subjects saw the person more often than they saw the object. In addition, dozens of experiments confirm that women are much better than men at judging emotions based on the expression on a stranger's face.[41]

These differences have motivated the gender specialists at the Harvard Graduate School of Education, the Wellesley Center, the Boys' Project at Tufts, and McLean Hospital's Center for Men to recommend that we all try to "reconnect" boys. But there is no evidence that boys need what they are offering. Would boys be improved if they were taught to be comfortable playing with Talk with Me Barbie? Are their preferences and attitudes signs of insensitivity and repression, or just innocent and healthy expressions of their inner nature?

If, as the evidence strongly suggests, the characteristic preferences and behaviors of males and females are expressions of innate differences, the differences in emotional styles will be difficult or impossible to eliminate. In any case, why should anyone make it their business to eliminate them?

The gender experts will reply that boys' relative taciturnity puts them and others in harm's way; in support they adduce their own research. But that research is flawed. There is no good reason to believe that boys as a group are emotionally endangered; nor is there reason to think that the typical male reticence is some kind of disorder in need of treatment. In fact, the boy reformers such as Pollack, Gilligan, and their followers need to consider the possibility that male stoicism and reserve may well be traits to be encouraged, not vices or psychological weaknesses to be overcome.

A Plea for Reticence

The argument in favor of saving boys by reconnecting them emotionally rests on the popular assumption that repressing emotions is harmful, while giving discursive vent to them is, on the whole, healthy. Psychologists have recently begun to examine the supposition that speaking out and declaring one's feelings is better than holding them in. Jane Bybee, a psychologist at Suffolk University in Boston, studied a group of high school students, classifying them as "repressors" (those not focused on their inner states), "sensitizers" (those keenly aware of their moods and feelings), or "intermediates." She then had the students evaluate themselves and others using these distinctions. She also had the teachers evaluate the students. She found that the "repressors" were less anxious, more confident, and more successful academically and socially. Bybee's conclusion is tentative: "In our day-to-day behavior it may be good not to be so emotional and needy. The moods of repressed people may be more balanced."[42]

In 2012, University of Missouri psychologist Amanda Rose and her coauthors published a study in *Child Development* that tested the Gilligan/Pollack assumption that boys were fearful and ashamed of sharing their feelings with others.[43] Rose and her colleagues surveyed and observed nearly two thousand children and adolescents and found that boys and girls have very different expectations about the *value* of problem talk. Girls were more likely to report that personal disclosure made them feel cared for and understood. Boys, overall, found it to be a waste of time—and "weird." Contra Pollack and Gilligan, boys did not feel embarrassed about sharing feelings and were not filled with angst about being ridiculed or teased for being weak or unmasculine. Instead, said the lead author Amanda Rose, "boys' responses suggest they just don't see talking about problems to be a particularly useful activity." [44] Rose has sound advice for parents. If you want your son to be more forthcoming, it won't help to make him feel "safe" about sharing confidence. You will have to persuade him that it serves a practical purpose. As for daughters, she warns, excessive problem talk is linked to anxiety and depression. "So girls should know that talking about problems isn't the only way to cope."

It is worth noting that in most past and present societies, "repression" of private feelings has often been regarded as a social virtue. From a historical perspective, the burden of proof rests on those who believe that being openly expressive makes people better and healthier. That view has become a dogma of contemporary American popular culture, but in most cultures— including, until quite recently, our own—reticence and stoicism are regarded as commendable, while the free expression of emotions is often seen as self-centered and immature.

Pollack, who is a champion of emotional expressiveness, instructs parents, "Let boys know that they don't need to be 'sturdy oaks.'" To encourage boys to be stoical, says Pollack, is to harm them: "The boy is often pushed to 'act like a man,' to be the one who is confident and unflinching. No boy should be called upon to be the tough one. No boy should be harmed in this way." [45]

But Pollack needs to show, not merely assert, that it harms a child to be "called upon to be tough." Why shouldn't boys—or for that matter, girls—try to be sturdy oaks? All of the world's major religions place stoical control of emotions at the center of their moral teachings. For Buddhists, the ideal is emotional detachment; for Confucianism, dispassionate control. Nor is "Be in touch with your feelings" one of the Ten Commandments. Judeo-

Christian teaching enjoins attentiveness to the emotional needs and feelings of others—not one's own.

The insights of the save-the-male psychologists into the inner world of boys are by no means self-evident; nor is it at all obvious that their emotivist proposals would benefit boys. Boys' aggressive tendencies do need to be checked. But the boy reformers have not proved that they have the recipe for civilizing boys and restraining their rough natures. Before the gender experts at the Harvard Graduate School of Education and the practitioners of the new male psychology are given broad license to reprogram our sons to be "sensitizers" rather than repressors, they should first be required to show that the repairs they are so anxious to make are beneficial and not injurious.

These reform-minded experts should seriously consider the possibility that American children may in fact need more, not less, self-control and less, not more, self-involvement. It may be that American boys don't need to be more emotional—and that American girls do need to be less sentimental and self-absorbed.

The Culture of Therapy

The British writer and social critic Fay Weldon has coined the useful, if somewhat ungainly, term *therapism* for the popular doctrine that almost all personal troubles can be cured by talk.[46] Weldon is more concerned with therapism as a pop phenomenon than an educational practice; but in either sphere, talk therapy, once primarily a private therapeutic technique, has gone public in ways undreamed of in Sigmund Freud's philosophy.[47]

Strangers, proudly in touch with their feelings, share their innermost thoughts and experiences with one another. Talk-show participants make intensely personal disclosures to wildly applauding audiences. The endless stream of confessional memoirs, the self-esteem movement, the textbooks and questionnaires that probe children's innermost feelings are all manifestations of a profound and rampant therapism.

The contemporary faith in the value of openness and the importance of sharing one's feelings is now so much a part of popular culture that we find even such staid organizations as the Girl Scouts of America giving patches for being open about grief. *Lingua Franca* writer Emily Nussbaum reports that "a Girl Scout troop in New York instituted a 'grief patch' in 1993— troop members could earn this epaulette by sharing a painful feeling with one another, writing stories and poems about death and loss and meeting with bereavement counselors."[48]

One sector in our society has so far been highly resistant to therapism: little boys are no more interested in earning "grief patches" than they are eager to interact personally with dolls. When homework assignments require them to explore their deeper feelings about a text, it is likely that they will not engage. I suspect that efforts to get little boys to be more overtly emotional rarely succeed. But I do not discount the powers of the would-be reformers to wreak a great deal of harm and grief by trying.

All through the 1990s, *self-esteem* was the education buzzword. Everyone needed it; many demanded it for their children or pupils as a basic human right. But the excesses of those who promoted techniques for increasing students' self-esteem provide a cautionary example of what can happen when teachers, counselors, and education theorists, armed with good intentions and specious social science (for one thing, no one agrees on what self-esteem is or how to measure it), turn classrooms into encounter groups.

It has never been shown that "high self-esteem" is a good trait for students to possess. Meanwhile, researchers have uncovered a worrisome correlation between inflated self-esteem and juvenile delinquency. As Brad Bushman, an Iowa State University psychologist, explains, "If kids develop unrealistic opinions of themselves and those views are rejected by others, the kids are potentially dangerous."[49]

John Hewitt, a University of Massachusetts sociologist, has examined the morality of the self-esteem movement in a fine scholarly book called *The Myth of Self-Esteem*. Hewitt documents the exponential growth of self-esteem articles and programs from 1982 to 1996.[50] He points to the ethical hazards of using the classroom for therapeutic purposes. In a typical class-room self-esteem exercise, students complete sentences beginning "I love myself because . . ." or "I feel bad about myself because . . ." Hewitt explains that children interpret these assignments as *demands* for self-revelation. They feel pressed to complete the sentences "correctly" in ways the teacher finds satisfactory. As Hewitt acutely observes, "Teachers . . . no doubt regard the exercises as being in the best interest of their students. . . . Yet from a more skeptical perspective these exercises are subtle instruments of social control. The child *must* be taught to like himself or herself. . . . The child *must* con-fess self-doubt or self-loathing, bringing into light the feelings that he or she might prefer to keep private"[51] (emphasis in original).

Far from being harmless, these therapeutic practices are unacceptably prying. Surely school children have a right not to be subjected to the psycho-logical manipulations of both self-esteem educators and the reformers intent on getting boys to disclose their emotions in the way girls often do.

Therapism versus Stoicism

The vast majority of American boys and girls are psychologically healthy. On the other hand, there is strong evidence that they are morally and academi-cally undernourished. Every society confronts the difficult and complex task of civilizing its children, teaching them self-discipline and instilling in them a sense of right and wrong. The problem is old, and the workable solution is known—character education in a sound learning environment. The known, tested solution does not include therapeutic pedagogies.

Children need to be moral more than they need to be in touch with their feelings. They need to be well educated more than they need classroom self-esteem exercises and support groups. Nor are they improved by having their femininity or masculinity "reinvented." Emotional fixes are not the answer. Genuine self-esteem comes with pride in achievement, which is the fruit of disciplined effort.

American boys do not need to be rescued. They are not pathological. They are not seething with repressed rage or imprisoned in "straitjackets of masculinity." American girls are not suffering a crisis of confidence; nor are they being silenced by the culture. But when it comes to the genuine problems that do threaten our children's prospects—their moral drift, their cognitive and scholastic deficits—the healers, social reformers, and confidence builders don't have the answers. On the contrary, they stand in the way of genuine solutions.

7

Why Johnny Can't, Like, Read and Write

There is a much-told story in education circles about a now-retired Chicago public school teacher, Mrs. Daugherty. She was a dedicated sixth-grade teacher who could always be counted on to bring out the best in her students. But one year she found her class nearly impossible to control. The students were noisy, unmanageable, and seemingly unteachable. She began to worry that many of them had learning disabilities. When the principal was out of town, she did something teachers were not supposed to: she went to his office and looked in a special file where students' IQ scores were recorded. To her amazement, she discovered that a majority of the students were significantly above average in intelligence. A quarter of the class had IQs in the high 120s (124, 127, 129), several in the 130s, and one of the worst classroom culprits was in fact brilliant: he had an IQ of 145.

Mrs. Daugherty was angry at herself for having felt sorry for them and for expecting so little from them. Things soon changed. She increased the difficulty of the work, doubled the homework, and ran the class with uncompromising discipline. Slowly but perceptibly, the students' performance improved. By the end of the year, this class of former ne'er-do-wells was among the best behaved and highest performing of the sixth-grade classes.

The principal was delighted. He was well aware of this infamous sixth-grade class and its less-than-stellar reputation, so at the end of the year he called Mrs. Daugherty into his office to ask what she had done. She felt compelled to tell him the truth. The principal listened attentively and immediately forgave her. He congratulated her. But then he said, "I think you should know, Mrs. Daugherty, those numbers next to the children's names—those are not their IQ scores. Those are their locker numbers." [1]

The moral of the story: Strict standards are good. Demanding and expecting excellence can only benefit the student. These were once truisms of education. Even today, setting and enforcing high standards for students is uncontroversial, at least as a general principle. Who would question the need for challenging work, high expectations, and strict discipline? The sad answer is that a lot of education experts are skeptical about what they see as old-fashioned pedagogy, and their theories have the effect of relaxing standards and expectations. Rousseauian romanticism, in the form of progressive education, remains a powerful force in American schools. The departure from structure, competition, discipline, and skill-and-fact-based learning has been harmful to all children—but it appears to have exacted an especially high toll on boys.

Knowledge Acquisition versus Jazz Improvisation

Progressive pedagogues pride themselves on fostering creativity and enhancing children's self-esteem. Strict discipline and the old-fashioned "dry-knowledge" approach are said to accomplish the opposite: to inhibit creativity and leave many students with feelings of inadequacy. Progressives frown on teacher-led classrooms with fact-based learning, memorization, phonics, and drills. Trainees in the schools of education are enjoined to "Teach the student, not the subject!" and are inspired by precepts like "[Good teaching] is not vase-filling; rather it is fire-lighting." [2]

In this "child-centered" model, the teacher is supposed to remain in the background so that students have the chance to develop as "independent learners." Drill and rote have no place in a style of education focused on freeing "the creative potential of the child." One prominent champion of progressivism, Alfie Kohn, author of *The Schools Our Children Deserve* and *Punished by Rewards*, suggests the modern cooperative classroom should resemble a musical jam session: "Cooperative learning not only offers instruments to everyone in the room, but invites jazz improvisation."[3]

Child-centered, progressive education has been prevalent in American schools of education since the 1920s. According to University of Virginia education scholar E. D. Hirsch Jr., the "knowledge-based approach currently employed in the most advanced nations [has been] eschewed in our own schools for more than half a century."[4] With the exception of a brief period in the late 1950s and early 1960s (when the Soviet Union's success with Sputnik generated fears that an inadequate math and science curriculum was a threat to national security), the fashion in education has been to downplay basic skills, knowledge acquisition, competitive grading, and discipline. This fashion has opened a worrisome education gap that finds American students falling behind their counterparts in other countries.[5]

In recent years, a growing number of British and Australian educators became convinced that progressive methods in education are a prime reason that their male students are so far behind the girls. There is now a concerted movement in both countries to improve boys' educational prospects by going back to a traditional pedagogy. Many British educational leaders believe that the modern classroom fails boys by being too unstructured and permissive and hostile to the spirit of competition that so often provides boys with the incentive to learn and excel.

Why the special focus on boys in Britain and Australia? Leaders in both countries view widespread male underachievement as a threat to their national futures. The workplace has changed radically in the past few decades. Today, solid math and reading skills are prerequisites for success. Boys who lack them will face a bleak future, and nations with too many languishing males risk losing their economic edge. As Gavin Barwell, British MP, explained in a 2012 report on male literacy: "Literacy is a significant issue for us all . . . due to the demands of an increasingly complex workplace. We need to act to ensure all our children fulfill their potential and contribute to making the UK economy globally competitive."[6] Closing the boy achievement gap has been at the forefront of Britain's and Australia's national agendas for more than a decade.

By contrast, the looming prospect of an underclass of badly educated, barely literate American boys has yet to become a cause for open concern among American educators or political leaders. In a 1995 article in *Science*, University of Chicago education researchers Larry Hedges and Amy Nowell discussed the bleak employment outlook for the "generally larger number of males who perform near the bottom . . . in reading and writing."[7] That employment outlook is even bleaker today. In March 2010 the Center on Education Policy, an independent research center that advocates for public education, released a comprehensive, state-by-state analysis:

> Consistent with other recent research, our analysis of state test results by gender suggests that the most pressing issue related to gender gaps is the lagging performance of boys in reading. . . . Researchers and state officials might investigate ways in which the school environment may be changed to better address the needs of boys.[8]

So far, neither state nor federal officials seem inclined to take that suggestion. That must change. As Massachusetts Institute of Technology economist Lester Thurow has pointed out, "Within the developed world, the under-educated and under-skilled are going to be left out, or perhaps more accurately, thrown out of the global game."[9] How do we turn things around? The first thing we should do is to follow the example of the British and the Australians. Their efforts can be summarized in a few words: Bring back teachers like Mrs. Daugherty.

British and Australian Initiatives

In the mid-1990s, British newspapers were full of stories about the distressing scholastic deficits of the nation's schoolboys. The *Times* of London warned of the prospect of "an underclass of permanently unemployed, unskilled men." [10] "What's Wrong with Boys?" asked the *Glasgow Herald*. [11] The *Economist* referred to boys as "tomorrow's second sex." [12] In Britain, the public, the government, and the education establishment are well aware of the increasing numbers of underachieving young males and they started looking for ways to help them. They had a name for them—the "sink group"—and they called what ails them "laddism."

A council of British headmasters and headmistresses organized a clearinghouse for information on effective classroom practices and programs for boys. *Can Boys Do Better?* is its 1997 summary of what works best for boys. [13] Here is a partial list of the approaches that these practitioners deemed effective for boys:

- More teacher-led work
- A structured environment
- High expectations
- Strict homework checks
- Consistently applied sanctions if work is not done
- Greater emphasis on silent work
- Frequent testing
- Single-sex classes

The British headmasters called for "silent" (solitary) reflection and study and warned against collaborative learning. The headmasters advised schools to avoid fanciful, "creative" assignments, noting, "Boys do not always see the intrinsic worth of 'Imagine you're a sock in a dustbin.' They want relevant work." [14] Nor are the British headmasters focused on students' self-esteem. They know that boys do better than girls on self-esteem questionnaires—but that gender gap does not strike them as evidence that the girls are being shortchanged. As Peter Downes, a former Scottish headteacher, dryly notes: "Boys swagger . . . while girls win the prizes." [15] He urges teachers to be brutally honest with boys about what life has in store for them if they continue to underperform academically.

Coed public schools throughout Great Britain also began experiment-

ing with all-male classes. In 1996, Ray Bradbury, the headteacher of Kings'
School in Winchester, was alarmed by the high failure rate of his male students. Seventy-eight percent of the girls were getting passing grades or better, compared with 56 percent of the boys. Bradbury identified the thirty
or so boys he thought to be at risk for failure and placed them together
in a class. He chose an athletic young male teacher he thought the boys
would like. The class was not "child-centered"; the pedagogy was strict and
old-fashioned. As Bradbury explained, "We consciously planned the teaching methodology. The class is didactic and teacher-fronted. It involves sharp
questions and answers and constantly checking for understanding. Discipline is clear-cut—if homework isn't presented, it is completed in a detention. There is no discussion." [16]

Here is how one visiting journalist describes a typical class: "Ranks of
boys in blazers face the front, giving full attention to the young teacher's
instructions. His style is uncompromising and inspirational. 'People think
that boys like you won't be able to understand writers such as the Romantic
poets. Well, you're going to prove them wrong. Do you understand?'" [17]

The teacher found that the boys in his single-sex class actively supported
one another with genuine team spirit. "When girls are present, boys are
loath to express opinions for fear of appearing sissy." He chose challenging
but male-appropriate readings: "Members of my group are football mad and
quite 'laddish.' In the mixed classes they would be turned off by *Jane Eyre,*
whereas I can pick texts such as *Silas Marner* and the War Poets." The initial
results were promising. In 1996, the boys were far behind the girls. By 1997,
after only a year in the special class, the boys had nearly closed the gap. As
one of the boys said, "We are all working hard to show we can be just as successful as the other groups." [18]

The authors of *Can Boys Do Better?* were careful not to claim too much.
"It should be stressed that many of these strategies [to help boys do better]
have only recently been implemented, and it is too early in many cases
to fully evaluate their effectiveness." [19] However, a follow-up study by the
National Foundation for Educational Research in 1999 (*Boys' Achievement,
Progress, Motivation and Participation*) supported the headmasters' key

propositions: "The following items all emerge as being important: highly structured lessons, more emphasis on teacher-led work, clear and firm deadlines, and short-term targets."[20] The same report noted that all-male classes and all-male schools may be "singularly well-placed to raise achievement among boys, as they could tailor their strategies directly to the needs of boys."[21]

The British are now well into a second generation of research and activism on the boy gap. They have not solved the problem of male underachievement, but they are closing in on solutions. Addressing boys' literacy is now at the top of the list—even for high government officials. In 2012, the Boys' Reading Commission issued a major, evidence-based report on how to engage more boys with the written word. The commission included ten members of Parliament, suggesting how seriously the British take the problem to be. Among its recommendations:

- Every teacher should have an up-to-date knowledge of reading materials that will appeal to disengaged boys;

- Every boy should have weekly support from a male reading role model;

- Parents need access to information on how successful schools are in supporting boys' literacy.[22]

To those who say that the main factor in literacy is social class, not gender, the report stated outright that "within like-for-like social class groupings, a gender gap of 10 percentage points is sustained."[23] And the report readily acknowledges sex differences: "It is clear from research, and to most people observing children, that there are cognitive differences between girls and boys."[24]

The British learned long ago that phonics (teaching beginning readers to learn the relationship between symbols and sounds) works better for boys than the "whole language" approach (where children learn to read "naturally" by seeing words in context). The report cites a now-famous 2005 seven-year study in the Scottish town of Clackmannanshire, which found that "after receiving an early grounding in synthetic phonics, boys significantly surpassed girls in word reading, and stayed ahead through the end of primary school. The same was true for the children's progress in spelling."[25] But phonics is only the first step. Further research revealed that though the phonics program taught boys the mechanics of reading, it did not improve their comprehension. For that, they need to be motivated to care about what they are reading. So the report stresses the importance of showing boys that reading is pleasurable.[26]

A color-coded chart in the commission report indicates children's reading preferences: girls prefer fiction, magazines, blogs, and poetry; boys like comics, nonfiction, and newspapers. "Boys were significantly more likely than girls to read science-fiction/fantasy, sports-related and war/spy books."[27] Such findings will be unsurprising to many, but the report notes that in a survey of 1,200 primary school teachers in the United Kingdom, only one teacher could name a significant writer for boys.[28] That was the reason for the commission's arresting recommendation that teachers should actually have knowledge of reading materials of interest to boys.[29]

In 2002, the Australian House of Representatives Standing Committee on Education and Training published *Boys: Getting It Right: Report on the Inquiry into the Education of Boys.* The report notes that earlier government inquiries on gender equity focused only on the needs of girls. That has to change, says the committee. What is more, the committee dismissed prior reports that called for transforming boys' masculinity. Like the British headmasters, the Australian committee members specifically rejected "the progressiveness of the 1970s" in favor of old-fashioned pedagogy.[30] Among the committee's recommendations:

- More structured activity;
- Greater emphasis on teacher-directed work;
- Clearly defined objectives and instructions;
- A return to the traditional phonics-based teaching of reading;
- More male role models.[31]

Australia has since launched an aggressive campaign on behalf of boys' education. In 2006, for example, it initiated Success for Boys. This program provided grants to 1,600 schools to incorporate boy-friendly methods into their daily practice.[32] In both England and Australia there are now websites and clearinghouses where teachers can find out what is working for boys. The British and Australians have not yet found a complete solution to the boy gap, but they are more than a decade ahead of us in the effort.

Back in the USA

American boys have a lot in common with their counterparts in England and Australia. In all three countries, boys are on the wrong side of an education gender gap. But there is one major difference: it is inconceivable that reports on the US boy gap would emanate from the US Congress. A Success for Boys campaign would create havoc in the United States. The women's lobby would rise in fury. The ACLU would find someone to sue. Legislators would face an avalanche of angry faxes, emails, petitions, and phone calls for taking part in a "backlash" against girls.

And imagine the uproar if the US Department of Education were to compile a list of boy-friendly reading materials, or even suggest that teachers might familiarize themselves with such things. That would be an affront to decades of "nonsexist" curriculum development. Mark Bauerlein, former director of research at the National Endowment for the Arts, and Sandra Stotsky, professor of education at the University of Arkansas, summed up "Why Johnny Won't Read" in a 2005 *Washington Post* op-ed:

> Unfortunately, the textbooks and literature assigned in the elementary grades do not reflect the dispositions of male students. Few strong and active male role models can be found as lead characters. Gone are the inspiring biographies of the most important American presidents, inventors, scientists and entrepreneurs. No military valor, no high adventure. On the other hand, stories about adventurous and brave women abound. Publishers seem to be more interested in avoiding "masculine"

perspectives or "stereotypes" than in getting boys to like what they are assigned to read.[33]

American legislators who followed the back-to-basics leadership of their British and Australian counterparts would enrage not only our women's lobby but our education establishment as well. According to a 2007 report by the Thomas B. Fordham Institute (an education think tank), all the best evidence shows that students need focused instruction in phonics, grammar, spelling, and punctuation. But an overwhelming number of schools of education—85 percent!—refuse to instruct future teachers in these methods.[34] Collaborative writing groups, creative self-expression, and "journaling"— soporifics for many boys—still take precedence.

The debate between traditionalists and progressives over how to teach language skills is an old one. Particularly frustrating, however, is that this debate has proceeded for decades in the United States without anyone taking serious notice of the fact that American boys are significantly less literate than girls. In an annual survey of college freshmen conducted by the Higher Education Research Institute at UCLA, students are asked how many hours per week they spent reading for pleasure during the preceding year. The 2010 results were consistent with other years: 36 percent of males answered "none." Among females, the figure was 22 percent.[35] Surely this pattern is worth attention; surely the question of "best practices" in teaching reading and writing should consider what works best for boys.

The federal government, state departments of education, and women's groups have spent many millions of dollars addressing a surreal self-esteem problem that allegedly afflicts girls more than boys. But in the matter of basic literacy, where we have a real and alarming difference between boys and girls, initiatives to close the gap are nowhere to be found. In education circles, it is acceptable to say that boys are psychologically distressed and in need of rescue from their emergent masculinity, but it is not acceptable to say that our schools are failing to teach boys how to read and write. The women's lobby is one thing, but it is dismaying that those professionally responsible for the education of our children should be so heedless of the needs of boys.

The Wider Background

A frieze on the façade of Horace Mann Hall of Columbia Teachers College celebrates nine great education pioneers. Among them are Johann Heinrich Pestalozzi (1746–1827), Johann Friedrich Herbart (1776–1841), and Friedrich Froebel (1782–1852). Few Americans know much about the profound influence that these eighteenth-century German and Swiss theorists have had on American education. Froebel, for example, is credited with inventing the concept of a kindergarten. The German word *kindergarten* literally means a garden whose plants are children. Froebel regarded children as fragile young plants and the ideal teacher as a gentle gardener:

> To young plants and animals we give space, and time, and rest, knowing that they will unfold to beauty by laws working in each. We avoid acting upon them by force, for we know that such intrusion upon their natural growth could injure their development. . . . Education and instruction should from the very first be passive, observant, protective, rather than prescribing, determining, interfering. . . . All training and instruction which prescribes and fixes, that is interferes with Nature, must tend to limit and injure.[36]

Froebel wrote these words almost two hundred years ago, but his plant child metaphor continues to inspire American educators. In the most straightforward sense, the plant metaphor is profoundly antieducational; after all, you can't teach a plant—all you can do is help it develop. Progressive educators oppose "interference" with the child's nature and look for ways to release its creative forces. Teachers are urged to build on the "natural curiosity children bring to school and ask the kids what they want to learn."[37] All this is antithetical to classical education and, if the British and Australian reformers are right, antithetical to the needs of many boys. Consider the contents of a leading American teacher-training book.

Best Practice: Today's Standards for Teaching and Learning in America's Schools is a 2005 summary of the "state-of-the art of the teaching methods."[38] Its authors, three university curriculum experts, base their recommendations on what "good teachers do." Their list of "Best Practices" reflects what they say is the "unanimous" opinion of leading education experts and teaching associations.[39] Many of them are the opposite of what the British headmasters recommend for boys:

- "LESS rote memorization of facts and details."
- "LESS emphasis on competition and grades in school."
- "MORE cooperative, collaborative activity; developing the classroom as an interdependent community."
- "LESS whole-class, teacher-directed instruction."[40]

According to *Best Practice*, these recommendations are the expression of an "unrecognized consensus" stemming from a "remarkably consistent, harmonious vision of 'best educational practice.'"[41] That vision may work for many students, but as the British and Australians have found, it is clearly not working for millions of disengaged boys. Referring to such boys, *New York Times* writer David Brooks says:

> Schools have to engage people as they are. That requires leaders who insist on more cultural diversity in school: not just teachers who celebrate cooperation, but other teachers who celebrate competition; not just teachers who honor environmental virtues, but teachers who honor military virtues; not just curriculums that teach how to share, but curriculums that teach how to win and how to lose; not just programs that work like friendship circles, but programs that work like boot camp.[42]

The British are heeding Brooks's counsel. Along with the Australians, they are developing a new academic discipline: male-specific pedagogy. There is no such broad-based effort in the United States. Although there are signs of hope at some vocational and technical schools such as Aviation High School (recounted in chapter 1), these efforts are now themselves at risk.

Our Tinkerers, Ourselves

Sumitra Rajagopalan, an adjunct professor of biomechanics at McGill University, has developed a program for teenage boys in Montreal, where one in three male students drops out of high school. Rajagopalan explains that the male students she met were bored by their classroom instruction and starved for hands-on activities. She was shocked to find that many had never held a hammer or screwdriver before. At first they fumbled around, but they quickly gained competence. Under Rajagopalan's supervision, the boys have now built a solar-driven Sterling engine from Coca-Cola cans and straws. "[B]oys are born tinkerers," she said. "They have a deep-seated need to rip things apart, decode their inner workings, create stuff."[43]

There are millions of languishing young men in the United States just like the ones Rajagopalan is trying to help. In their 2011 *Pathways to Prosperity* report, Harvard education researchers note the dismal prospects of underachieving young men and suggest that a revival of vocational education in secondary schools may be a partial solution to their problem.[44] They cite several such programs and suggest we use them as a model for education reform. The Massachusetts system is singled out for special mention.

Massachusetts has a network of twenty-six academically rigorous vocational-technical high schools serving 27,000 male and female students. Students in magnet schools such as Worcester Technical, Madison Park Technical Vocational, and Blackstone Valley Regional Vocational Technical take traditional academic courses but spend half their time apprenticing in a field of their choice. These include computer repair, telecommunications networking, carpentry, early childhood education, plumbing, heating, refrigeration, and cosmetology. In former times, vocational high schools were often dumping grounds for low achievers. Today, in Massachusetts, they are launching pads into the middle class. The Massachusetts program is so successful it has become known as the "Cadillac of Career Training Education (CTE)."[45]

Blackstone Valley Tech in Upton, Massachusetts, should be studied by anyone looking for solutions to the boy problem. It is working wonders with girls (who comprise 44 percent of the student body), but its success with boys is astonishing.[46] According to a study of vocational education by the commonwealth's Pioneer Institute, "[O]ne in four Valley Technical students enter their freshman year with a fourth-grade reading level."[47] The school immerses these students in an intense, individualized remediation program until they read proficiently at grade level. Like Aviation High, otherwise disaffected students put up with remediation as well as a full load of college preparatory courses (including honors and Advanced Placement classes), because otherwise they could not spend half the semester apprenticing in diesel mechanics, computer repair, or automotive engineering. One hallmark of the school is the novel way it combines academics with job training. As the Pioneer Institute report explains, "[P]roportions might be reinforced in auto shop with algebra problems asking students to figure the rate at which a car is burning oil or losing tire tread, and a machine shop instructor might ask students for daily written reflections of their work."[48]

These Massachusetts technical high schools have long waiting lists (seven hundred students applied for three hundred places in the Blackstone Valley Class of 2015).[49] The Pioneer Institute calls the Massachusetts technical school program "a true American success story."[50] And the success can be measured in concrete results. According to the Harvard *Pathways* report,

> These [Massachusetts] schools boast a far lower dropout rate than the state average, and have some of the state's highest graduation rates. Well over half of the graduates go on to postsecondary education. Perhaps most remarkably, in 2008, 96% of students at these high schools passed the state's rigorous MCAS high-stakes graduation test, surpassing the average of students at more conventional comprehensive high schools.[51]

Not only do schools like Aviation High and Blackstone Valley Tech help their students secure a better life, they also address a looming national skills shortage. As the *New York Times* reported in 2010, "domestic manufacturers . . . are looking to hire people who can operate sophisticated computerized machinery, follow complex blueprints and demonstrate higher math proficiency than was previously required of the typical assembly line worker." [52] But they cannot find them. Countries like Austria, Germany, the Netherlands, and Switzerland have sophisticated programs to prepare their young people for today's job market. The United States is lagging behind. "[W]hile we have been standing still, other nations have leapfrogged us," say the *Pathways* authors. [53]

The Women's Lobby Strikes Back

Despite their success and promise, vocational academies like Aviation High School and Blackstone Valley Tech face harsh opposition from the women's lobby. In a 2007 report, the National Coalition for Women and Girls in Education (NCWGE) condemned high school vocational training schools as hotbeds of "sex segregation." [54] (The NCWGE is a consortium of more than fifty groups that lobby for girls' rights in education; members include the AAUW, the National Women's Law Center, the ACLU, NOW, the Ms. Foundation, and the National Education Association.) Girls and boys enroll in these programs in roughly the same numbers, but they tend to pursue different fields. According to one NCWGE report, "Girls are largely absent from traditional male courses, comprising only 4% of heating, A/C and refrigeration students, 5% of welding students, 6% of electrical and plumber/pipefitter students and 9% of automotive students." [55] At the same time, they account for 98 percent of students enrolled in cosmetology, 87 percent of child-care students, and 86 percent of health-related fields. [56] Such enrollment patterns, they say, "reflect, at least in part, the persistence of sex stereotyping and sex discrimination." [57]

But what if they reflect preferences? What if girls are not that interested in refrigeration or welding, compared to early childhood education or nursing? We can all agree that career and technical programs should do what they can to attract and engage female (and male) students in nontraditional occupations. Electricians can earn more than child-care workers. The girls should know this—indeed, they probably know it all too well. According to Alison Fraser, a curriculum specialist at Blackstone Valley Tech (and author of the

Pioneer Institute study on Massachusetts programs), recruiting more girls into nontraditional fields ("nontrads" for short) is an overwhelming preoccupation at schools like hers. "It is all we think about," Fraser told me. She describes Blackstone Valley Tech girls, pressured to sign up for auto body and machine shop programs, who then come to her in tears saying they just don't want those careers. Says Fraser,

> We do *everything* we can to promote nontraditional fields. We bring in successful women welders and electricians; we counsel the girls and their parents about the benefits of traditional male fields. We *force* them to explore fields outside their interests. But we cannot force them into a career they don't want (Fraser's emphasis).[58]

Why are vocational schools going to such lengths to persuade girls to become welders rather than nurses? Because state and federal equity officials require them to. Under the Carl D. Perkins Career and Technical Education Act, first enacted in 1984, the US Department of Education disburses $1.1 billion annually through the states to secondary schools and colleges for vocational and technical training. The act requires schools to take aggressive measures to persuade young women to enter nontraditional fields. Career and technical schools live in fear that with too few "nontrads," they will fall short of their "Perkins number"—an illusive, nonspecific, and ever-changing gender quota. As Fraser told me, it is not enough to get girls to explore new areas, we have to "get them to sign up, and get them to stay there." And the requirements are about to become even tougher—moving toward precisely defined gender goals and quotas.

In April 2012, US Secretary of Education Arne Duncan sent out a "Blueprint" for reforming the Perkins Act when it is reauthorized in 2013. "This is not a time to tinker with [Career and Technical Education]," said the secretary, "it is time to transform it."[59] One proposed transformation is equity for women and girls. "This commitment," explains the Duncan Blueprint, "stems from the fact that the everyday educational experience of women . . . violate[s] the belief in equity at the heart of the American promise." [60] To fulfill the commitment, the Perkins Act will "ensure equity in access, participation and *outcomes*" by providing "wrap around supports" (my emphasis). [61] Such vagueness will be more than enough for the girl-power lobby to set up shop at the heart of Perkins Act grant making and enforcement.

The National Women's Law Center is already prepared to wrap around. It has developed state-by state litigation guides—*Tools of the Trade: Using the Law to Address Sex Segregation in High School Career and Technical Education.* The toolkit informs readers that the "data show a stark pattern of under-representation of girls in non-traditional CTE course in every region of the country." [62] To wit:

- In Massachusetts, "120 girls are enrolled in electrician courses, compared to 1,717 boys"; and "1,605 girls are enrolled in cosmetology courses, compared to 36 boys." [63]

- In Maryland, "189 girls are enrolled in automotive courses, compared to 2,425 boys." [64]

Interested parties are advised: "Contact the National Women's Law Center if you want to take action to address the under-representation of female students in CTE in your school or state." [65] Note the use of *under-representation* as a synonym for *discrimination*. The new Perkins Act will further empower the women's lobby to threaten schools like Aviation and Blackstone Valley with lawsuits.

Why pursue this course? Instead of spending millions of dollars in a dubious effort to change aspiring cosmetologists into welders, education officials should concentrate on helping young people, male and female, enter careers that interest them. "What we do not need," said Alison Fraser from Blackstone Valley Tech, "is having the state say, you have to force these round pegs into square holes." [66]

The Perkins Act is not the only reason pressure is increasing on Alison Fraser and her colleagues to change their students' preferences. On the fortieth anniversary of the Title IX equity law in June 2012, the White House announced that the Department of Education would be adopting a new and more rigorous application of Title IX to high school and college technology, engineering, and science programs. According to the White House press release, "The Department of Education will announce the revision of its Title IX Technical Assistance presentation, made available nationwide to state and local education agencies across the country, to include information on how institutions receiving federal financial assistance are also required to ensure equal access to educational programs and resources in STEM (science, technology, engineering and math) fields." President Obama explained the rationale in a *Newsweek* op-ed:

> Let's not forget, Title IX isn't just about sports. From addressing inequality in math and science education to preventing sexual assault on campus to fairly funding athletic programs, Title IX ensures equality for our young people in every aspect of their education. It's a springboard for success: it's thanks in part to legislation like Title IX that more women graduate from college prepared to work in a much broader range of fields, including engineering and technology. I've said that women will shape the destiny of this country, and I mean it.

It is admirable for President Obama to encourage young women to shape our country's destiny—but that is already happening. It is our underachieving young men that destiny is leaving behind, and they are being discouraged rather than encouraged by our political elites.

Introducing divisive gender politics into schools like Aviation High and Blackstone Valley Tech is the last thing we should be doing. While it is true that fewer young women than men enter fields like engineering, aviation, and automobile repair, young women are soaring in areas such as biology, psychology, and veterinary medicine.[67] In 2010, women held 64 percent of seats in graduate programs in the social sciences, 75 percent in public administration, 78 percent in veterinary medicine, and 80 percent in health sciences.[68] Will the federal government demand Title IX investigations in those female-dominated programs? Will our high schools and colleges be taken to task for doing a far better job educating girls than boys? Not likely. There is no National Coalition for Boys in Education, no lobby promoting changes in the Perkins Act or Title IX to help them. And, unlike in England and Australia, no political leader has spoken out publicly on their behalf.

Between the Perkins Act reauthorization and the new application of Title IX to technology and engineering programs, schools will be forced to adopt gender quotas in those few programs that seem to be working for at-risk boys. Women's groups vehemently deny that quotas are in the offing. "Title IX does not require quotas," says the NCWGE. "It simply requires that schools allocate participation opportunities nondiscriminatorily."[69] But over the years, this diffuse requirement has been interpreted by judges, Department of Education officials, college administrators, and women's groups to mean that women are entitled to "statistical proportionality." What does that mean? Consider what happened in sports.

If a college's student body is 60 percent female, then 60 percent of the athletes should be female—even if far fewer women than men are interested in playing sports at that college. But many athletic directors have been unable to attract the same proportions of women as men. To avoid government harassment, loss of funding, and lawsuits, they have simply eliminated men's teams. Vocation and technical schools won't get rid of their "male teams" in welding, engineering, or automotive repair, but they are likely to cut them back and practice reverse discrimination in favor of girls. More resources will be deployed to change the preferences of young women to suit the ideology of groups like the AAUW and the National Women's Law Center. School leaders have no matching incentive to develop programs that could attract great numbers of disengaged young men. On the contrary, they are well advised to avoid them. Such programs will put them at risk of a federal investigation and loss of funds.

The Montreal professor, Sumitra Rajagopalan, is surely right. Boys, more than girls, are natural tinkerers, builders, and systematizers. There are a few colleges that have no trouble attracting males—schools whose names include "tech." If you build them, males will come: Georgia Tech (69 percent male), Rochester Institute of Technology (67 percent); South Dakota School of Mines and Technology (74 percent), and Embry Riddle Aeronautical (85 percent). The Department of Education and the president should be doing all they can to help young men become the builders, engineers, and techies so many of them want to be. Instead, they are creating powerful obstacles to thwart them.

Temple Grandin, professor of animal science at Colorado State, is an advocate for those who, like herself, are afflicted with a type of autism known as Asperger's syndrome. She once told an interviewer:

> Who do you think made the first stone spear? That wasn't the yakkity yaks sitting around the campfire. It was some Asperger sitting in the back of a cave figuring out how to chip rocks into spearheads. Without some autistic traits you wouldn't even have a recording device to record this conversation on.[70]

But we know that autistic traits are far more common in males than females. Scientists such as Cambridge University's Simon Baron-Cohen believe autism offers insight into the typical male mind.[71] It helps explain the universal male fixation on gadgets, technology, and engineering. Why war against this reality? Why try to change tinkerers into yakkity yaks, or vice versa? To thrive as a society, we need both. By neglecting the needs and interests of boys, we not only sacrifice their life prospects, but our society's technological future.

Are There More Girl Geniuses?

A 2010 *New York Times* report carries more bad news for boys. A significant gender gap favoring girls has arisen inside New York City's gifted and talented programs. According to the article, "Around the city, the current crop of gifted kindergarteners . . . is 56 percent girls, and in the 2008–2009 year, 55 percent were girls."[72] In some of the most elite programs, almost three-fifths of the prodigies are girls. Could it be that girls are simply smarter than boys?

In fact, males and females appear to be equally intelligent on average. But on standardized intelligence tests, more males than females get off-the-chart scores in *both* directions. The greater variance of males on intelligence tests is one of the best-established findings in psychometric literature. Males predominate among the mentally deficient and the abnormally brilliant. The difference in variation isn't huge, but it is large and consistent enough that a fair selection process for a gifted-and-talented program will generally produce more boys than girls.

To give just one example of the difference in IQ distribution, here is what a group of Scottish psychologists found in 2002 when they analyzed the results of IQ tests given to nearly all eleven-year-olds in Scotland in 1932.

Figure 12: IQ Scores in Scotland, 1932, Gender Percent by IQ Score
Sample size: 79,376 11-year-olds

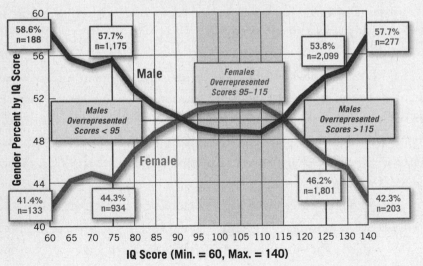

Source: Scottish Mental Survey, 1932.

This study, one of the most comprehensive in the literature, shows that for the highest IQ score of 140, boys outnumbered girls 277 to 203 (or 57.7 percent boys versus 42.3 percent girls), and for the lowest IQ boys also outnumber girls, by 188 to 133 (or 58.6 percent boys versus 41.4 percent girls).[73]

Little appears to have changed in the cognitive profile of men and women since prewar Scotland. Those with IQs above 140 or below 70 are still very much the exception. They can be male or female, but males have a statistically significant edge at both extremes. How did things get turned around with New York City's kindergarteners? Here is how the *Times* describes playtime for a group of five-year-old braniacs:

> Four of the boys went to the corner to build an intricate highway structure and a factory from wooden blocks, while two others built trucks. One girl helped them, by creating signs on Post-its to stick on the buildings. Another kindergarten girl, Tamar Greenberg, stood to announce to the class her own activity, a Hebrew lesson. "We're moving to the green table because it's too distracting with the computers" in the back, she told the other children. On a roster, she neatly recorded the names of the three children who joined her for the lesson: Skyler, Isabelle and Bayla. "No boys were interested," Tamar said.[74]

Highly gifted boys and girls are just like other children in one respect: in both groups, the girls are more mature, more verbal, and more capable of sitting still. Until a few years ago, admissions directors for New York City's gifted programs took account of these differences and through a series of tests, interviews, and observations managed to recruit roughly equal numbers of budding engineers and linguists.

But the old practice of taking equal numbers of boys and girls was phased out a few years ago when Mayor Michael Bloomberg and his administration sought to make the application process more fair, open, and uniform. Reforms were needed because, for many years, admission procedures were haphazard and varied from school to school. Parents who knew how to work the system had a huge advantage. Many average children with assertive parents found their way into the city's elite programs—and many bright but socially disadvantaged children never had a chance. The Bloomberg administration imposed a uniform and transparent admission process so that all applicants (about fifteen thousand four- and five-year-olds) now take the same two standardized tests. Only children who score in the 90th percentile or above can enter the programs. This approach leaves little room for parental lobbying.

The reformers believed this open and consistent procedure would yield a more ethnically diverse group of students. So far it has not. It *has* yielded more girls than boys. As the *Times* reports, the test is "more verbal than other tests" and it plays to girls' strengths. Boys are especially disadvantaged by the necessity to sit quietly for one hour and focus exclusively on the test.[75] Pre-kindergarten boys with mental abilities three or four standard deviations above the mean have astonishing talents. But as Terry Neu, an expert on gifted boys, told me, sitting still for an extended period of time is not one of them. The capacity to remain seated for a long test does not reliably measure brilliance, but requiring pre-K children to do it is a sure way of securing more places for girls than boys in a gifted program.[76]

The developing gender gap in the gifted programs of New York City does not indicate that girls are smarter than boys. Rather, it shows how well-intentioned government officials and educators—adults with the standard adult preferences for order and quiet—can disregard boys' needs and abilities and unwittingly adopt policies stacked against them. It is a small part of the long story of how boys have become the have-nots in American education.

The Road to Recovery

American educators and government officials should follow the example of the British and Australians. We are kindred spirits—inclusive, fractious democracies. We all embrace and insist upon the social and political equality of the sexes, and we all contend with the sometimes excessive pressures for political correctness and multiculturalism. Yet, somehow, the British and Australians openly acknowledge the plight of boys and are unapologetically taking steps to help them. The mood in Great Britain and Australia is constructive and informed by good research and common sense. The mood in the United States is contentious, ideological, and cowed by gender politics. The British have their parliamentary "toolkit of effective practices" for educating boys,[77] while Americans have the National Women's Law Center's *Tools of the Trade: Using the Law to Address Sex Segregation in High School Career and Technical Education.*

We should pay close attention to the advice dispensed by the British Boys' Reading Commission and the Australians' Success for Boys. That means more experiments with single-sex classes and academies. That means more schools of education offering special courses on boy-friendly pedagogy. Old-fashioned, structured, competitive, teacher-directed classrooms work best for many boys. Too many get lost in jazz improvisations. We must make room for more boy-enthralling, job-directed schools like Aviation High School and Blackstone Valley Tech, and more boy-effective teachers like Chicago's Mrs. Daugherty and Montreal's Professor Rajagopalan.

Most of all, we need a change of attitude. The women's lobby, the Department of Education, the gender theorists in our schools of education, the ACLU, the authors of the Perkins Act Reauthorization, and the president of the United States are so carried away with girl power they have forgotten about our male children. They have distracted themselves and the nation from acknowledging a plain and simple fact: American boys across the ability spectrum and in all age groups have become second-class citizens in the nation's schools. The Australians and British are coping with this reality. If they can do it, so can we.

8

The Moral Life of Boys

Boys who are morally neglected have unpleasant ways of getting themselves noticed. All children need clear, unequivocal rules. They need structure. They thrive on firm guidance and fair discipline from the adults in their lives. But boys need these things even more than girls do.

The Josephson Institute of Ethics conducts surveys on the moral attitudes of young people. Girls routinely far outperform boys in every measure of honesty and self-control. As part of the 2010 *Report Card on the Ethics of American Youth*, Josephson researchers polled a sample of more than forty thousand high school students. They found that significantly more boys "agree" or "strongly agree" with the following statements:

- "A person has to lie or cheat sometimes in order to succeed" (47.4 percent of males versus 29.8 percent of females).[1]

- "It's not cheating if everyone's doing it" (19.1 percent of males, 9.8 percent of females).[2]

- "It's sometimes okay to hit or threaten a person who makes me angry" (36.7 percent of males, 19.1 percent of females).[3]

The American Psychiatric Association defines a "conduct disorder" as "a repetitive and persistent pattern of behavior in which the basic rights of others, or other major age-appropriate societal norms or rules, are violated."[4] According to the APA, the prevalence of conduct disorder has increased since the 1960s. Far more males than females fit the pattern. "Rates vary depending on the nature of populations sampled and the methods of ascertainment: for males under age 18 years, rates range from 6 percent to 16 percent; for females, rates range from 2 percent to 9 percent."[5] For conduct disorders severe enough to gain the attention of the police, boys also predominate. According to the Justice Department's Office of Juvenile Justice and Delinquency Prevention Center, 62 percent of children younger than age eighteen arrested for property crimes in 2009 were boys; of those arrested for violent crimes, 82 percent were boys.[6]

The male's greater propensity for antisocial behavior is cross-cultural. A 1997 University of Vermont study compared parents' reports of children's behavior in twelve countries. The populations studied (which included the United States, Thailand, Greece, Jamaica, Puerto Rico, and Sweden) differed greatly in how they raised children and defined gender roles. Yet in every case boys were more likely than girls to fight, swear, steal, throw tantrums, and threaten others.[7]

Every new generation enters society unformed. Princeton University demographer Norman B. Ryder speaks of "a perennial invasion of barbarians who must somehow be civilized . . . for societal survival."[8] Ryder views the problem from the vantage point of society. But when socialization is inadequate, the children also suffer. A society that fails in its mission to humanize and civilize its children fails its male children in uniquely harmful ways.

Janet Daley, the education writer at the *Daily Telegraph* in London, has written at length about how the lack of directive moral education harms boys more than girls:

There is one indisputable fact with which anyone who is serious about helping young men must come to terms: boys need far more discipline, structure and authority in their lives than do girls. . . . Boys must be actively constrained by a whole phalanx of adults who come into contact with them—parents, teachers, neighbors, policemen, passers-by in the streets—before they can be expected to control their asocial, egoistic impulses.[9]

What happens when boys never encounter that "phalanx of adults"? We don't have to look far. In the middle and late decades of the twentieth century, the United States experimented with value-free education. Stanford education scholar William Damon has described the era:

> Educators found themselves embedded in a . . . postmodern world. Most responded by concluding that the moral part of their traditional mission had become obsolete. Moral relativism was in, *in loco parentis* was out. . . . This thinking was a misconception that caused so many readily apparent casualties among the young that it was bound to be abandoned sooner or later.[10]

Today, most schools have abandoned once popular laissez-faire attitudes toward behavior. As we saw in earlier chapters, many now err in the opposite direction, with draconian zero-tolerance policies for even harmless behavior. But it is instructive to go back a few decades to a time when large numbers of adults defected altogether from the central task of civilizing the children in their care.

When the "Barbarians" Don't Get Civilized

In the late 1980s and early 1990s, newspapers carried shocking stories about adolescent boys exploiting, assaulting, and terrorizing girls. In the South Bronx, a group of boys known as the "whirlpoolers" surrounded girls in public swimming pools and sexually assaulted them. In Glen Ridge, New Jersey, popular high school athletes raped a mentally disabled girl. In Lakewood, California, a gang of high school boys known as the Spur Posse turned the sexual exploitation of girls into a team sport.[11]

Women's groups seized on these incidents as symptomatic of a violent misogyny pervading American culture. The cause? Stereotypical male socialization. Referring to the Glen Ridge case, feminist pioneer Betty Friedan noted somberly that, "machismo is a fertile ground for the seeds of evil."[12] Columnist Judy Mann wrote that the Spur Posse case "contains all the ingredients of patriarchal culture gone haywire."[13] For Susan Faludi, the Spurs were "ground zero of the American masculinity crisis."[14]

Author Joan Didion wrote a lengthy piece on the Spur Posse for the *New Yorker*, and Columbia University journalism professor Bernard Lefkowitz spent six years researching the Glen Ridge case for his 1997 book, *Our Guys: The Glen Ridge Rape and the Secret Life of the Perfect Suburb*. Didion and Lefkowitz offer detailed portraits of the lives of the young male predators. We can see for ourselves some of the forces that turned seemingly normal boys into criminals. Were they desensitized by being separated from their mothers at too early an age, as William Pollack and Carol Gilligan suggest? Are they products of conventional male socialization? Are they the offspring of what Judy Mann calls the "machocracy"?[15] The narrative evidence points, albeit unintentionally, to an entirely different cause.

"Our Guys"

The Glen Ridge rape was reported on May 25, 1989. Several popular high school athletes had lured a mentally disabled girl into a basement, removed her clothes, and penetrated her with a broomstick. Lefkowitz was intrigued by the question of how seemingly normal American boys had come to commit such acts: "This wasn't about just a couple of oddballs with a sadistic streak. . . . Thirteen males were present in the basement where the alleged rape occurred. There also were reports that a number of other boys had tried to entice the young woman into the basement a second time to repeat the experience. . . . I wanted to know more about how this privileged American community raised its children, especially its sons."[16]

According to Lefkowitz, these boys were "pure gold, every mother's dream, every father's pride. They were not only Glen Ridge's finest, but in their perfection they belonged to all of us. They were Our Guys." [17] To find out what had gone wrong, he undertook "an examination of the character of their community and of the young people who grew up in it." [18]

Lefkowitz shares with Friedan and Mann the view that machismo created much of the evil:

> The Jocks didn't invent the idea of mistreating young women. The ruling clique of teenagers adhered to a code of behavior that mimicked, distorted and exaggerated the values of the adult world around them. . . . But these misguided and ultimately dehumanizing values were not exclusive to this one small town. As the continuing revelations of sexual harassment and abuse in the military, in colleges, in the workplace . . . suggest, these values have deep roots in American life. [19]

Lefkowitz presents the Glen Ridge story as a modern morality tale about misogyny and the oppression of women. But the facts he powerfully reports sustain a very different interpretation. The real story is about how a group of adults—parents, teachers, coaches, and community leaders—failed massively and tragically to carry out their responsibility to civilize the children in their care. The problem with these young male predators was not conventional male socialization, but its absence.

All through elementary school and junior high, Chris Archer and twins Kevin and Kyle Scherzer, the three boys who would later be convicted of first-degree sexual assault, had bullied other students and mistreated teachers. The "jocks," as their group was called, routinely disrupted class with outbursts and obscenities. They smashed up the science laboratory, trashed the Glen Ridge Country Club (surely a redoubt of the suburban patriarchy), stole from other students, and vandalized homes. All these actions apparently went unpunished. No charges were filed. No arrests were made. No athletic privileges were rescinded. No apologies were demanded or received. According to Lefkowitz, the jocks had such a bad reputation that twenty families withdrew their children from the school system during their reign. [20]

The history of abuse of the mentally disabled girl, known as Leslie, went back to Kevin and Kyle's early childhood. The girl's mother reports that when the twins were in kindergarten, they tricked her daughter into eating dog feces. Later, they fed her mud, pinched her arm until it was covered with welts, and routinely referred to her in public as "Brain-Les," "Head-Les," and "retard."

Again, it seems the boys were never reprimanded or punished. Leslie's parents chose not to tell Kevin and Kyle's parents about the feces, the mud, and the welts. No one seemed to see the behavior in moral terms. Leslie's parents did consult a child psychologist, who blamed the incidents on the girl's immaturity—something she would grow out of. The active malice and cruelty of the boys was never regarded as a serious problem to be disciplined and stopped.

From the time they were small children, the boys who would later take part in the rape were opportunistically abusive and cruel to nearly anyone who crossed their paths. This pattern persisted through adolescence. It affected their peers regardless of sex. Later on, it affected their teachers and schoolmates. The glaring absence of any firm discipline, the failure of the adults in their lives to punish them for their egregious actions, turned them into monsters.

By the time the Glen Ridge boys assaulted Leslie in the basement, they had had years of experience with mayhem and abuse without suffering any consequences. Where were their parents? The school officials? The police? According to David Maltman, principal of the Glen Ridge Middle School, "These kids would act up in class, disrupt the learning situation, set other kids up, get in fights with them, go after them back and forth to school. By the fifth grade, they already had had a bad name for a long time."[21] Officials did attempt to intervene. Just before the unruly cohort entered high school, Maltman and the teachers developed a plan to introduce more discipline and order into the school. It had several features that are standard in many schools:

- Students with learning and behavior disorders would be identified and put in special classes, and, where necessary, would be given professional treatment. (Kevin Scherzer, for example, had been classified as "neurologically impaired" in second grade. But his parents always insisted he be mainstreamed and treated as normal.)

- The school would hire a crisis-intervention counselor and institute an alcohol awareness program.

- The school would draw up a new code of discipline, which it would strictly enforce.

Many Glen Ridge parents were incensed by these plans. They argued that hiring crisis-intervention counselors and having alcohol programs would give Glen Ridge a bad reputation. The very idea of having their children "classified" under some category of disorder made these parents angry. When Maltman presented the seemingly mild code of discipline at a parents meeting, "all hell broke loose." According to the principal, "The parents thought these were Gestapo methods."[22]

Lefkowitz, Friedan, and Mann draw the wrong lesson. This is not a story about an American "patriarchal culture gone awry"; it is about what happens to children in a moral wasteland. These boys were raised so permissively, with so little moral guidance, and with adult passivity even in the face of the most loathsome conduct, that they ended up sociopaths. It is a tale of young barbarians who were never civilized—a suburban *Lord of the Flies*. The difference is that the feral English boys in William Golding's novel committed their atrocities when they were isolated from adults and civil society, stranded on an island after a shipwreck. What is so chilling about Glen Ridge is all the timid, doting adults who presided for years over their children's moral disintegration. The lesson of the Lakewood Spur Posse is the same.

"What's Not to Like About Me?"

The Spur Posse, a high school clique that took its name from the San Antonio Spurs basketball team, consisted of twenty to thirty middle-class boys who competed with one another in "scoring" with girls, especially underage girls. In March 1993, nine members were arrested and charged with a variety of crimes ranging from sexual assault to rape. One of the alleged victims was a ten-year-old girl.

Eventually, most of the charges were dropped, but these swaggering, ignorant, predatory boys from "Rapewood" enjoyed a temporary celebrity. "We didn't do nothing wrong 'cause it's not illegal to hookup," an indignant nineteen-year-old, Billy Shehan, told the *New York Times*.[23] The boys appeared on the *Dateline, Maury Povich, Jane Whitney,* and *Jenny Jones* television shows, telling fascinated audiences about their sexual adventures.

Orthodox feminist writers like Betty Friedan, Judy Mann, and Susan Faludi saw in the Spur Posse an embodiment of macho-patriarchal ideals. Less encumbered by a feminist framework, novelist and social critic Joan Didion saw them more conventionally as a group of proto-sociopathic boys. When Didion visited Lakewood in 1993 to do her story for *The New Yorker*, she noted that contempt for women was not the only thing the members of the Spur Posse had in common. Like the Glen Ridge jocks, these boys had been permitted to terrorize a town with impunity for years. A member of the school board told Didion stories of Spurs approaching nine- and ten-year-old children in playgrounds, stealing their baseball bats, and saying, "If you tell anyone, I'll beat your head in." The group had a long history of antisocial behavior, including burglary, credit card fraud, assault, arson, and even an attempted bombing.

Like the jocks, the Spur Posse had little sense of the harm and suffering they were causing and no feelings of remorse or shame. One thing they did have was high self-esteem. Didion writes in her *New Yorker* piece: "The boys seemed to have heard about self-esteem, most recently at the 'ethics' assemblies . . . the school had hastily organized after the arrests, but hey, no problem. 'I'm definitely comfortable with myself and my self-esteem,' one said on *Dateline*."[24] When another interviewer asked a member of the group if he liked himself, the surprised boy replied, "Yeah, why wouldn't I? I mean, what is not to like about me?"[25]

The mayor of Lakewood, Marc Titel, rightly saw in this group of boys a deplorable failure of moral education: "We need to look at what kind of values we are communicating to our kids."[26] Because boys are by nature more physically aggressive, less risk-averse, and more prone to rule breaking, the communication has to be clear and explicit. Boys, as a rule, require a form of character education that places strong behavioral constraints on them—constraints that many progressive educators feel we have no right to impose on any child.

It is absurd to talk of the Glen Ridge and Lakewood outrages in terms of "patriarchal culture gone haywire" or "ground zero of a masculinity crisis." They are instead evidence of what can happen when adults withhold elementary moral instruction from the young males in their charge, and punishment from acts of youthful terrorism. The more one faults masculinity for such acts, the further one strays from acknowledging the failures of moral education in the last decades of the twentieth century.

A Socratic Dialogue

Unfortunately, even some moral philosophers are reluctant to talk plainly about right and wrong and to pronounce judgment on clear cases of moral callowness and immaturity. In the fall of 1996, I took part in a televised "Socratic dialogue" on moral dilemmas with another ethics professor, a history teacher, and seven high school students. The program, *Ethical Choices: Individual Voices*, was shown on public television and is still circulated to high schools for use in classroom discussions of right and wrong.[27] Its message still troubles me.

In one typical exchange, the moderator, Stanford law professor Kim Taylor-Thompson, posed this dilemma to the students: Your teacher has unexpectedly assigned you a five-page paper. You have only a few days to do it, and you are already overwhelmed with work. Would it be wrong to hand in someone else's paper?

Two of the girls found the suggestion unthinkable and spoke about responsibility, honor, and principle. "I wouldn't do it. It is a matter of integrity," said Elizabeth. "It's dishonest," said Erin. But two of the boys saw nothing wrong with cheating. Eleventh grader Joseph flatly said, "If you have the opportunity, you should use it." Eric concurred. "I would use the paper and offer it to my friends."

I had taught moral philosophy to college freshmen for more than fifteen years, so I was not surprised to find students on the PBS program defending cheating. There are some in every class who play devil's advocate with an open admiration for the devil's position. But at least that evening, in our PBS "Socratic dialogue," I expected to have a professional ally in fellow panelist William Puka, a philosophy professor at Rensselaer Polytechnic Institute. Surely he would join me in making the case for honesty.

Instead, the professor told the students that it was the *teacher* who was immoral for having given the students such a burdensome assignment. He was disappointed in us for not seeing it his way. "What disturbs me," he said, "is how accepting you all seem to be of this assignment. To me it's outrageous from the point of view of learning to force you to write a paper in this short a time."[28]

For most of the session, the professor focused on the hypocrisy of parents, teachers, and corporations but had little to say about the moral obligations of students. When we discussed the immorality of shoplifting, he implied that stores were in the wrong for their pricing policies and talked about "corporations deciding on a twelve percent profit margin . . . and perhaps sweatshops."[29]

The professor was friendly and to all appearances well-meaning. Perhaps his goal was to embolden students to question authority and rules. That, however, is something contemporary adolescents are already good at. Too often, we teach students to question principles before they understand them. And in this case the professor was advising school students to question moral teachings and behavioral guidelines that are crucial to their well-being.

Professor Puka's "hands-off" style was fashionable in public schools for more than thirty years. It has gone under various names: values clarification, situation ethics, self-esteem education. These value-free approaches to ethics have flourished at a time when many parents fail to give children basic guidance in right and wrong. The decline of directive moral education has been bad for all children, but is has been especially bad for boys.

Value-Free Kids

In 1970, Theodore Sizer, then dean of the Harvard School of Education, coedited with his wife, Nancy, a collection of ethics lectures entitled *Moral Education*.[30] The preface set the tone by condemning the morality of the "Christian gentleman," "the American prairie," the McGuffey Readers, and the hypocrisy of teachers who tolerate a grading system that is the "terror of the young."[31] The Sizers were critical of the "crude and philosophically simpleminded sermonizing tradition" of the nineteenth century. They referred to directive ethics education in all its guises as "the old morality." According to the Sizers, leading contemporary moralists agree that that kind of morality "can and should be scrapped."[32]

Some twenty-four hundred years ago, Aristotle articulated what children need: clear guidance on how to be moral human beings. Aristotle compared moral education to physical training. Just as we become strong and skillful by doing things that require strength and skill, so too do we become good by practicing goodness. Ethical education, as he understood it, was training in emotional control and disciplined behavior. First, children must be socialized by inculcating into them habits of decency and using suitable punishments and rewards to discipline them to behave well. Eventually they will understand the reasons for and advantages of being moral human beings. Aristotle's principles for raising moral children were unquestioned through most of Western history; even today his teachings represent commonsense opinion about child rearing. What Aristotle advocated became the default model for moral education over the centuries. He showed parents and teachers how to civilize the invading hordes of child barbarians. Only in the last decades of the twentieth century did large numbers of parents and educators begin to denigrate his teachings.

The Sizers, for example, favored a "new morality" that gives primacy to students' autonomy and independence. Teachers should never preach or attempt to inculcate virtue; rather, through their actions, they should demonstrate a "fierce commitment" to social justice. In part, that means democratizing the classroom: "Teacher and children can learn about morality from each other."[33]

The Sizers preached a doctrine that was already being practiced in many American schools. Schools were scrapping the "old morality" in favor of alternatives that gave primacy to the children's moral autonomy. "Values clarification" was popular in the 1970s. Proponents of values clarification consider it inappropriate for a teacher to encourage students, however subtly or indirectly, to adopt the values of the teacher or the community. The cardinal sin is to impose values on the student. Instead, the teacher's job is to help the students discover "their own values." In *Readings in Values Clarification* (1973), two of the leaders of the movement, Sidney Simon and Howard Kirschenbaum, explain what is wrong with traditional ethics education: "We call this approach 'moralizing,' although it has also been known as inculcation, imposition, indoctrination, and in its most extreme form, 'brainwashing.'"[34]

However, the purpose of moral education is not to preserve our children's autonomy but to develop a character they will rely on as adults. Children who receive guidance and develop good moral habits find it easier to become autonomous adults. Conversely, children who are left to their own devices will flounder.

Lawrence Kohlberg, a Harvard moral psychologist, developed "cognitive moral development," another favored approach during the laissez-faire years. Kohlberg shared the Sizers' low opinion of traditional morality, referring disdainfully to the "old bags of virtues" that earlier educators had sought to inculcate.[35] Kohlbergian teachers were more traditional than the proponents of values clarification. They sought to promote a Kantian awareness of duty and responsibility in students. They were also traditional in their opposition to the moral relativism that many progressive educators found congenial. But they shared with other progressives a scorn for any form of top-down inculcation of moral principles. They, too, believed in "student-centered teaching," where the teacher acts less as a guide than as a "facilitator" of the student's development.

Kohlberg himself would later change his mind and concede that his rejection of "indoctrinative" moral education had been a mistake.[36] But his admirable recantation had little effect. Throughout the 1980s and 1990s, the traditional directive approach to moral education had fallen into desuetude in most public schools.

Ironically, the next fashion in progressive pedagogy, "student-centered learning," was soon to leave the Kohlbergians and the values clarifiers far behind. The new buzzword was *self-esteem*, and by the late 1980s it had become all the rage. Ethics was superseded by attention to the child's personal sense of well-being; the school's primary aim was to teach children to prize their rights and self-worth. In the old days, teachers would assign seventh graders to write about "The Person I Admire Most"; now students were assigned to write essays celebrating themselves. In one popular middle school English text, an assignment called "The Nobel Prize for Being You" informs students that they are "wonderful" and "amazing" and instructs them to "create two documents in connection with your Nobel Prize. Let the first document be a nomination letter written by the person who knows you best. Let the second be the script for your acceptance speech, which you will give at the annual award ceremony in Stockholm, Sweden." For extra credit, students can award themselves a trophy "that is especially designed for you and no one else." [37]

Throughout most of human history, children learned about virtue and honor by hearing or reading the inspiring stories of great men and women. During the 1970s and 1980s, the practice was replaced by practices that suggested to students that they were their own best guides in life. This turn to the autonomous subject as the ultimate moral authority is a notable consequence of the triumph of the progressive style over traditional directive methods of education.

It's hard to see how the Harvard theorists who urged teachers to jettison the "crude and philosophically simpleminded sermonizing tradition" can today defend the crude egoism that has replaced it. Apart from the philosophical niceties, there are concrete behavioral consequences. The moral deregulation that the progressive educators called for took hold in the very decades that saw a rise in conduct disorders among boys in the nation's schools.[38] No doubt much, perhaps most, of this trend can be ascribed to the large social changes that weakened families, such as the disappearance of fathers. But some of the blame can be laid at the doors of the well-intentioned professors who helped to undermine the schools' traditional mission of morally edifying their pupils.

Few thinkers have written about liberty and individual autonomy with greater passion and good sense than the nineteenth-century philosopher John Stuart Mill. But Mill makes it clear he is talking about adults. "We are not speaking of children," he says in *On Liberty*. "Nobody denies that people should be so taught and trained in youth as to know and benefit by the ascertained results of human experience."[39]

Mill could not foresee the advent of thinkers like the Sizers and the values clarificationists who would glibly recommend "scrapping" the old morality. From the loftiest of progressive motives, many schools were robbed of the ability to enforce society's codes and rules.

The Courts Enter the Fray

The courts also played a role in eroding teachers' and school officials' power to enforce traditional moral standards and discipline. In 1969, in *Tinker v. Des Moines Independent Community School District*, the US Supreme Court ruled that Iowa school authorities violated students' rights by denying them permission to wear protest armbands to school. Justice Abe Fortas, in the majority opinion, found the action of the school authorities unconstitutional: "It can hardly be argued that students shed their constitutional rights to freedom of speech or expression at the schoolhouse gate."[40] Justice Hugo Black dissented. Though a great champion of the First Amendment, he noted that schoolchildren "need to learn, not teach." He wrote, presciently: "It is the beginning of a new revolutionary era of permissiveness in this country fostered by the Judiciary. . . . Turned loose with lawsuits for damages and injunctions against their teachers . . . it is nothing but wishful thinking to imagine that young, immature students will not soon believe it is their right to control the schools."[41]

Abigail Thernstrom, a political scientist at the Manhattan Institute, cites *Tinker* as the beginning of the end of effective school discipline. She also sees it as an unfortunate example of Rousseauian romanticism in the courts. According to Thernstrom, "[Fortas's majority] opinion was a romantic celebration of conflict and permissiveness, even within the schoolhouse walls—as if the future of democratic government and American culture could be placed in jeopardy had the students been told to stage their demonstration elsewhere."[42]

In 1975, a second case that would further diminish the authority of school officials to correct student behavior reached the high court. In *Goss v. Lopez*, the Supreme Court ruled it unconstitutional for schools to suspend students without due process. Justice Byron White, who wrote the majority opinion, strongly favored extending students' rights. Justice Lewis Powell opposed the ruling, fearing it would ultimately be harmful to students.

Justice White prevailed, and the judiciary thus joined the progressive educationists and many parents in holding that "student rights" trump the traditional prerogative of teachers to require compliance with school discipline. The *Goss* ruling helped bring on the era of permissiveness that Justice Black had warned about.

A Stanford education scholar explains what happened next: "In response to the threat of such lawsuits, schools have felt forced to institute increasingly formal and rigid procedures that cannot be challenged in court because they allow for no discretion or flexibility in the way they are administered."[43] Enter the zero-tolerance policies we discussed in chapter 2. Schools gradually augmented value-free education with judgment-free discipline. But punishment without discretion and judgment angers students and further undermines the moral authority of the school.

Where the Reformers Go Wrong

Those who oppose directive moral education often call it a form of brainwashing or indoctrination. That is sheer confusion. To brainwash children undermines their autonomy and rational self-mastery, and diminishes their freedom. To educate them and to teach them to be competent, self-controlled, and morally responsible in their actions increases their freedom and deepens their humanity. The Greeks and Romans understood this well, as did most of the great scholastic and Enlightenment thinkers. It is a first principle of every great religion and high civilization. To know what is right and act on it is the highest expression of freedom and personal autonomy.

What Victorians had in mind when they extolled the qualities of a "gentleman" are the virtues we need to teach our children: honesty, integrity, courage, decency, politeness. These are as important to the well-being of a young male today as they were in nineteenth-century England. Even today, despite several decades of moral deregulation, most young men (and women) understand the term *gentleman* and approve of the ideals it connotes.

Far from being oppressive, the manners, instincts, and virtues we recognize in decent human beings—in the case of males, the manners, instincts, and virtues we associate with being a "gentleman"—are liberating. To civilize a boy is to allow him to make the most of himself. And good manners and good morals benefit the community more than even the best of laws. As Edmund Burke advised, "Manners are of more importance than laws. Upon them, in a great measure, the laws depend. The law touches us but here and there and now and then. Manners are what vex and soothe, corrupt or purify, exalt or debase, barbarize or refine us by a constant, steady uniform insensible operation."[44]

Common sense, convention, tradition, and modern social science research converge in support of the Aristotelian tradition of directive character education.[45] Children need clear standards, firm expectations, and adults in their lives who are loving and understanding but who insist on responsible behavior. But all of this was out of fashion in education circles for more than thirty years. By the mid-1970s, we were on our way to becoming the first society in history to use high principle to weaken the moral authority of teachers. Soon, local officials throughout the country, from Principal Maltman at Glen Ridge High in New Jersey to Mayor Titel of Lakewood, California, would be powerless in the face of delinquent students and litigious parents.

Value-free education declined slowly, then came to an abrupt end on April 20, 1999, when two boys walked into Columbine High School in Littleton, Colorado, and murdered twelve students and a teacher.

Evil Boys

The Columbine massacre shocked the nation. How could it happen? The usual explanations failed. Poverty? The killers, Eric Harris and Dylan Klebold, were middle class. Easy access to weapons? True, but young men, especially in the West, have always had access to guns. Broken families? Both boys' families were intact. A nation of emotionally repressed boys? Boys were much the same back in the '50s and '60s when nobody brought guns to school. Bullies drove them to it? As journalist Dave Cullen showed in his meticulously researched *Columbine*, the killers were not bullied; nor were they members of an outcast Goth cult called the Trench Coat Mafia—that was all a media fiction.[46]

One week after the Colorado shootings, Secretary of Education Richard Riley talked to a group of students at a high school in Annapolis, Maryland. After the secretary rounded up the usual causes and reasons for the atrocity, a student asked him about one he had not mentioned: "Why haven't students been offered ethics classes?" Secretary Riley seemed taken aback by the question.

Sad to say, it is not likely that an ethics curriculum would have stopped boys like Harris and Klebold from their murderous rampage. Harris was a cold-blooded sociopath; Klebold, an enraged, suicidal follower. They planned their assault for more than a year, and the goal was not to shoot a few students. Their plan (which fortunately failed when their bombs did not detonate) was to rival Timothy McVeigh and to blow up the entire school. They were domestic terrorists.

As noted in chapter 2, many social critics cited the Columbine debacle as a metaphor for all boys. William Pollack, director of the Center for Men at McLean Hospital and author of the bestselling *Real Boys: Rescuing Our Sons from the Myths of Boyhood*, told audiences around the country, "The boys in Littleton are the tip of the iceberg. And the iceberg is *all* boys" [47] (his emphasis). More recently, feminist sociologist Jessie Klein opined:

Eric and Dylan were affirming, rather than rejecting, some of the prevailing social moral standards at their school. These expectations push boys to achieve a certain kind of status at all costs—and in particular link the achievement of this status to a narrow definition of masculinity that values power and dominance above all else.[48]

There were hundreds of boys at Littleton's Columbine High. Some behaved heroically. Senior Seth Houy threw his body over a terrified girl to shield her from the bullets. Scores of grief-ridden boys attended the memorial services. At one service, two brothers performed a song they had written for their lost friends. Other young men read poems. To take two morbid killers as representative of "the nature of boyhood" is profoundly misguided and unjust.

Certainly, the school could have done a better job protecting itself. When Harris and Klebold appeared in school with T-shirts with the words "Serial Killer" emblazoned on them, the principal should have taken notice. An English teacher at Columbine, Cheryl Lucas, told *Education Week* that both boys had written short stories about death and killing "that were horribly, graphically, violent" and that she had notified school officials. According to Lucas, the officials had taken no action because nothing the boys wrote had violated school rules. Speaking with painful irony, the frustrated teacher explained, "In a free society, you can't take action until they've committed some horrific crime because they are guaranteed freedom of speech."[49] Harris and Klebold exposed the madness of deploying that sort of logic with adolescents.

But one of the lessons of the Columbine story is to be careful drawing lessons. In the first edition of this book, I cited the case as an example of a breakdown in character education. But the more we learn about the events at Columbine or Sandy Hook Elementary, why those killers did what they did is as mysterious and complex as the problem of evil itself. We need to do all we can to identify deviants such as Klebold, Harris, and Adam Lanza; and we need to protect ourselves from their malice. But they should not be confused with normal boys. Most boys don't need therapeutic interventions, gender resocialization, or draconian punishments; what they need are basic ethics.

In sum: Columbine brought an abrupt end to the "value-free" progressive pedagogy of 1970–1999, but it also led to serious errors in the opposite direction: the zero-tolerance movement. Both were errant extremes that proved particularly harmful to boys. At the same time, Columbine produced positive and productive responses. It invigorated a burgeoning character education movement. Such a movement may never protect us from sociopaths like Harris, Klebold, and Lanza, but its prospects for normal, healthy children are bright.

The Quiet Revival of Character Education

In the early 1990s, even before the Columbine shootings, a hitherto silent majority of parents, teachers, and community activists were beginning to agitate in favor of old-fashioned moral education. In July 1992, a group called the Character Counts Coalition (organized by the Josephson Institute of Ethics and made up of teachers, youth leaders, politicians, and ethicists) gathered in Aspen, Colorado, for a three-and-a-half-day conference on character education. The program was initiated by Michael Josephson, a former law professor and entrepreneur. His texts were Aristotle, St. Augustine, and the *Boy Scout Handbook*—the "old morality."

At the end of the conference, the group put forward "The Aspen Declaration on Character Education." Among its principles:

- The present and future well-being of our society requires an involved, caring citizenry with good moral character.

- Effective character education is based on core ethical values that form the foundation of democratic society, in particular, respect, responsibility, trustworthiness, caring, justice, fairness, civic virtue, and citizenship.

- Character education is, first and foremost, an obligation of families: it is also an important obligation of faith communities, schools, youth, and other human service organizations.[50]

Over the years, the Character Counts Coalition has attracted a wide and politically diverse following. Its council of advisors has included liberals such as Marian Wright Edelman and conservatives such as William Bennett. Several United States senators from both political parties have joined, along with a number of governors, mayors, and state representatives. The new character-education movement has been embraced by dozens of youth-serving organizations, including the National Association of Secondary School Principals, the YMCA of the USA, Boys & Girls Club of America, and the National PTA. Members also include schools, municipalities, and businesses. "Together we reach more than seven million young people every day," says the Josephson Institute.[51] Today most states mandate some form of moral education.

Individual schools have testified to its effectiveness. Fallon Park Elementary School in Roanoke, Virginia, for example, saw a dramatic change in its students after the principal adopted the Character Counts program in 1998.[52] Every morning the students recite the Pledge of Allegiance. This is followed by a pledge written by the students and teachers: "Each day in our words and actions we will persevere to exhibit respect, caring, fairness, trustworthiness, responsibility, and citizenship." These core values were integrated into the daily life of the school. According to the principal, suspensions declined, attendance and grades improved, and—*mirabile dictu*—misbehavior on school buses all but disappeared.[53] That was in 1998; in 2012 the program was still going strong.

Character Counts is the most widely used character education program. So far there is little research proving its efficacy, but dozens of evidence-based programs have flourished over the years, and many received strong federal support for a time. Among the most successful are PATHS (South Deerfield, Massachusetts), Roots of Empathy (Toronto, Canada), Caring School Community (Oakland, California), and Positive Action (Twin Falls, Idaho). Stanford's William Damon reports, "Federal support for such programs was authorized under the Clinton administration and tripled in size during the Bush administration."[54] According to Damon, the Obama administration has "reduced or eliminated support . . . with the lone exception of a new bullying initiative."[55]

Members of the Obama administration may have recoiled from the conservative connotations of "character." But it is also possible they were reacting to the muddled state of research surrounding such programs. There are hundreds of different programs, and the research on their effectiveness is mixed. In *What Works in Character Education*, a 2005 survey, University of Missouri–St. Louis education scholar Marvin Berkowitz and his colleague Mindy Bier identified "sixty-nine scientifically rigorous studies showing the effectiveness of a wide range of character education initiatives."[56] Thirty-three programs were cited for having "scientifically demonstrated positive student outcome." However, these results were contradicted by a major 2010 Department of Education study, which examined seven typical character education programs and found them ineffective.[57] Researchers randomly assigned programs to eighty-four schools in six states and then measured their impact on student behavior and achievement. When compared to the results of a control group, they could find no evidence of improvement.

The latter study has proved controversial. According to Berkowitz, the research design was so rigorous that it likely made it difficult to implement the programs effectively. Such comprehensive school initiatives usually require strong commitment from school leaders and staff, and randomly assigning programs to schools and classrooms is therefore an obstacle to effectiveness. William Damon judged it to be "a poor test of how real character education influences students."[58] Allen Ruby, the coauthor of the Department of Education study, conceded that "this is one study, so people shouldn't just say, 'We're done, let's move on.'"[59] All the same, the findings were sobering and remind us that the task of finding our way back to moral education is not going to be easy. Needless to say, we have to keep trying. Too many children, boys most of all, are morally adrift. And there are some programs that have been judged effective by other researchers. Consider Positive Action.

Aristotle in Idaho

Positive Action is a character education program founded in 1982 by education scholar Carol Gerber Allred. Today more than eleven thousand schools, twenty-five hundred districts, and two thousand community groups have adopted it. The K–12 curriculum consists of teachers' guides and scripted lessons, along with a variety of age-appropriate games, music, posters, stories, and activities. Lessons are taught fifteen minutes a day throughout the school year. When the Department of Education carried out an evaluation of forty-one leading character education programs in 2007, Positive Action was the only one to receive its seal of approval. Positive Action is the one ethics program included in the department's influential What Works Clearinghouse (WWC). "The WWC considers the extent of evidence for Positive Action to be moderate to large for behavior and for academic achievement." [60]

In the late 1970s, Allred was teaching high school in Idaho and became discouraged by her students' lack of engagement and ambition. Many were confused about basic ethics and had little understanding of work ethic. "I just knew they could do better," she told me. In response, Allred developed a character education system based on her readings in psychology, philosophy, and her appreciation of "Idaho farm values." She asked herself, "What do these hardworking, self-reliant, and honorable farmers know, and how can I teach it to my students?" She came up with a simple formula, which she named Positive Action. According to several carefully designed studies, her formula works. [61] These studies found that Positive Action improved behavior, increased academic achievement, reduced suspension rates, and, according to the WWC, reduced "serious violence among boys." [62] A third, more recent study found that Positive Action had "favorable program effects on reading for African American males." [63]

The Positive Action curriculum is based on the old-fashioned idea that "you feel good about yourself when you think and do positive actions, and there is a positive way to do everything." Its philosophy was crisply expressed by Abraham Lincoln: "When I do good I feel good, and when I do bad I feel bad." [64] Children as young as three or four are able to grasp this simple truth. The program teaches them how to stay inside the "Success Circle" (or "Happy Circle" for the younger children). The key is to fix on and hold positive thoughts and then act on them. Good feelings follow.

But Positive Action is not an "I love myself" self-esteem program. Allred became disillusioned with the self-esteem movement when she realized it lacked moral substance. Positive Action directs children toward a set of core values: specifically, trustworthiness, industry, kindness, and achievement. Children learn to pay close attention to how they feel when they are honest, hardworking, and kind; and they learn to avoid the vicious cycle that comes from cultivating bad thoughts, taking destructive actions, and feeling self-loathing. They become their own moral mentors.

One goal of the program is to get kids hooked on self-improvement—physical, moral, and intellectual. They are taught that it can be hard to stay inside the Success Circle but intrinsically very rewarding. It may be tempting to shirk a demanding task, lie to a friend, or steal something from someone. But children learn to monitor the toll it takes on their psyches. They also learn the central lesson that comes down to us from the ancient Stoics: you don't have to be at the mercy of your thoughts and ideas—you can change them and improve them. As the first-century Greek philosopher Epictetus said, "What upsets people is not things themselves, just their judgment about things."[65] Through Positive Action, children learn to be mindful and careful of their judgments.

Older students also study the lives of great individuals—George Washington, Thomas Jefferson, Florence Nightingale, Susan B. Anthony, Albert Einstein, the Dalai Lama, Gandhi, Martin Luther King Jr., Mother Teresa, or Rosa Parks—with a focus on "the thoughts that lead them to take great actions." Allred's program is practical, mundane, and homespun, but it somehow captures the insights of the world's great moral traditions. What's more, it resonates with children. "It is intuitive in them," Allred told me. Aristotle and Epictetus could not agree more. This Idaho educator may have found a way to equip children with a moral compass—and the means to find their way back to true north when they stray.

In June 2011, an eleven-year-old boy at Monterey Heights Elementary School in California gave a speech at graduation about how Positive Action had changed his life. He had once been a bully and a troublemaker and was failing his classes. "The lunch lady tried to keep me from recess so I cursed her out," he told his audience. "School was a prison to me and teachers were just trying to keep me locked in." But something in the Positive Action curriculum reached him. He is now a Positive Action "Sumo." His grades are good, he has more friends, and he has emerged as a school leader. "To all my future lunch ladies—I will not cuss you out."

When a Michigan state official visited a Positive Action class at Tustin Elementary in Tustin, Michigan, she remarked to a coworker, "I can use this in my own life."[66] We can all use it in our lives, but too many parents and schools simply fail to impart basic worldly wisdom to children. Positive Action appears to be effective with both girls and boys; but today, with so many boys clueless about right and wrong, misdirected by the self-esteem movement, and lacking ambition—it is just the sort of instruction they desperately need.

How to Be Successful

The movement to restore directive moral education to the schools has been fiercely resisted by many educators since its inception. Amherst professor Benjamin DeMott wrote a piece for *Harper's Magazine* in 1994 jeering at the revived character education movement. Like Professor Puka, DeMott asked how we can hope to teach ethics in a society where CEOs award themselves large salaries "in the midst of the age of downsizing."[67] Alfie Kohn, a popular education speaker and writer, wrote a long critical piece in the education magazine *Phi Delta Kappan* accusing character education programs of indoctrinating children and making them obedient workers in an unjust society where "the nation's wealth is concentrated in fewer and fewer hands."[68] Reactionary values, he claims, are already a powerful force in our nation's schools: "Children in American schools are even expected to begin each day by reciting a loyalty oath to the Fatherland, although we call it by a different name."[69] Kohn's comparison—likening the Pledge of Allegiance to a loyalty oath to Hitler's Reich—is a fair example of the mind-set one still finds among some progressives.

Thomas Lasley, former dean of the University of Dayton School of Education and another foe of the "old morality," denounces the "values juggernaut" for its hypocrisy:

Teachers tell students to cooperate, but then they systematically rank students in terms of their class performance. . . . Teachers tell students that respect is essential for social responsibility, but then they call on boys a majority of the time. . . . And finally students are informed that they should be critical thinkers, but then they are evaluated on whether they think the same way that their teachers do.[70]

Jerry Harrington (now retired) taught math at the Woodland Park Middle School, located in a poor neighborhood of San Diego, for more than thirty years. During his time at Woodland Park, Harrington taught a fifteen-minute morning class to students called How to Be Successful. It's a course on what Aristotle called the practical virtues. But it is also the kind of course critics like Kohn and Lasley deplore. In Harrington's class, the kids learn the "Eleven B's": Be responsible. Be on time. Be friendly. Be polite. Be a listener. Be a tough worker. Be a goal setter. And so on. Children are taught all about the work ethic and how to integrate it into their lives.[71]

Writer Tim Stafford described what happened when Harrington ran into a former pupil.[72] The student, Philip, then in high school, was bagging groceries, and Harrington asked him how he got his job. Philip said he got it by applying what he had learned in class. First, he set a goal: "I set a goal that I needed to earn six hundred dollars in the summer because my mother could not afford to buy me clothes for school." Adhering closely to the method taught in the course, Philip then broke the goal down into small parts. Next he had taken what are called "action steps." Step one: He listed twenty businesses that were within walking or biking distance of his house. Step two: He went to each one to apply for a job. After sixteen rejections, the seventeenth place—the grocery store—hired him.

Two years later, Mr. Harrington ran into Philip's older brother, who told him that Philip was still working. The older brother told Mr. Harrington, "You saved my life too." He explained that their mother was an alcoholic who had had a series of boyfriends. Their home life was chaotic. Philip had told his brother about what he had learned in his How to Be Successful class. Now both brothers were putting their lives together.[73]

I spoke with Harrington in the fall of 1999. He told me that, on average, middle school boys are less mature than the girls: "The boys have difficulties at the level of basic organization: being responsible for their backpacks, their homework." Most of the girls understand the idea of personal responsibility and are ready to move on to the idea of being responsible for others. At Harrington's school, it is girls who are active in school events and who hold the leadership positions in student government. The male students are preoccupied with skateboarding, surfing, and roller blading—activities with few rules, little structure, no responsibilities. When he asks his male students about their long-term goals, many of them confidently assert that they plan to become sports stars. But when he inquires about what steps they are taking to realize even that unrealistic goal, he finds that they have a very poor understanding of the relationship of means to ends. Harrington has two daughters and assures me that "girls are very dear to my heart." But, he points out, no one seems to be focused on boys: "Every time I turn around, if there is an event or program where someone is going to be lifted up and encouraged, it's for girls." Harrington was unusual in recognizing and talking about boys, their insufficiencies, and how badly we neglect them. He was doing what he could to help them, but in too many schools the moral needs of boys are disregarded and unmet.[74]

There are millions of American boys who could greatly benefit from courses like Harrington's and from programs like Positive Action—and not just poor and neglected boys. Of course, girls need directive moral education as well. But when we consider that boys are more likely to fail at school, to become disengaged, to get into trouble, and generally to lose their way to a viable future, it is reasonable to conclude that boys need it more. When two University of Pennsylvania researchers tried to determine why girls do so much better in school than boys, one glaring but simple difference stood out: "Self-discipline gives girls the edge."[75]

What real-world help do the DeMotts, Kohns, Lasleys, and Pukas have to offer boys such as Philip and his brother? What do they propose the schools do about boys with serious character disorders, such as Kyle and Kevin Scherzer and Chris Archer, the Glen Ridge ringleaders, and the Lakewood boys? How would Philip and his brother have fared under the latter-day romantic permissive philosophy of these progressive educators? At the other extreme, too many schools have adopted zero-tolerance policies and simply suspend or expel troubled boys and leave them to cope on their own. The evidence on current character education is mixed, but the extremes—value-free education, gender resocialization, and zero tolerance—have no empirical basis whatsoever.

Lacking guidance and discipline and ignorant of their moral heritage, many American public school children, especially boys, are ill prepared for real life, confused about how to manage their personal lives, and ethically challenged. Some, indeed, are lethally dangerous. In the war against moral education, it is boys who suffer most of the casualties.

9

War and Peace

There have always been societies that favored boys over girls. Ours may be the first to deliberately throw the gender switch. If we continue on our present course, boys will be tomorrow's second sex.

The preeminence of girls is gratifying to those who believe that, even now, many girls are silenced and diminished. At long last, it is boys who are learning what it is like to be "the other sex." Recall Peggy Orenstein's approval of a women-centered classroom, whose walls were filled with pictures and celebrations of women, with men conspicuously absent: "Perhaps for the first time, the boys are the ones looking in through the window." [1]

But reversing the positions of the sexes in an unfair system should be no one's idea of justice. A lopsided educational system in which boys—finally—are on the outside looking in is inherently unjust and socially divisive. The public has given no one a mandate to pursue a policy of privileging girls. Nor is anyone (outside exotic gender equity circles) demanding that boys be resocialized away from their boyishness.

The Great Relearning

Recently, there have been signs of resistance. New groups, such as the Boys Initiative, have formed to promote the cause of boys. [2] Several excellent books on the struggles of boys have materialized. Chicago public schools have dared to introduce an ambitious boy-focused ethics program with a blatantly gendered name: Becoming a Man—Sports Edition.[3] Indeed, with respect to boys, we may now be entering the era of "The Great Relearning." I borrow the phrase from the novelist Tom Wolfe, who first applied it to lessons learned in the late 1960s by a group of hippies living in the Haight-Ashbury district of San Francisco. What happened to Wolfe's iconoclast hippies is instructive.

The Haight-Ashbury hippies had collectively decided that hygiene was a middle-class hang-up. So they determined to live without it. For example, baths and showers, while not actually banned, were frowned upon as retrograde. Wolfe was intrigued by these hippies who, he said, "sought nothing less than to sweep aside all codes and restraints of the past and start out from zero."[4] After a while their principled aversion to modern hygiene had consequences that were as unpleasant as they were unforeseen. Wolfe describes them thus: "At the Haight-Ashbury Free Clinic there were doctors who were treating diseases no living doctor had ever encountered before, diseases that had disappeared so long ago they had never even picked up Latin names, diseases such as the mange, the grunge, the itch, the twitch, the thrush, the scroff, the rot."[5] The itching and the manginess eventually began to vex the hippies, leading them individually to seek help from the local free clinics. Step by step, they had to rediscover for themselves the rudiments of modern hygiene. That rueful process of rediscovery is Wolfe's Great Relearning. A Great Relearning is what has to happen whenever reformers go too far— whenever, in order to start over "from zero," they jettison basic values, well-proven social practices, and plain common sense.

Wolfe's story is both true and amusing. We are, however, familiar with more consequential, less amusing twentieth-century experiments with re-building humankind from zero: Today, more than twenty years after the fall of communism, Eastern Europeans are still in the midst of their own Great Relearning. The United States has also had its share of radical social experiments. By recklessly denying the importance of giving young people moral guidance, parents and educators have cast great numbers of them morally adrift. In defecting from the crucial duties of moral education, we have placed ourselves and our children—especially boys—in serious jeopardy.

We are at the tail end of an extraordinary period of moral deregulation that has left many tens of thousands of our boys academically deficient and without adequate guidance. Too many American boys are floundering, unprepared for the demands of family and work. Many have only a vague sense of right and wrong. Many are still being taught by Rousseauian romantics, which is to say they have been left to "find their own values." Leaving children to discover their own values is a little like putting them in a chemistry lab full of volatile substances and saying, "Discover your own compounds, kids."

In the pursuit of a misguided radical egalitarian ideal, many in our society have insisted the sexes are the same. In our schools, boys and girls are treated as if they are cognitively and emotionally interchangeable. We must now relearn what previous generations never doubted: the sexes are different. It is much more challenging to educate males than females. Just like the British and Australians, we must find out way back to fair-minded, gender-specific policies and practices that acknowledge difference.

Between Mothers and Sons is a wonderful book about feminist mothers coping with an unforeseen and startling event—the birth of a *son*.[6] One might expect the book to be full of advice to mothers on how to resocialize their male child in the direction of androgyny. Instead, it offers a poignant glimpse of women rediscovering the ineradicable nature of boys. These mothers came to question cherished antimale dogmas when these conflicted with something far stronger and deeper—motherly love. Some of the mothers confess to having tried to educate their sons to conform with strict feminist precepts, stopping only when it became evident their boys were suffering. In these accounts, Mother Nature, not Social Construction, gets the last word.

Deborah Galyan, a short-story writer and essayist, describes what happened when she sent her son Dylan to a Montessori preschool "run by a goddess-worshiping, multiracial women's collective on Cape Cod"[7]:

> [S]omething about it did not honor his boy soul. I think it was the
> absence of physical competition. Boys who clashed or tussled with each

other were separated and counseled by the peacemaker. Sticks were confiscated and turned into tomato stakes in the school garden. . . . It finally came to me. . . . I had sent him there to protect him from the very circuitry and compulsions and desires that make him what he is. I had sent him there to protect him from himself.[8]

Galyan then posed painful questions to which she found a liberating answer: "How could I be a good feminist, a good pacifist, and a good mother to a stick-wielding, weapon-generating boy?" And "What exactly is a five-year-old boy?" "A five-year-old boy, I learned from reading summaries of various neurological studies . . . is a beautiful, fierce, testosterone-drenched, cerebrally asymmetrical humanoid carefully engineered to move objects through space, or at very least, to watch others do so."[9]

Janet Burroway, a poet, novelist, and self-described pacifist-liberal, has a son, Tim, who grew up to become a career soldier. She is not sure how exactly he came to move in a direction opposite to her own. She recalls his abiding fascination with plastic planes, toy soldiers, and military history, noting that "his direction was early set."[10] Tim takes her aback in many ways, but she is clearly proud of him: throughout his childhood she was struck by his "chivalric character": "He would, literally, lay down his life for a cause or a friend." And she confesses, "I am forced to be aware of my own contradictions in his presence: a feminist often charmed by his machismo."[11]

Galyan and Burroway discarded some common antimale prejudices when they discovered that boys have their own distinctive charm. The love and respect they shared with their sons left them chastened, wiser, and free of the fashionable resentments that many women harbor toward males. All the same, such stories are sobering. They remind us of the strong disapproval with which many women initially approach boys.

Mary Gordon, perhaps the most orthodox and inveterate feminist in this instructive anthology, is another mother with a disarming son. On one occasion, her son David defends his older sister from a bully. "I thought it was really nice of him to stand up for me," said the sister. For a moment, the mother is also moved by David's gallantry. "But after a minute, I didn't want to buy the idea that a woman needs a man to stand up for her." Gordon says that this incident "expressed for me the complexities of being a feminist mother of a son."[12]

Gordon realizes that she cannot be fair to her son unless she overcomes her prejudices: "Would I take my generalized anger against male privilege out on this little child who was dependent upon me for his survival, physical to be sure, but mental as well?" Nevertheless, Gordon remains torn between her principled animosity against "the male" and her maternal love: "We can't afford wholesale male-bashing, nor can we afford to see the male as the permanently unreconstructable gender. Nor can we pretend that things are right as they are. . . . We must love them as they are, often without knowing what it is that's made them that way."[13] Gordon still firmly believes that males need to be "reconstructed." In saying "We can't afford wholesale male-bashing," she implies that a certain amount of bashing is proper.

An unacknowledged animus against boys is loose in our society. The women who design events such as Son's Day, who write antiharassment guides, who gather in workshops to determine how to change boys' "gender schema" barely disguise their disapproval. Others, who bear no malice to boys, nevertheless do not credit them with sanity and health, for they regard the average boy as alienated, lonely, emotionally repressed, isolated, and prone to violence. These "save-the-male" critics start out by giving boys a failing grade. They join the girl partisans in calling for radical change in the way American males are socialized: only by raising boys to be more like girls can we help them become "real boys."

It is also unfortunate that so many popular writers and education reformers think ill of American boys. The worst-case sociopathic males—gang rapists, mass murderers—become instant metaphors for everyone's sons. The vast numbers of decent and honorable young men, on the other hand, never inspire disquisitions on the inner nature of the boy next door. The false and corrosive doctrine that equates masculinity with violence has found its way into the mainstream.

Now, it is the fashion to celebrate "The End of Men." The male declinists like *Slate*'s Hanna Rosin and ABC legal analyst Dan Abrams seem to imagine a world of busy, consensus-building women, happily and competently interacting and managing the new economy.[14] Rosin points to the explosion of jobs in the nurturing and communicating professions: boys are going to have to adapt to this new women-centered world, or perish. While it is true that family therapists, website designers, personal coaches, dance therapists, home health assistants, and executive producers are in high demand, it is not clear that this network of nurturers and communicators can be sustained without someone paying for it. Society still needs hard-driven innovators.

Women are joining men as partners in running the world and even moving ahead of them in many fields, but they are not replacing them. After almost forty years of gender-neutral pronouns, men are still more likely than women to run for political office, start businesses, file for patents, tell jokes, write editorials, conduct orchestras, and blow things up. Males succeed and fail more spectacularly than females: More males are Nobel laureates and CEOs. But more are also in maximum-security prisons, and males commit most acts of wanton violence. But it usually takes other men to stop them. "Are Men Necessary?" asks *New York Times* writer Maureen Dowd. Yes, they are.

Not because women lack the talent to do the things men do—women can be just as formidable and enterprising as men when they set their minds to it. But fewer women than men do set their minds to it. The sexes are equal, but they exercise their equality in different ways. There is a well-known complementarity between the two sexes. They need each other. They have even been known to love one another. How did we forget about these simple truths? And how have we allowed our society to become so badly rigged against boys?

As part of our Great Relearning, we must again recognize and respect the reality that the sexes are different but equal. Each has its distinctive strengths and graces. We must put an end to all the crisis mongering that pathologizes children: we must be less credulous when sensationalistic experts talk of girls as drowning Ophelias or of boys as anxious, isolated Hamlets. Neither sex needs to be "revived" or "rescued"; neither needs to be "reinvented." Instead of doing things that do not need doing and should not be done, we must dedicate ourselves to the hard tasks that are both necessary and possible:

improving the moral climate in our schools and providing our children with first-rate schooling that equips them for the good life in the new century.

We have created a lot of problems, both for ourselves and for our children. Now we must resolutely set about solving them. I am confident we can do that. American boys, whose very masculinity turns out to be politically incorrect, badly need our support. If you are an optimist, as I am, you believe that good sense and fair play will prevail. If you are a mother of sons, as I am, you know that one of the most agreeable facts of life is that boys will be boys.

Acknowledgments

I could not have written this book without the unstinting support of the American Enterprise Institute. AEI is the ideal scholarly environment where I was able to devote more than a year to this new version of *The War Against Boys*. I am especially grateful to the late Elizabeth Lurie. She believed in this book from its beginning in the late 1990s and was partly responsible for bringing me to AEI, where I wrote the first edition. She is dearly missed. I also want to thank Sue Koffel for her vital encouragement and support.

I am heavily indebted to several research assistants and interns who have contributed so much to this project: Caroline Kitchens, Keriann Hopkins, Riva Litman, Emily Jashinsky, and Geneva Ruppert. Special thanks are also owed to two AEI colleagues and good friends who have been so generous with their time: Mark Perry and Karlyn Bowman.

I owe a particular debt of gratitude to my editor at Simon & Schuster, Robert Bender, who encouraged me to write this second edition. Many thanks to Karyn Marcus, Jessica Chin, and Patricia Romanowski Bashe for shepherding this book through the production process.

There is no adequate way to thank my husband, Fred Sommers. He is more interested in formal logic and metaphysics, but he patiently discussed every page with me. If he is tired of hearing about the plight of American boys, he never let on.

My sons, David and Tamler, were at the forefront of my consciousness when I first wrote *The War Against Boys*. They have grown up to become wonderful men, but they were the paradigmatic boys whose cause this book defends. I dedicate it to them.

Notes

Preface

1. Success for Boys, "Outline," Australian Government Department of Education, Employment, and Workplace Relations, www.deewr.gov.au/Schooling/BoysEducation/Pages/success_for_boys.aspx (accessed September 19, 2012).

2. Boys' Reading Commission, *All Party Parliamentary Literacy Group Final Report*, National Literacy Trust, July 2, 2012, www.literacytrust.org.uk/assets/0001/4056/Boys_Commission_Report.pdf (accessed September 19, 2012).

3. Carolyn Abraham, "Failing Boys and the Power Keg of Sexual Politics," *Globe and Mail*, October 15, 2010.

1. *Where the Boys Are*

1. Laura Zingmond, "H.S. 610 Aviation High School," Insideschools.org, a Project of the Center for New York City Affairs, The New School, http://insideschools.org/index12.php?fs=1035 (accessed June 15, 2012). Statistic regarding college enrollment is dated January 2009. (The New York State average graduation rate is 72 percent.)

2. New York City, Department of Education, Progress Overview, 2010–2011, http://schools.nyc.gov/OA/SchoolReports/2010-11/Progress_Report_Overview_2011_HS_Q610.pdf (accessed June 20, 2012).

3. Aviation High website: www.aviationhs.net/site_res_view_template.aspx?id=a057d48e-a5d4-4049-86df-12ff765a9577 (accessed June 20, 2012).

4. New York Department of Education website: http://schools.nyc.gov/SchoolPortals/24/Q610/AboutUs/Statistics/register.htm (accessed July 6, 2012).

5. Marcia C. Greenberger, Leslie T. Annexstein, and Kathleen M. Keller to Chancellor Harold O. Levy, New York City Board of Education, August 16, 2001, in the possession of the author.

6. Ibid.

7. Betsy Gotbaum, Public Advocate for the City of New York, *Blue School, Pink School: Gender Imbalance in New York City CTE High Schools*, January 2008, p. 7.

8. Whitehouse, *Title IX at the White House*, 1 hr., 1 min., 41 sec.; video recording. Uploaded June 26, 2009, www.youtube.com/watch?v=MqLeg7eunsA (accessed July 26, 2011).

9. Yupin Bae, Susan Choy, Claire Geddes, Jennifer Sable, and Thomas Snyder, *Trends in Educational Equity of Girls and Women*, NCES 2000-030 (Washington, DC: US Government Printing Office, 2000).

10. Gender Equity in Education Act of 1993, HR 1793, 103rd Cong. Library of Congress THOMAS. Available at: http://thomas.loc.gov/cgi-bin/bdquery/z?d103:H.R.1793: (accessed June 20, 2012).

11. *A Call to Action: Shortchanging Girls, Shortchanging America* (Washington, DC: American Association of University Women, 1991), p. 4.

12. US Department of Health and Human Services, "Secretary Shalala Unveils New Girl Power!–Girl Scouts Partnership," news release, June 23, 1997. A Ford Foundation grant made it possible for *How Schools Shortchange Girls: The AAUW Report* to be translated into French, Spanish, and Chinese and made available to UN conference delegates. According to PR Newswire (September 1, 1995), "Over a hundred AAUW members are meeting in Beijing and Hauirou at the UN Conference, [to] bring its concerns about access to education for women and girls to the table . . . *How Schools Shortchange Girls*, a groundbreaking report of gender bias in America's schools, will be addressed during education reform discussion." See also Anne Bryant, "Education for Girls Should Be Topic A in Beijing," *Houston Chronicle*, August 30, 1995, p. 17.

13. American Association of University Women, *How Schools Shortchange Girls: The AAUW Report* (Washington, DC: American Association of University Women, 1992).

14. Here I am referring to the much-quoted study by David and Myra Sadker in which they claim to have found that boys in elementary and middle school called out answers eight times more often than girls. Allegedly, when boys called out, their teachers listened, but when girls called out they were instructed to raise their hands. However, David Sadker presented the finding in an unpublished paper at a symposium sponsored by the American Educational Research Association (AERA) and now it seems neither he nor AERA has a copy. He has also conceded that the eight-to-one ratio he announced might have been inaccurate. See: Amy Saltzman, "Schooled in Failure?," *U.S. News & World Report*, November 7, 1994, p. 90. See also Judith Kleinfeld, "Student Performance: Males Versus Females," *National Affairs*, Winter 1999, p. 14.

15. Carol Gilligan, "Prologue," in *Making Connections: The Relational Worlds of Adolescent Girls at Emma Willard School*, eds. Carol Gilligan, Nona Lyons, and Trudy Hanmer (Cambridge, MA: Harvard University Press, 1990), p. 4.

16. Ibid.

17. Mary Pipher, *Reviving Ophelia: Saving the Selves of Adolescent Girls* (New York: Penguin Group, 2005), p. 19.

18. Bae, Choy, Geddes, Sable, and Snyder, *Trends in Educational Equity of Girls and Women*, p. 22.

19. J. H. Pryor, S. Hurtado, L. DeAngelo, L. Palucki Blake, and S. Tran, *The American Freshman: National Norms Fall 2010* (Los Angeles: Higher Education Research Institute, UCLA, 2010), pp. 43, 67. Relevant data from aggregates of male and female responses to the question "What was your average grade in high school?," in which a larger percentage of females than males received A's and a larger percentage of males

than females received C's. The gap in percentage receiving A's and percentage receiving C's has remained constant since 1970. See also US Department of Education, Institute of Education Sciences, National Center for Education Statistics, *High School Transcript Study (HSTS), 2000, 1998, 1994, 1990.*

20. Ibid. Relevant data from aggregates of male and female responses to the question "During your last year in high school, how much time did you spend during a typical week doing the following activities? Studying/homework," pp. 56, 80.

21. US Department of Education, National Center for Education Statistics, *Education Longitudinal Study of 2002* (ELS:2002/2004), "First Follow-Up, 2004."

22. Pryor, Hurtado, DeAngelo, Palucki Blake, and Tran, *The American Freshman: National Norms Fall 2010*, pp. 58, 82.

23. National Center for Education Statistics, *The Nation's Report Card: Arts 2008 Music & Visual Arts* (Washington, DC: National Center for Education Statistics, 2009), executive summary, p. 2.

24. For suspension rates in 2006, see US Department of Education, *The Condition of Education 2009* (Washington, DC: US Department of Education, 2009), p. 206. For information on dropouts, see US Department of Education, *The Condition of Education 2006* (Washington, DC: US Department of Education, 2006), p. 163. Boys are three times as likely as girls to be enrolled in special education programs and four times as likely as girls to be diagnosed with attention deficit/hyperactivity disorder (AD/HD). Males win the day when it comes to partying, watching video games, and drinking beer. Pryor, Hurtado, DeAngelo, Palucki Blake, and Tran, *The American Freshman: National Norms Fall 2010.*

25. Lisa Wolf, "Boys' Self-Esteem Problems," *Daily Beast*, November 11, 2010, www.thedailybeast.com/articles/2010/11/11/boys-self-esteem-problems.html.

26. College Board, *2010 College-Bound Seniors Total Group Profile Report*, "Total Group Mean SAT Scores: College-Bound Seniors, 1972–2010," 2010, http://professionals.collegeboard.com/profdownload/2010-total-group-profile-report-cbs.pdf (accessed July 11, 2012).

27. College Board, *College Bound Seniors: 1992 Profile of SAT and Achievement Test Takers* (Princeton, NJ: Educational Testing Service, 1992), p. iv. See also *Introduction to the 1998 College-Bound Seniors, a Profile of SAT Program Test Takers*, www.collegeboard.org/sat/cbsenior/yr1998/nat/intrcb98; and Warren Willingham and Nancy Cole, *Gender and Fair Assessment* (Mahwah, NJ: Erlbaum, 1997).

28. *The Condition of Education 1997*, "Women in Mathematics and Science," US Department of Education, p. 6, http://nces.ed.gov/pubs97/97982.pdf (accessed June 20, 2012).

29. According to the Centers for Disease Control and Prevention (CDC), in a 2007 parent-reported survey of attention deficit/hyperactivity disorder among children ages four to seventeen, boys were much more likely to have been diagnosed with AD/HD (13.2 percent of boys and 5.6 percent of girls). This means boys constitute 73 percent of AD/HD diagnoses. See Centers for Disease Control and Prevention, "Increasing Prevalence of Parent-Reported Attention-Deficit/Hyperactivity Disorder Among Children—United States, 2003 and 2007," *Morbidity and Mortality Weekly Report* 59, no. 44 (November 12, 2010), pp. 1439–1443.

30. Christina Hoff Sommers, "The War Against Boys," *The Atlantic Monthly* 285, no. 5 (May 2000), pp. 59–74; Peg Tyre, "The Trouble with Boys," *Newsweek* (January 30, 2006). See also Marcia Vickers, "Why Can't We Let Boys Be Boys?," *BusinessWeek*, no. 3834 (May 26, 2003), p. 84. See also Richard Whitmire, "Boy Trouble," *The New*

Republic 234, no. 2 (January 23, 2006), p. 15. See also Brendan I. Koerner, "Where the Boys Aren't," *U.S. News & World Report*, 126, no. 5 (February 8, 1999), pp. 46–55. See also "The Gender Gap: Boys Lagging," report by Leslie Stahl, *60 Minutes*, CBS, February 11, 2009. See also "Author Richard Whitmire Examines the Gender Gap in Education," *ABC News*, ABC, January 15, 2010. See also Richard Whitmire, *Why Boys Fail: Saving Our Sons from an Educational System That's Leaving Them Behind* (New York: American Management Association, 2010). See also Angela Phillips, *The Trouble with Boys: A Wise and Sympathetic Guide to the Risky Business of Raising Sons* (New York: Basic Books, 1994).

31. See, for example, Duncan Chaplin and Daniel Klasik, *Gender Gaps in College and High School Graduation by Race, Combining Public and Private Schools* (Fayetteville: Education Working Paper Archive, Department of Education Reform, University of Arkansas, November 16, 2006). See also Arizona State University Center for Community Development and Civil Rights, *Pathways to Prevention: The Latino Male Dropout Crisis* (2007). See also Krista Kafer, *Taking the Boy Crisis in Education Seriously: How School Choice Can Boost Achievement Among Boys and Girls* (Washington, DC: Women for School Choice: A Project of the Independent Women's Forum, April 2007).

32. Celine Coggins, *Are Boys Making the Grade? Gender Gaps in Achievement and Attainment* (Cambridge, MA: Rennie Center for Education Research and Policy, October 2006), p. 9.

33. Ibid., p. 2.

34. California Postsecondary Education Commission, *The Gender Gap in California Higher Education: Commission Report 06-08* (Sacramento: California Postsecondary Education Commission, June 2006), and California Postsecondary Education Commission, *The Gender Gap in California Higher Education: Commission Report: A Follow-Up* (Sacramento: California Postsecondary Education Commission, September 2006).

35. Ibid., p. 2.

36. Ibid., p. 5.

37. Linda Hallman, *AAUW Current Topics Briefing #5: Breaking Through Barriers Briefing*, American Association of University Women, June 30, 2008, www.aauw.org/member_center/briefings/briefingUnifyingFocus_063008.cfm (accessed August 9, 2011).

38. Linda Hallman, "Strength in Numbers," *AAUW Outlook* (Washington, DC: AAUW Publications Office, Spring/Summer 2008), p. 3.

39. Turner Strategies Inc., *AAUW "Where the Girls Are" Report* soundbites from AAUW President Linda Hallman, 7 min., 31 sec.; video recording, uploaded May 18, 2008, www.youtube.com/watch?v=BdPkKgM2kfw (accessed August 9, 2011). Quote begins at 1:18.

40. It was also featured in several influential education publications and websites such as the National Council of Teachers of English Blog and Inside Higher Education.

41. Christianne Corbett, Catherine Hill, and Andresse St. Rose, *Where the Girls Are: The Facts About Gender Equity in Education* (Washington, DC: AAUW Educational Foundation, May 2008), p. 6.

42. Ibid., p. 55.

43. Ibid., p. 2.

44. Ibid., p. 9.

45. Caryl Rivers and Rosalind Chait Barnett, "The Myth of the Boys Crisis," *Washington Post*, April 9, 2006, www.washingtonpost.com/wp-dyn/content/article/2006/04/07/

AR2006040702025.html (accessed June 20, 2012). See also Sara Mead, *The Evidence Suggests Otherwise: The Truth About Girls and Boys* (Washington, DC: Education Sector, June 2006).

46. Tamar Lewin, "Girls' Gains Have Not Cost Boys, Report Says," *New York Times*, May 20, 2008, www.nytimes.com/2008/05/20/education/20girls.html (accessed June 20, 2012).

47. Corbett, Hill, and St. Rose, *Where the Girls Are: The Facts About Gender Equity in Education*, p. 55.

48. US Department of Education, National Center for Education Statistics, *Earned Degrees Conferred, 1869–70 through 1964–65*; Projections of Education Statistics to 2019; Higher Education General Information Survey (HEGIS), *Degrees and Other Formal Awards Conferred* surveys, 1965–66 through 1985–86; and 1986–87 through 2008–09 Integrated Postsecondary Education Data System, *Completions Survey* (IPEDS-C:87-99), and Fall 2000 through Fall 2009. (This table was prepared September 2010.)

49. *PBS NewsHour*, "Forum: Education Experts on Gender Gap," PBS, www.pbs.org/newshour/forum/education/jan-june08/gendergap_05-21.html (accessed August 4, 2011).

50. US Census Bureau, Current Population Survey, 2008 Annual Social and Economic Supplement (internet release date: April 2009).

51. Valerie Strauss, "No Crisis for Boys in Schools, Study Says," *Washington Post*, May 20, 2010, www.washingtonpost.com/wp-dyn/content/article/2008/05/19/AR2008051902798.html (accessed July 11, 2012).

52. According to statistics from 2009 Department of Education data cited by forbes.com, the gender ratio at Fisk University is 64 percent female, 35 percent male, www.forbes.com/colleges/fisk-university/ (accessed July 11, 2012); *U.S. News & World Report*'s profile of Howard University includes a student body that is 67 percent female and 33 percent male, http://colleges.usnews.rankingsandreviews.com/best-colleges/howard-university-1448 (accessed July 11, 2012); *U.S. News & World Report* shows a gender ratio of 72 percent female and 28 percent male for Clark Atlanta University, http://colleges.usnews.rankingsandreviews.com/best-colleges/clark-atlanta-university-1551 (accessed July 11, 2012).

53. Andrew Sum et al., "The Gender Gaps in High School Graduation, Post-Secondary Education/Training Program Enrollment, and Four-Year College Enrollment Rates of Boston Public School Graduates, Class of 2007" (Boston: Center for Labor Market Studies, Northeastern University, 2009), p. 16.

54. See Victor B. Saenz, "The Vanishing Latino Male in Higher Education," *Journal of Hispanic Higher Education* 8, no. 1 (2009), pp. 54–89. See also Jerlando F. Jackson, "African-American Males in Education: Endangered or Ignored?," *The Teachers College Record* 108, no. 2 (February 2006), pp. 201–205. See also Arizona State University Center for Community Development and Civil Rights, "Pathways to Prevention: The Latino Male Dropout Crisis" (2007).

55. John Michael Lee Jr. and Tafaya Ransom, *The Educational Experience of Young Men of Color: A Review of Research, Pathways and Progress* (New York: College Board Advocacy and Policy Center, June 2011), p. 50.

56. Pryor, Hurtado, DeAngelo, Palucki Blake, and Tran, *The American Freshman: National Norms, Fall 2010*, pp. 43, 67. Data comes from number of respondents who answered "A or A+" to the question "What was your average grade in high school?"

57. Judith Kleinfeld, *Five Powerful Strategies for Connecting Boys to Schools*, paper for White House Conference on Helping America's Youth, Indianapolis, IN (June 6, 2006), pp. 1–2.

58. Corbett, Hill, and St. Rose, *Where the Girls Are: The Facts About Gender Equity in Education*, p. 9.

59. Colleen Leahey, "Update: Fortune 500 Women CEOs Hits a Record 20," *Fortune*, July 18, 2012, http://postcards.blogs.fortune.cnn.com/2012/07/18/fortune-500 -women-ceos-2/ (accessed January 24, 2013). Library of Congress, "Members of the US Congress," http://beta.congress.gov/members?pageSize=25&Legislative_ Source=Member+Profiles&Congress=113th+Congress+%282013-2014%29 (accessed January 22, 2013); Martha S. West and John W. Curtis, "AAUP Faculty Gender Equity Statistics, 2005," *American Association of University Professors*, www.aaup.org/NR/rdonlyres/63396944-44BE-4ABA-9815-5792D93856F1/0/ AAUPGenderEquityIndicators2006.pdf (accessed April 25, 2012); www.bls.gov/news .release/empsit.t16.htm; Bureau of Labor Statistics, Economic News Release, January 4, 2014; James J. Stephan, "Census of State and Federal Correctional Facilities, 2005," *Bureau of Justice Statistics*, October 2008, www.bjs.gov/content/pub/pdf/csfcf05.pdf (accessed April 25, 2012).

60. "An Analysis of Reasons for the Disparity in Wages Between Men and Women," CONSAD Research Group, available at www.consad.com/content/reports /Gender%20Wage%20Gap%20Final%20Report.pdf (accessed March 9, 2012).

61. Midwest Pharmacy Workforce Research Consortium, *2009 National Pharmacies Workplace Survey* (Alexandria, VA: Pharmacy Manpower Project, 2010).

62. Eduardo Porter, "Motherhood Still a Cause of Pay Inequality," *New York Times*, June 12, 2012, www.nytimes.com/2012/06/13/business/economy/motherhood-still-a -cause-of-pay-inequality.html?_r=1 (accessed June 20, 2012).

63. AAUW, *Behind the Pay Gap*, 2007, p. 18. Buried in the report is this statement: "After accounting for all factors known to affect wages, about one-quarter of the gap remains unexplained and *may* be attributed to discrimination" (emphasis added). As Steve Chapman noted in *Reason*, "Another way to put it is that three-quarters of the gap clearly has innocent causes—and that we actually don't know whether discrimination accounts for the rest," http://reason.com/archives/2010/08/19/the-truth-about-the -pay-gap (accessed June 20, 2012).

64. Ibid., p. 3.

65. National Organization for Women, "Women Deserve Equal Pay," www.now.org/ issues/economic/factsheet.html (accessed June 20, 2012).

66. Kevin Wack and Beth Quinby, "Boys in Jeopardy at School," *Portland Press Herald*, March 18, 2010, www.pressherald.com/archive/boys-in-jeopardy-at -school_2008-02-07.html (accessed January 25, 2013).

67. Ibid.

68. Tom Mortenson, "What's Wrong with Guys?," *Postsecondary Education Opportunity* 39, article 1 (September 1995), www.postsecondary.org/articlesyearlist .asp?cat5=%271995%27# (accessed June 20, 2012).

69. Scott Jaschik, "Is There a Crisis in Education of Males?," insidehighered.com, May 21, 2008, www.insidehighered.com/news/2008/05/21/gender (accessed June 20, 2012).

70. US Department of Health and Human Services, "Secretary Shalala Unveils New Girl Power!–Girl Scouts Partnership," news release, June 23, 1997.

71. According to the book description, Pipher's *Reviving Ophelia* spent three years on the *New York Times* bestseller list.

72. William C. Symonds, Robert B. Schwartz, and Ronald Ferguson, *Pathways to Prosperity: Meeting the Challenge of Preparing Young Americans for the 21st Century* (Pathways to Prosperity Project, Harvard Graduate School of Education, February 2011), p. 2.

73. Ibid.

74. Michael Greenstone and Adam Looney, "Trends: Reduced Earnings for Men in America," *The Milken Institute Review* (3rd qtr., 2011), p. 8, www.milkeninstitute.org/publications/publications.taf?function=detail&ID=38801273&cat=MIR (accessed June 20, 2012).

75. Ibid., p. 14.

76. Mark Mather, "In US, a Sharp Increase in Young Men Living at Home," Population Reference Bureau, September 2011, www.prb.org/articles/2011/us-young-adults-living-at-home.aspx (accessed June 15, 2011).

77. The Coalition includes the AAUW and the National Women's Law Center.

78. National Coalition for Women and Girls in Education (NCWGE), *Title IX at 40: Working to Ensure Gender Equity in Education* (Washington, DC: NCWGE, 2012), p. 30. Available at www.ncwge.org/PDF/TitleIXat40.pdf (accessed July 11, 2012).

79. Ibid., p. 35.

80. Linda Hallman, "Strength in Numbers." *AAUW Outlook* (Washington, DC: AAUW Publications, Spring/Summer 2008), p. 13.

81. William Brozo and Richard Whitmire, "Boys Aren't Learning to Read—and It's a Global Problem," *New York Daily News*, December 20, 2010, http://articles.nydailynews.com/2010-12-20/news/27084903_1_reading-literacy-skills-boys (accessed June 20, 2012).

82. Office for Civil Rights and US Department of Education, *Gender Equity in Education: A Data Snapshot,* June 2012, www2.ed.gov/about/offices/list/ocr/docs/gender-equity-in-education.pdf (accessed January 22, 2013).

83. College Board, *Program Summary Report 2012*, http://media.collegeboard.com/digitalServices/pdf/research/program_summary_report_2012.pdf (accessed January 22, 2013).

84. Christopher Cornwell et al., "Non-cognitive Skills and the Gender Disparities in Test Scores and Teacher Assessments: Evidence from Primary School," *Journal of Social Resources* (Winter 2013), pp. 236–264.

85. Matt Weeks, "New UGA Research Helps Explain Why Girls Do Better in Schools," *UGA Today*, January 2, 2013, http://news.uga.edu/releases/article/why-girls-do-better-in-school-010212/ (accessed January 22, 2013).

2. *No Country for Young Men*

1. Amanda Rose et al., "How Girls and Boys Expect Disclosure About Problems Will Make Them Feel: Implications for Friendships," *Child Development*, February 2012, pp. 844–866.

2. See, for example, Carrie Stetler, " 'Tug of War' now 'Tug of Peace,' " June 12, 2008, http://blog.nj.com/parentalguidance/2008/06/tugopeace.html (accessed June 20, 2012). Additional examples of students playing "tug of peace" are found at Avon Elementary School in Albany, MN: http://www.albany.k12.mn.us/LinkClick.aspx?fileticket=PS7Sr0Jb9-s%3D&tabid=541&mid=2790&language=en-US; Frost Valley YMCA Summer Camp in Claryville, NY: http://fvsummercamp.wordpress.com/2008/12/29/tug-of-peace/; Friends School of Portland in Falmouth, ME: http://friendsschoolofportland.org/photos/tug-peace; and Connelly School of the Holy Child

in Potomac, MD: http://www.holychild.org/HAPPENINGS_FEBRUARY152012 (all accessed January 24, 2013).

3. Janet Cromley, "Tag, You're Out!," *Los Angeles Times*, November 6, 2006, http://articles.latimes.com/2006/nov/06/health/he-tag6 (accessed June 20, 2012).

4. Martin Miller, "Principal Says the Game of Tag Lowers Students' Self-esteem," *Chicago Tribune*, June 26, 2002, http://articles.chicagotribune.com/2002-06-26/features/0206260054_1_tag-self-esteem-chase-games (accessed July 11, 2012).

5. Sandy Coleman, "Dodgeball Sparks Debate in Schools," *Dayton Daily News*, April 3, 2001.

6. Thomas Murphy, physical education teacher at Tobin Elementary School, in ibid.

7. Paul Zientarski, department chairman for Naperville Central High School, in Karen Brandon, "Foul Ball: Childhood Game Picking Up More Enemies; Some PE Teachers Say Dodgeball Sends Harmful Message," *Chicago Tribune*, March 18, 2001, sec. C, p. 1.

8. Neil F. Williams, "The Physical Education Hall of Shame," *Journal of Physical Education, Recreation & Dance* 65, no. 2, (February 1994), pp. 57–60.

9. For a review of the literature, see A. D. Pellegrini and Peter K. Smith, "Physical Activity Play: The Nature and Function of a Neglected Aspect of Play," *Child Development* 69, no. 3 (June 1998), pp. 577–598.

10. Eleanor Emmons Maccoby and Carl Nagy Jacklin, *The Psychology of Sex Differences* (Stanford, CA: Stanford University Press, 1974), p. 352. Janet Lever, "Sex Differences in the Games Children Play," *Social Problems* 23 (1967), pp. 478–487. See also Deborah Tannen, *You Just Don't Understand: Women and Men in Conversation* (New York: Ballantine, 1990), pp. 43–47.

11. Deborah Tannen, op. cit., p. 47.

12. Anthony Pellegrini and Jane Perlmutter, "Rough-and-Tumble Play on the Elementary School Playground," *Young Children*, January 1998, pp. 14–17.

13. Ibid., p. 15.

14. Ibid.

15. Mary Ellin Logue and Hattie Harvey, "Preschool Teachers' Views of Active Play," *Journal of Research in Childhood Education* 24, no. 1 (December 2009), p. 35.

16. Ibid., p. 35.

17. Ibid., p. 45.

18. Ibid., p. 42.

19. Walter S. Gilliam, "Prekindergarteners Left Behind: Expulsion Rates in State Prekindergarten Systems," *Foundation for Child Development Policy Brief Series* no. 3 (May 2005).

20. Logue and Harvey, "Preschool Teachers' View of Active Play," p. 43.

21. Mary Ellin Logue and Hattie Shelton, "The Stories Bad Guys Tell: Promoting Literacy and Social Awareness in Preschool," *The Constructivist*, National Journal for the Association of Constructivist Teaching, September 2008. Also see Jane Klatch, *Under Deadman's Skin* (Boston: Beacon Press, 2001).

22. Logue and Harvey, "Preschool Teachers' View of Active Play," p. 35.

23. Megan Rosenfeld, "Reexamining the Plight of Young Males," *Washington Post*, March 26, 1998, p. A1.

24. Ibid.

25. "The War on Boys," National Desk, PBS, April 9, 1999.

26. "Daily School Recess Improves Classroom Behavior," sciencedaily.com, January 26, 2009, www.sciencedaily.com/releases/2009/01/090126173835.htm (accessed June 20, 2012).

27. Dirk Johnson, "Many Schools Putting an End to Child's Play," *New York Times*, April 7, 1998, www.nytimes.com/1998/04/07/us/many-schools-putting-an-end-to-child-s -play.html?pagewanted=all&src=pm (accessed June 20, 2012).

28. Ibid.

29. A. D. Pellegrini, Patti David Huberty, and Ithel Jones, "The Effects of Recess Timing on Children's Playground and Classroom Behaviors," *American Educational Research Journal* 32, no. 4 (Winter 1995), pp. 845–864.

30. Gopal K. Singh and Michael D. Kogan, "Childhood Obesity in the United States, 1976–2008," US Department of Health and Human Services, www.hrsa.gov/healthit/ images/mchb_obesity_pub.pdf (accessed June 20, 2012); and Cynthia L. Ogden et al., "Prevalence of Obesity in the United States, 2009–2010," US Department of Health and Human Services, www.cdc.gov/nchs/data/databriefs/db82.pdf (accessed June 20, 2012).

31. Carlin DeGuerin Miller, "Two-Inch Lego Gun Gets 4th-Grader Patrick Timoney in Trouble; Where's the NRA?," cbsnews.com, February 4, 2010, www.cbsnews .com/8301-504083_162-6173526-504083.html (accessed June 20, 2012).

32. Andy Cordan, "Boy Disciplined After Waving a Gun-shaped Pizza Slice," wkrn.com, December 14, 2011, www.wkrn.com/story/16325409/gun-shaped-pizza-slice (ac- cessed June 20, 2012); Kathryn Sotnik, "Coventry School Bans Army Men Hat," wpri.com, June 17, 2010, www.wpri.com/dpp/news/local_news/coventry-school-bans -army-men-hat (accessed June 20, 2012); Ian Urbina, "Boy's Camping Utensil Vio- lates 'Zero Tolerance,'" *New York Times*, October 12, 2009, www.sfgate.com/cgi-bin/ article.cgi?f=/c/a/2009/10/11/MNM21A4B2T.DTL (accessed September 20, 2012).

33. "Boy Suspended Over Utensil Gets Reprieve," today.com, October 14, 2009, http:// today.msnbc.msn.com/id/33289924/ns/today-today_news/t/boy-suspended-over -utensil-gets-reprieve/#.T9uACHngf5w (accessed September 20, 2012).

34. Department of Education, *Condition of Education*, 2009, p. 206. See also Steven Teske, "A Study of Zero Tolerance Polices in Schools: A Multi-Integrated Systems Approach to Improve Outcomes for Adolescents," *Journal of Child and Adolescent Psychiatric Nursing* 24 (2011), p. 89.

35. National Center for Education Statistics, *Youth Indicators 2011*, December 2011, p. 38.

36. James Comer and Alvin Poussaint, *Raising Black Children* (New York: Plume Books, 1992), pp. 197–198.

37. Marianne Bertrand and Jessica Pan, "The Trouble with Boys: Social Influences and the Gender Gap in Disruptive Behavior," National Bureau of Economic Research, Working Paper No. 17541, October 2011, www.nber.org/papers/w17541 (accessed August 20, 2012).

38. Ibid., p. 2.

39. Carolyn Evertson and Carol Weinstein, eds., *Handbook of Classroom Management: Research, Practice and Contemporary Issues* (Mahwah, NJ: Erlbaum, 2006), pp. 1068– 1069.

40. Zero Tolerance Task Force, "Are Zero Tolerance Policies Effective in the Schools?," *American Psychologist* (December 2008), p. 856, www.apa.org/pubs/info/reports/zero -tolerance-report.pdf (accessed September 20, 2012).

41. Crime Lab, University of Chicago, "BAM—Sports Edition," July 2012, https://crimelab.uchicago.edu/sites/crimelab.uchicago.edu/files/uploads/BAM_FINAL%20Research%20and%20Policy%20Brief_20120711.pdf. (accessed January 22, 2013).

42. Zero Tolerance Task Force, "Are Zero Tolerance Policies Effective in the Schools?"

43. Ibid., p. 54. See also Linda Raffaele Mendez, "Predictors of Suspension and Negative School Outcomes: A Longitudinal Study," *New Directions for Youth Development* 99 (Fall 2003), pp. 17–33.

44. Zero Tolerance Task Force, "Are Zero Tolerance Policies Effective?," p. 853.

45. Ibid.

46. Richard Zoglin, Sam Allis, and Ratu Kamlani, "Now for the Bad News: A Teenage Time Bomb," *Time*, January 15, 1996.

47. James Q. Wilson, "Crime and Public Policy," in James Q. Wilson and Joan Petersilia, eds., *Crime* (San Francisco: Institute for Contemporary Studies, 2005), pp. 489–507.

48. John J. DiIulilo Jr., "The Coming of the Super-Predators," *Weekly Standard* 1, no. 11, November 27, 1995.

49. John J. DiIulio Jr., *How to Stop the Coming Crime Wave* (New York: Manhattan Institute, 1996), p. 1.

50. William J. Bennett, John J. DiIulio Jr., and John P. Walters, *Body Count: Moral Poverty . . . and How to Win America's War Against Crime and Drugs* (New York: Simon & Schuster, 1996), pp. 26–27.

51. Dewey Cornell, *School Violence: Fears Versus Facts* (Mahwah, NJ: Erlbaum, 2006), p. 16.

52. Sarah Glazer, "Boys' Emotional Needs: Is Growing Up Tougher for Boys Than for Girls?," *Congressional Quarterly Researcher*, June 18, 1999, p. 521.

53. Ibid., p. 523.

54. Charles Puzzanchera and Benjamin Adams, "Juvenile Arrests 2009," US Department of Justice, December 2011, www.ojjdp.gov/pubs/236477.pdf (accessed June 20, 2012).

55. Ibid., pp. 9–11.

56. Richard Redding and Barbara Mrozoski, "Adjudicatory and Dispositional Decision Making in Juvenile Justice," in Kirk Heilbrun et al., eds., *Juvenile Delinquency: Prevention, Assessment and Intervention* (Oxford, UK: Oxford University Press, 2005), pp. 17–33.

57. Zero Tolerance Task Force, "Are Zero Tolerance Policies Effective?," p. 853.

58. Simone Robers, Jijun Zhang, and Jennifer Truman, "Indicators of School Crime and Safety: 2011," National Center for Education Statistics, Institute of Education Sciences, US Department of Education, and Bureau of Justice Statistics, Office of Justice Programs, US Department of Justice, 2012, p. iv.

59. Cornell, *School Violence: Fears Versus Facts*, p. 30.

60. See National Center for Education Statistics, *Indicators of School Crime and Safety: 2011*, Institute of Education Sciences, US Department of Education, February 2012, p. 96. http://nces.ed.gov/programs/crimeindicators/crimeindicators2011/tables/table_02_1.asp (accessed January 23, 2013). See also National School Safety and Security Services, "School Associated Violent Deaths and School Shootings," http://www.schoolsecurity.org/trends/school_violence.html (accessed January 23, 2013).

61. Lydia Saad, "Parents' Fear for Children's Safety at School Rises Slightly," *Gallup Politics,* December 28, 2012, www.gallup.com/poll/159584/parents-fear-children-safety -school-rises-slightly.aspx (accessed January 23, 2013).

62. Elizabeth Becker, "As Ex-Theorist on Young 'Superpredators,' Bush Aide Has Regrets," *New York Times*, February 9, 2001, www.nytimes.com/2001/02/09/us/as-ex-theorist -on-young-superpredators-bush-aide-has-regrets.html?pagewanted=all&src=pm (accessed September 20, 2012).

63. Cornell, *School Violence,* p. 15.

64. Becker, "As Ex-Theorist on Young 'Superpredators,' Bush Aide Has Regrets."

65. Barry O'Neill, "The History of a Hoax," *New York Times Magazine*, March 6, 1994.

66. Phillip Matier and Andrew Ross, "Center for Gender Equity Makes Some More Equal Than Others," *San Francisco Chronicle*, April 27, 2005, www.sfgate.com/bayarea/ matier-ross/article/Center-for-Gender-Equity-makes-some-more-equal-2638931.php (accessed June 20, 2012).

67. Ms. Foundation, *Youth, Gender and Violence: Building a Movement for Gender Justice*, Ms. Foundation for Women Symposium Report, September 2008, p. 3.

68. Memo from Marie Wilson, Ms. Foundation for Women, to groups and individuals working on Son's Day, March 29, 1996.

69. Ibid.

70. Ibid.

71. Elizabeth Gleick, "The Boys on the Bus," *People*, October 30, 1992, p. 125. Quoted in Ruth Shalit, "Romper Room: Sexual Harassment—by Tots," *The New Republic*, March 29, 1993, p. 13.

72. Nan Stein, "Secrets in Public: Sexual Harassment in Public (and Private) Schools," Working Paper No. 256 (Wellesley, MA: Wellesley College, Center for Research on Women, rev. 1993), p. 4.

73. Merle Froschl et al., grant proposal to Department of Education for *Quit It!* Available through Educational Equity Concepts, New York, NY, 1997.

74. Education Equity Concepts and Wellesley College Center for Research on Women, *Quit It! A Teacher's Guide on Teasing and Bullying for Use with Students in Grades K–3* (New York and Wellesley, MA: Educational Equity Concepts and Wellesley College Center for Research on Women, 1998), p. 2.

75. Ibid., p. v.

76. "WEEA History," www.edc.org/WomensEquity. The site is no longer active. The WEEA office was closed in 2003.

77. Katherine Hanson, "WEAA Equity Center Update," memo, February 27, 1998.

78. Katherine Hanson, opening statement in *1999 Catalogue: WEEA Equity Center* (Washington, DC: US Department of Education, 1999).

79. Katherine Hanson and Anne McAuliffe, "Gender and Violence: Implications for Peaceful Schools," *The Fourth R* (Newsletter of the National Center for Mediation in Education) 52 (August/September 1994).

80. Ibid., p. 1.

81. Katherine Hanson, "Gendered Violence: Examining Education's Role," Working Paper Series (Newton, MA: Center for Equity and Cultural Diversity, 1995), p. 1.

82. Ibid.

83. Hanson and McAuliffe, "Gender and Violence," p. 1.

84. Ibid., p. 2.

85. Ibid., p. 4.

86. Ibid., p. 3.

87. Centers for Disease Control and Prevention, "Deaths: Final Data for 2009," *National Vital Statistics Report*, www.cdc.gov/nchs/data/dvs/deaths_2009_release.pdf (accessed June 20, 2012).

88. Federal Bureau of Investigation and Department of Justice, *Crime in the United States: 1996* (Washington, DC: US Government Printing Office, 1996). In 2009, the number of women who died by homicide was 3,673. See Division of Vital Statistics, "Deaths: Final Data for 2009," *National Vital Statistics Reports* 60, no. 3 (2011), p. 100.

89. Katherine Hanson, interview with author.

90. This is based on 1996 data, available in Division of Vital Statistics, "Deaths: Final Data for 1996," *National Vital Statistics Reports* 47, no. 9 (1998), p. 28.

91. See US Bureau of Justice Statistics, *Violence-Related Injuries Treated in Hospital Emergency Departments* (Washington, DC: US Bureau of Justice Statistics, 1999). See also Centers for Disease Control and Prevention, *Injury Visits to Hospital Emergency Departments, United States, 1992–1995* (Hyattsville, MD: US Department of Health and Human Services, 1998). Of course, not every battered woman goes to an emergency room for treatment, and among those women who go to emergency rooms because of battery, some attribute their injuries to other causes. For a sober and reliable assessment of the incidence and severity of domestic violence, see Cathy Young, *Ceasefire: Why Women and Men Must Join Forces to Achieve True Equality* (New York: Free Press, 1999). Noting that the Bureau of Justice study and the CDC study have underreported the incidence of domestic violence, Young says, "Even if we assume that four out of five such cases are missed, domestic violence would still be ranked far behind falls (27 percent of injuries) and automobile accidents (13 percent)," p. 105.

92. Federal Bureau of Investigation, *Crime in the United States, 1991* (Washington, DC: Federal Bureau of Investigation, 1992), pp. 23–24. According to the FBI, "An estimated 106,593 forcible rapes were reported to law enforcement agencies across the nation during 1991. The 1991 total was 4 percent higher than the 1990 level" (p. 24). For more recent data, see www.fbi.gov/about-us/cjis/ucr/crime-in-the-u.s./2010/crime-in-the-u.s.-2010/tables/10tb101.xls.

93. Hanson and McAuliffe, "Gender and Violence," p. 3.

94. Ibid.

95. Katherine Hanson et al., *More Than Title IX: How Equity in Education Has Shaped the Nation* (Lanham, MD: Rowman and Littlefield, 2009). Biography on back cover.

96. Ms. Foundation, *Youth, Gender & Violence: Building a Movement for Gender Justice*, p. 4.

97. Jessie Klein, *The Bully Society: School Shootings and the Crisis of Bullying in America's Schools* (New York: New York University Press, 2012), p. 5.

98. Ibid., p. 79.

99. Ibid., p. 76.

100. Mayo Clinic, "Women's Health: Preventing the Top 7 Threats," www.mayoclinic.com/health/womens-health/WO00014/ (accessed July 4, 2012).

101. Klein, p. 71.

102. Centers for Disease Control and Prevention, "Youth Behavior Risk Surveillance— United States 2009," *Surveillance Summaries*, MMWR 2010: 59 (No. SS-5905).

103. US Department of Education, *1999 Catalogue: WEEA Equity Center* (Washington, DC: US Department of Education, 1999), inside cover. The WEEA Center offered an online course for Title IX coordinators, www.gpo.gov/fdsys/pkg/GAOREPORTS -PEMD-95-6/pdf/GAOREPORTS-PEMD-95-6.pdf.

104. "Boy Suspended for Kiss on Cheek," shortnews.com, February, 26, 2004, www .shortnews.com/start.cfm?id=37334 (accessed June 20, 2012).

105. Scott James, "A Touch During Recess, and Reaction Is Swift," *New York Times*, January 26, 2012, www.nytimes.com/2012/01/27/education/boy-6-suspended-in-sexual -assault-case-at-elementary-school.html (accessed June 20, 2012).

106. "North Carolina Principal Forced to Retire After Suspending 9-Year-Old for Calling Teacher 'Cute,'" foxnews.com, December 8, 2011, www.foxnews.com/us/2011/12/07/ north-carolina-principal-forced-to-retire-after-suspending-nine-year-old-for/ (accessed June 20, 2012).

107. Sharon Lamb, "Sex—When It's Child's Play," *Boston Globe*, April 13, 1997.

108. Author interviews with parents, January and February 1998.

109. In talking about sex differences, it is important to bear in mind that the characterizations do not apply to all children. But the exceptions prove the rule. Although there are any number of gentle and shy boys who shrink from violence, it is said that boys are more aggressive than girls because *on the whole* they are. And although there are many girls who are less nurturing than the average boy, it is said that girls are more nurturing than boys because, on average, they are.

110. Eleanor Emmons Maccoby and Carol Nagy Jacklin, *The Psychology of Sex Differences*, vol. 1 (Palo Alto, CA: Stanford University Press, 1974), p. 352.

3. *Guys and Dolls*

1. *Fox News in Depth*, June 5, 1997.

2. *Providence Journal Bulletin*, September 12, 1995.

3. See, for example, David Geary, *Male, Female: The Evolution of Human Sex Differences* (Washington, DC: American Psychological Association, 2010); Steven Rhoads, *Taking Sex Differences Seriously* (San Francisco: Encounter Books, 2004); Simon Baron-Cohen, *The Essential Difference: The Truth About the Male and Female Brain* (New York: Basic Books, 2003); Jerre Levy and Doreen Kimura, "Men, Women and the Sciences," in Christina Hoff Sommers, ed., *The Science on Women and Science* (Washington, DC: AEI, 2010); Marco Del Giudice, Tom Booth, and Paul Irwing, "The Distance Between Mars and Venus: Measuring Global Sex Differences in Personality," *PLoS ONE*, January 4, 2012, available at www.plosone.org/article/info:doi/10.1371/ journal.pone.0029265 (accessed August 20, 2012).

4. WEEA Publishing Center, *Gender Equity for Educators, Parents, and Community* (Newton, MA: WEEA Publishing Center, 1995), p. 1.

5. See, for example, Janet Hassett et al., "Sex Differences in Rhesus Monkey Toy Preferences Parallel Those of Children," *Journal in Hormone and Behavior* 54, no. 3 (August 2008), pp. 359–364. See also Sonya M. Kahlenberg and Richard W. Wrangham, "Sex Differences in Chimpanzees' Use of Sticks as Play Objects Resemble Those of Children," *Current Biology* 20, no. 24 (December 21, 2010), pp. R1067–R1068.

6. Doreen Kimura, "Sex Differences in the Brain," *Scientific American*, Spring 1999, p. 27.

7. Ibid., p. 27.

8. Bonnie Raines, *Creating Sex-Fair Family Day Care: A Guide for Trainers* (Philadelphia and Washington, DC: Office of Educational Research and Improvement, 1991). The guide points out that the report was funded by the Department of Education and distributed under the auspices of its Women's Educational Equity Act, however, "no official endorsement of the Department should be inferred." Nevertheless, with "Office of Educational Research & Improvement, US Department of Education" on the front cover, most readers will naturally assume the booklet has the imprimatur of the government. Indeed, it is easy to mistake it for an official government document.

9. Ibid., p. 80.

10. Ibid., p. 114.

11. Ibid., p. 113.

12. Ibid., p. 87.

13. Ibid., p. 26.

14. Myra Sadker and David Sadker, *Failing at Fairness: How America's Schools Cheat Girls* (New York: Charles Scribner's Sons, 1994), p. 224.

15. Charlotte Zolotow, *William's Doll* (New York: HarperCollins, 1972), p. 5.

16. Sadker and Sadker, *Failing at Fairness*, p. 224.

17. "The War on Boys," National Desk, PBS, April 9, 1999.

18. Marie Franklin, "The Toll of Gender Roles," *Boston Sunday Globe,* November 3, 1996, p. H9.

19. Abigail J. Stewart, Janet Malley, Danielle LaVague, eds., *Transforming Science and Engineering: Advancing Academic Women* (Ann Arbor, MI: University of Michigan Press, 2007), p. 4.

20. ADVANCE website: www.portal.advance.vt.edu/index.php (accessed June 26, 2012).

21. Gender Equity Project website: www.hunter.cuny.edu/genderequity/ (accessed June 26, 2012).

22. Virginia Valian, *Why So Slow? The Advancement of Women* (Cambridge, MA: MIT Press, 1999), p. 13.

23. Ibid., p. 268.

24. Ibid., p. 34.

25. Ibid., p. 38.

26. Ibid., p. 332.

27. Ibid., p. 67.

28. Lise Eliot, *Pink Brain, Blue Brain* (New York: Mariner Books, 2010), p. 115.

29. Patricia Leigh Brown, "Supporting Boys or Girls When the Line Isn't Clear," *New York Times*, December 6, 2006.

30. Elizabeth Spelke, panel discussion, Impediments to Change: Revisiting the Women in Science Question, Radcliffe Institute for Advanced Study, Harvard University, March 21, 2005. Also cited here: www.edge.org/3rd_culture/debate05/debate05_index.html.

31. David Geary, *Male, Female: The Evolution of Human Sex Differences* (Washington, DC: American Psychological Association, 1998), p. 315.

32. See, for example, David Geary, *Male, Female*; Steven Rhoads, *Taking Sex Differences Seriously* (San Francisco: Encounter Books, 2004); Baron-Cohen, *The Essential Differ-*

ence; Jerre Levy and Doreen Kimura, "Men, Women and the Sciences," in Christina Hoff Sommers, ed., *The Science on Women and Science* (Washington, DC: AEI, 2010). See also OCED, *Pisa Results: What Students Know and Can Do—Student Performance in Reading, Mathematics and Science*, 2010, p. 14. In this study of student performance in seventy nations, girls outperformed boys in reading by large margin; boys outperformed girls in math by moderate margin. More girls than boys were among the top achievers in reading: 2.4 percent of girls and .05 percent of boys scored 90 percent or better; in math, 3.4 percent of girls and 6.6 percent of boys scored 90 percent or better.

33. Steven Pinker, *The Blank Slate: The Modern Denial of Human Nature* (New York: Viking Press, 2002), p. 350.

34. Marco Del Giudice, Tom Booth, and Paul Irwing, "The Distance Between Mars and Venus: Measuring Global Sex Differences in Personality," *PLoS ONE* 7, no. 1 (2012). See also David P. Schmitt et al., "Why Can't a Man Be More Like a Woman? Sex Differences in Big Five Personality Traits Across 55 Cultures," *Journal of Personality and Social Psychology* 94 (2008), pp. 168–182.

35. Simon Baron-Cohen, "The Extreme-Male-Brain Theory of Autism," Department of Experimental Psychology and Psychiatry, University of Cambridge (1999), available at www.autismresearchcentre.com/docs/papers/1999_BC_extrememalebrain .pdf.

36. Francis Wardle, "Men in Early Childhood: Fathers and Teachers," earlychildhoodnews .com, www.earlychildhoodnews.com/earlychildhood/article_view.aspx?ArticleID=400 (accessed July 11, 2012). Ninety-seven percent of teachers in pre-kindergarten programs are women, and only 13 percent of elementary school teachers are men.

37. National Association of Social Workers Center for Workforce Studies, "Licensed Social Workers in the United States, 2004," *NASW Center for Workforce Studies*, 2004, http:// workforce.socialworkers.org/studies/chapter2_0806.pdf (accessed July 12, 2012). In 2004, 81 percent of social workers in the United States were female.

38. "The Registered Nurse Population: Findings from the 2008 National Sample Survey of Registered Nurses," US Department of Health and Human Services, Health Resources and Services Administration, 2010, pp. 7.2–7.3.

39. Amy Cynkar, "The Changing Gender Composition of Psychology," *American Psychological Association*, June 2007, www.apa.org/monitor/jun07/changing.aspx (accessed July 11, 2012). In 2005, 72 percent of graduating PhDs and PsyDs were female.

40. " 'Nontraditional': A Video Makes a Car Job Seem Auto-Matic," ontheissuesmagazine .com, August 9, 2010, www.ontheissuesmagazine.com/cafe2/article/108. According to the Bureau of Labor Statistics, 98.2 percent of automotive service technicians and mechanics were male; 98.5 percent of automotive body and related repairers were male in 2009.

41. http://kosciuskocareers.com/careerclusters/details.cfm?JobTitle_id=187 (accessed July 12, 2012). At least 75 percent of oil drillers nationally are male.

42. National Science Foundation, *Women, Minorities, and Persons with Disabilities in Science and Engineering*, National Science Foundation, January 2012, table 9.5, www.nsf .gov/statistics/wmpd/pdf/tab9-5.pdf (accessed July 12, 2012). In 2006, 91.3 percent of all people in the United States employed as electrical engineers were male.

43. Marc Hauser, Steven Pinker, Armand Leroi et al., "The Assortative Mating Theory," edge.org, May 4, 2005, www.edge.org/3rd_culture/baron-cohen05/baron-cohen05_ index.html (accessed July 12, 2012).

44. Ibid.

45. Peggy Orenstein, *SchoolGirls: Young Women, Self-Esteem, and the Confidence Gap* (New York: Doubleday, 1994).

46. Ibid., p. 276.

47. Judy Logan, *Teaching Stories* (New York: Kodansha International, 1997). Endorsement by Mary Pipher on front cover.

48. Orenstein, *SchoolGirls*, p. 247.

49. Ibid., p. 248.

50. Ibid., p. 255.

51. Ibid., p. 263.

52. Ibid.

53. Ibid., pp. 267–270.

54. Ibid., p. 267.

55. Ibid., p. 273.

56. Ibid., p. 274.

57. Pinker, *The Blank Slate*, p. 351.

58. ABC News Special, "Men, Women and the Sex Difference," aired February 1, 1995.

59. Ibid.

60. Carolyn Rivers and Rosalind Barnett, cited in Cordelia Fine, *Delusions of Gender* (New York: W. W. Norton, 2010), p. xxviii.

61. Immanuel Kant, "Of the Distinction of the Beautiful and Sublime in the Interrelations of the Two Sexes," reprinted in Mary Briody Mahowald, *Philosophy of Woman: An Anthology of Classic to Current Concepts* (Indianapolis: Hackett, 1978), p. 103.

62. Quoted in Stephen J. Gould, *The Mismeasure of Man* (New York: W. W. Norton, 1981), pp. 104–105.

63. Ibid.

64. Leonard Sax, "Leonard Sax: Single-Sex Education Can Work," *Charleston Daily Mail*, June 5, 2012, www.dailymail.com/Opinion/Commentary/201206040082 (accessed July 12, 2012).

65. Cease and Desist Letter sent to J. Patrick Law, superintendent of Wood County Schools, May 21, 2012, www.aclu.org/files/pdfs/womensrights/teach/WoodCoSchoolsdemandletter.pdf, (accessed July 12, 2012).

66. Ibid.

67. Amy Novotney, "Coed Versus Single-Sex Ed," *American Psychological Association* 42, no. 2 (February 2011), p. 58, www.apa.org/monitor/2011/02/coed.aspx (accessed July 12, 2012).

68. Senator Hillary Clinton, *Congressional Record*, June 7, 2001, S5943.

69. Figures provided by National Association for Single-Sex Public Education (NASPE), www.singlesexschools.org/schools-schools.htm (accessed July 12, 2012).

70. Gregory Patterson, "Separating the Boys from the Girls," *Phi Delta Kappan*, February 2012, www.robinfogarty.com/documents/Kappan.Article.pdf (accessed July 12, 2012).

71. Irma Lerma Rangel Young Women's Leadership School, "School Profile 2011–2012," http://dallasisd.schoolwires.net/cms/lib/TX01001475/Centricity/Domain/6547/Irma%20L.%20Rangel%20YWLS%20Profile%202012-2013.pdf (accessed September 12, 2012).

72. Bill Zeeble, "Dallas All-Boys School Lets Young Men Shine," *Voice of America*, August 15, 2011, www.voanews.com/articleprintview/163616.html (accessed July 12, 2012).

73. ACLU Press Release, "ACLU Launches 'Teach Kids, Not Stereotypes' Campaign Against Single-Sex Classes Rooted in Stereotypes," May 21, 2012, www.commondreams.org/newswire/2012/05/21-0 (accessed July 12, 2012).

74. The boys in West Virginia score 13 points behind girls on the reading and 26 points in writing: http://nces.ed.gov/nationsreportcard/pdf/stt2011/2012454WV8.pdf (accessed January 23, 2013).

75. Gale Sherwin, " 'Science' Says No to Single-Sex Education," *ACLU Blog of Rights*, September 26, 2011, www.aclu.org/blog/womens-rights/science-says-no-single-sex-education (accessed July 12, 2012).

76. ACCES website: http://lives.clas.asu.edu/access/educators.html (accessed July 12, 2012).

77. Sarah Sparks, "Scholars Say Pupils Gain Social Skills in Coed Classes," *Education Week*, May 7, 2012, www.edweek.org/ew/articles/2012/05/07/30coed.h31.html?tkn=ZVTFyis8rJbJaOtgHu11xG33dXAowOwEiVZp&intc=es (accessed July 12, 2012).

78. Patterson, "Separating the Boys from the Girls."

79. Cease and Desist Letter sent to J. Patrick Law.

80. Diane Halpern, Lise Eliot, Rebecca Bigler, Richard Fabes et al., "The Pseudoscience of Same-Sex Schooling," *Science*, September 23, 2011, www.educ.ethz.ch/halpern-09-23-11_1_.pdf (accessed July 12, 2012).

81. Hyunjoon Park, Jere R. Behrman, Jaesung Choi, "Causal Effects of Single-Sex Schools on College Entrance Exams and College Attendance: Random Assignment in Seoul High Schools," *Demography*, October 2012, pp. 1–37.

82. US Department of Education, Office of Planning, Evaluation and Policy Development, Policy and Program Studies Service, *Single-Sex Versus Secondary Schooling: A Systematic Review*, Washington, DC, 2005.

83. Halpern, Eliot, Bigler, Fabes et al., "The Pseudoscience of Same-Sex Schooling," p. 1707.

84. Carol Lynn Martin and Richard Fabes, "The Stability and Consequences of Young Children's Same-Sex Play Interactions," *Developmental Psychology* 37, no. 3 (May 2001), pp. 431–446.

85. Diana Leonard, "Single-Sex and Co-educational Secondary Schooling: Life Course Consequences?," *Economic and Social Research Council*, 2007, pp. 18, 24.

86. Halpern, Eliot, Bigler, Fabes et al., "The Pseudoscience of Same-Sex Schooling," pp. 1706–1707.

87. Diane Halpern, Lise Eliot, Rebecca Bigler et al., "Letters," *Science* 35, January 13, 2012, p. 167.

88. See also ibid.

89. Amanda Datnow, Lea Hubbard, and Elisabeth Woody, "Is Single Gender Schooling Viable in the Public Sector? Lessons from California's Pilot Program. Final Report" (Toronto: Ontario Institute for Studies in Education, May 20, 2001), p. 11.

90. Ibid., p. 13.

91. Ibid., p. 40.

92. Tamar Lewin, "Single-Sex Education Is Assailed in Report," *New York Times*, September 22, 2011.

93. Lenora Lapidus, "Title IX: Means More Than Sports for My Daughter and All of Our Children," *ACLU Blog of Rights*, June 22, 2012, www.aclu.org/blog/womens-rights/title-ix-means-more-sports-my-daughter-and-all-our-children (accessed July 12, 2012).

94. Michael Erb, "Single-Gender Classes Could Cost Wood County Schools," *Parkersburg News and Sentinel*, June 27, 2012.

95. Michael Erb, "Wood Board of Education Votes to Keep Vandy Single-Gender Classes," *Parkersburg News and Sentinel*, July 3, 2012.

96. Debra Cassens Weiss, "School Concludes Bias Law Bars Father-Daughter Dances," *Education Weekly*, September 12, 2012, www.abajournal.com/mobile/article/school_concludes_discrimination_law_bars_father-daughter_dances/ (accessed September 20, 2012).

97. Vivian Gussin Paley, *Boys & Girls: Superheroes in the Doll Corner* (Chicago: University of Chicago Press, 1984), p. 1.

98. Ibid., p. 65.

99. Ibid., p. 67.

100. Ibid., p. 41.

101. Ibid., p. 90.

102. Ibid., p. 116.

4. *Carol Gilligan and the Incredible Shrinking Girl*

1. Francine Prose, "Confident at 11, Confused at 16," *New York Times Magazine*, January 7, 1990, p. 23.

2. Carol Gilligan, Nona Lyons, and Trudy University Hanmer, eds., *Making Connections: The Relational Worlds of Adolescent Girls at Emma Willard School* (Cambridge, MA: Harvard University Press, 1990).

3. Ibid., p. 4.

4. Ibid., p. 4.

5. Ibid., p. 23.

6. Ibid., p. 14.

7. Ibid.

8. Ibid., pp. 147–161.

9. Ibid., p. 154.

10. Ibid., p. 158.

11. Ibid., p. 147.

12. Ibid., p. 40.

13. Anna Quindlen, "Viewing Society's Sins Through the Eyes of a Daughter," *Chicago Tribune*, January, 1, 1991, p. 19.

14. Carolyn See, "For Girls the Hardest Lesson of All," *Washington Post Book World*, September 2, 1994, p. D3.

15. Myra Sadker and David Sadker, *Failing at Fairness: How America's Schools Cheat Girls* (New York: Charles Scribner's Sons, 1994), pp. 77–78.

16. Mary Pipher, *Reviving Ophelia: Saving the Selves of Adolescent Girls* (New York: Putnam, 1994), p. 19.

17. Anne C. Petersen et al., "Depression in Adolescence," *American Psychologist* 48, no. 2 (February 1993), p. 155.

18. Daniel Offer and Kimberly A. Schonert-Reichl, "Debunking the Myths of Adolescence: Findings from Recent Research," *Journal of the American Academy of Child & Adolescent Psychiatry* 31, no. 6 (November 1992), pp. 1003–1014.

19. Ms. Foundation for Women and Sondra Forsyth, *Girls Seen and Heard* (New York: Tarcher/Putnam, 1998), p. xiii.

20. Ibid., pp. xiv and xv.

21. Ms. Foundation, *Synopsis of Research on Girls* (New York: Ms. Foundation, 1995).

22. Ms. Foundation for Women and Sondra Forsyth, *Girls Seen and Heard*, p. xvii.

23. Ms. Foundation, *Synopsis of Research on Girls*, p. 1.

24. Ibid., p. 5.

25. Elizabeth Debold, Marie Wilson, and Idelisse Malave, *Mother Daughter Revolution: From Betrayal to Power* (Reading, MA: Addison-Wesley, 1993), p. 9.

26. American Association of University Women, *Shortchanging Girls, Shortchanging America*, Executive Summary (Washington, DC: AAUW, 1991), p. 7.

27. American Association of University Women, *A Call to Action* (Washington, DC: AAUW, 1991), p. 4.

28. Suzanne Daley, "Little Girls Lose Their Self-Esteem on Way to Adolescence, Study Finds," *New York Times*, January 9, 1991, p. B6.

29. Bruce Bower, "Teenage Turning Point," *Science News*, March 23, 1991, p. 184.

30. Ibid.

31. For other criticisms of the alleged self-esteem crisis, see William Damon, *Greater Expectations: Overcoming the Culture of Indulgence in America's Homes and Schools* (New York: Free Press, 1995), p. 74. See also Kristen C. Kling et al., "Gender Differences in Self-Esteem: A Meta-Analysis," *Psychological Bulletin* 125, no. 4 (1999), pp. 470–500; Kirk Johnson, "Self-Image Is Suffering from Lack of Esteem," *New York Times*, May 5, 1998, p. F7; my *Who Stole Feminism? How Women Have Betrayed Women* (New York: Simon & Schuster, 1994; Touchstone, 1995), pp. 136–50.

32. AAUW/Greenberg-Lake Full Data Report, *Expectations and Aspirations: Gender Roles and Self-Esteem* (Washington, DC: AAUW, 1990), p. 18.

33. Ibid., p. 13.

34. American Association of University Women, *How Schools Shortchange Girls: The AAUW Report*, p. 84.

35. Millicent Lawton, "AAUW Builds on History," *Education Week*, September 28, 1994, p. 17.

36. Susan Chira, "Bias Against Girls Is Found Rife in Schools, with Lasting Damages," *New York Times* February 12, 1992, p. 1.

37. Tamar Lewin, "How Boys Lost Out to Girl Power," *New York Times*, December 12, 1998, sec. 4, p. 1. See also Judith Kleinfeld, "Student Performance: Males Versus Females," *Public Interest*, Winter 1999, pp. 3–20.

38. American Association of University Women, *How Schools Shortchange Girls: The AAUW Report* (Executive Summary), p. 2.

39. Amy Saltzman, "Schooled in Failure?," *U.S. News & World Report*, November 7, 1994, p. 90. Psychologist Judith Kleinfeld had a similar experience when she attempted to locate the Sadker call-out study. Kleinfeld asked, "Is it possible for a study simply to disappear into thin air? Apparently it is: when I telephoned David Sadker to ask him for a copy of the research, he could not locate one." (In Judith Kleinfeld, "Student Performance: Males Versus Females," p. 14.)

40. See, for example, P. W. Hill, P. Smith-Homes, and K. J. Rowe, *School and Teacher Effectiveness in Victoria: Key Findings from Phase I of the Victoria Quality Schools Project* (Melbourne: Center for Applied Educational Research, 1993). University of Melbourne researchers studied fourteen thousand students: among their key findings were that (1) "attentiveness has a massive effect on student achievement" (p. 28), and (2) girls are more attentive than boys (pp. 18, 28).

41. Sadker and Sadker, *Failing at Fairness*, p. 279.

42. *Women's Research Network News* (New York: National Council for Research on Women, 1993), p. 11.

43. Emily Eakin, "Listening for the Voices of Women," *New York Times*, March 30, 2002, www.nytimes.com/2002/03/30/arts/listening-for-the-voices-of-women .html?pagewanted=all&src=pm (accessed September 20, 2012).

44. Metropolitan Life Insurance Company, *The American Teacher 1997: Examining Gender Issues in Public Schools* (New York: Metropolitan Life Insurance Company, 1997).

45. Ibid., p. 3.

46. Ibid., p. 131. A similar question was asked by the 1998–99 State of Our Nation's Youth Survey, *State of Our Nation's Youth 1998–1999* (Alexandria, VA: Horatio Alger Association, 1998): 71 percent of girls but only 64 percent of boys said they have an opportunity for open discussion in class.

47. The Search Institute is an educational foundation devoted to advancing the well-being of children and adolescents. See Search Institute, *Starting Out Right: Developmental Assets* (Minneapolis: Search Institute, 1997); also Search Institute, *A Fragile Foundation: The State of Developmental Assets Among American Youth* (Minneapolis: Search Institute, 1999).

48. Horatio Alger Association of Distinguished Americans, *State of Our Nation's Youth 1998–1999*. The survey conducted by NFO Research, Inc., was based on two small but carefully selected samples of students (a cross-section of 2,250 fourteen- to eighteen-year-olds as well as a computer-generated sample of 1,041 students; see p. 4). The researchers are careful to note that this study is not definitive and provides only a "snapshot in time."

49. Ibid., p. 31.

50. Bae, Choy, Geddes, Sable, and Snyder, *Trends in Educational Equity of Girls and Women*, p. 22.

51. Ibid., p. 28.

52. Susan Harter et al., "Predictors of Level of Voice Among High School Females and Males: Relational Context, Support and Gender Orientation," *Developmental Psychology* 34, no. 5 (1998), p. 892.

53. Susan Harter, Patricia Waters, and Nancy Whitesell, "Lack of Voice as a Manifestation of False Self-Behavior Among Adolescents: The School Setting as a Stage upon Which the Drama of Authenticity Is Enacted," *Educational Psychologist* 32, no. 3 (1997), pp. 153–173.

54. Ibid., p. 162.

55. Ibid., p. 153 (abstract).

56. Amy Gross, passage from *Vogue* cited in Carol Gilligan, *In a Different Voice* (Cambridge, MA: Harvard University Press, 1993).

57. Emily Eakin, "Listening for the Voices of Women," *New York Times*, March 20, 2002. Gilligan left Harvard soon after the donation, and the center never came into being. Harvard returned the funds to Ms. Fonda.

58. Lawrence J. Walker, "Sex Differences in the Development of Moral Reasoning: A Critical Review," *Child Development* 55 (1984), p. 681.

59. William Friedman, Amy Robinson, and Britt Friedman, "Sex Differences in Moral Judgments? A Test of Gilligan's Theory," *Psychology of Women Quarterly* 11 (1987), pp. 37–46.

60. See the exchange between Gilligan and me regarding the status (and whereabouts) of her research in *The Atlantic Monthly*, August 2000, Letters, vol. 286, no. 2, pp. 6–13. Available at www.theatlantic.com/past/docs/issues/2000/08/letters.htm (accessed September 12, 2012).

61. Zella Luria, "A Methodological Critique," *Signs*, no. 2 (1986), p. 318.

62. Faye J. Crosby, *Juggling: The Unexpected Advantages of Balancing Career and Home for Women and Their Families* (New York: Free Press, 1991), p. 124.

63. Gilligan is celebrated by some (mostly feminist) moral philosophers for her discovery of two approaches to morality: the (female) ethic of care and the (male) ethic of justice. The labeling of these as male and female is her doing, but the distinction is hoary. The tension between care and duty, between the personal and the impersonal, between abstract principle and contextual reality are familiar themes in moral philosophy that transcend gender. All standard theories (John Rawls's hypothetical contractarianism, for example) must assign proper places to care and duty, balancing, for example, considerations of justice with considerations of mercy. See George Sher, "Other Voices, Other Rooms? Women's Psychology and Moral Theory," and Marcia Baron, "The Alleged Repugnance of Acting from Duty," *Journal of Philosophy* 81, no. 4 (April 1984), pp. 197–220.

64. Lyn Mikel Brown and Carol Gilligan, *Meeting at the Crossroads: Women's Psychology and Girls' Development* (New York: Ballantine Books, 1992), p. 15.

65. Ibid., p. 10.

66. Francine Prose, "Confident at 11, Confused at 16," *New York Times Magazine*, January 7, 1990, p. 46.

67. Debra Viadero, "Their Own Voices," *Education Week*, May 13, 1998, p. 37.

68. Carol Gilligan, "Remembering Larry," *Journal of Moral Education* 27, no. 2 (May 1998), pp. 134–135.

69. Ruth Graham, "Carol Gilligan's Persistent 'Voice,'" *Boston Globe*, June 24, 2012, http://articles.boston.com/2012-06-24/ideas/32348040_1_psychology-gilligan -gender-studies/5 (accessed September 20, 2012).

70. Carol Gilligan, "The Centrality of Relationship in Human Development: A Puzzle, Some Evidence, and a Theory," in Gil Noam and Kurt Fischer, eds., *Development and Vulnerability in Close Relationships* (Mahwah, NJ: Erlbaum, 1996), p. 252.

5. *Gilligan's Island*

1. Carol Gilligan, "The Centrality of Relationship in Human Development: A Puzzle, Some Evidence, and a Theory," in Gil Noam and Kurt Fischer, eds., *Development and Vulnerability in Close Relationships* (Mahwah, NJ: Erlbaum, 1996), p. 258.

2. Ibid., p. 251.

3. Ibid., p. 250.

4. Gilligan, *In a Different Voice*, pp. 7–11.

5. Nancy Chodorow, *The Reproduction of Mothering: Psychoanalysis and the Sociology of Gender* (Berkeley: University of California Press, 1978), p. 9.

6. Ibid., p. 7.

7. Ibid., p. 180.

8. Ibid., p. 181.

9. Ibid., p. 214.

10. Gilligan, *In a Different Voice*, p. 8.

11. Ibid.

12. Chodorow, *The Reproduction of Mothering*, p. 219.

13. See chapter 3 for a review of literature on sex differences.

14. Michael Norman, "From Carol Gilligan's Chair," *New York Times Magazine*, November 9, 1997, p. 50.

15. Gilligan, "The Centrality of Relationship in Human Development," p. 251.

16. Ibid.

17. Norman, "From Carol Gilligan's Chair," p. 50.

18. Ibid.

19. Norman, "From Carol Gilligan's Chair," p. 50.

20. Gilligan, "The Centrality of Relationship in Human Development," p. 238; Franklin, "The Toll of Gender Roles," p. 9.

21. US Census Bureau, *Living Arrangements of Children 2009*, p. 4, www.census.gov/prod/2011pubs/p70-126.pdf (accessed September 21, 2012).

22. Ibid.

23. Daniel Patrick Moynihan, *The Negro Family: The Case for National Action* (Washington, DC: US Department of Labor, 1965). Quoted in National Fatherhood Initiative, *Father Facts* (Gaithersburg, MD: National Fatherhood Initiative, 1998), p. 57.

24. Elaine Ciulla Kamarck and William Galston, *Putting Children First: A Progressive Family Policy for the 1990s* (Washington, DC: Progressive Policy Institute, 1990), p. 14.

25. Cynthia Harper and Sara S. McLanahan cited in "Father Absence and Youth Incarceration," *Journal of Research on Adolescence* 14 (September 2004), pp. 369–397.

26. David Blankenhorn, *Fatherless America* (New York: HarperCollins, 1995).

27. Debra Viadero, "Their Own Voices," *Education Week*, May 13, 1998, p. 38.

28. Information sheet from Harvard Graduate School of Education, *Women's Psychology, Boys Development and the Culture of Manhood*, September 1995.

29. Gilligan, "The Centrality of Relationship in Human Development," p. 251.

30. Stephen Ambrose, *Citizen Soldiers* (New York: Simon & Schuster, 1997), p. 473.

31. Ibid.

32. Ibid., pp. 471–472.

6. *Save the Males*

1. McLean Hospital press release (www.mcleanhospital.org/PublicAffairs/boys1998.htm), June 4, 1998.

2. Ibid. In the study, as in the McLean press release, the word *healthy*, when applied to boys, is invariably encased in ironic scare quotes.

3. William Pollack, *Real Boys: Rescuing Our Sons from the Myths of Boyhood* (New York: Random House, 1998).

4. www.williampollack.com/talks.html, July 12, 1999.

5. William Pollack, "Listening to Boys' Voices," May 22, 1998, p. 28. (Available through McLean Hospital Public Affairs Office, Belmont, Massachusetts.)

6. McLean press release, p. 2.

7. Pollack, "Listening to Boys' Voices," p. 24.

8. Ibid., p. 10.

9. Ibid.

10. Ibid., p. 9.

11. Ibid., p. 17.

12. Ibid., p. 18.

13. American Psychiatric Association, *Diagnostic and Statistical Manual of Mental Disorders,* 4th ed. (Washington, DC: American Psychiatric Association, 1994), pp. 111–112. For an excellent critique of Pollack's work on boys, see Gwen Broude, "Boys Will Be Boys," *Public Interest* 136 (Summer 1999), pp. 3–17. It was Broude's article that brought the *DSM-IV* data on separation anxiety to my attention.

14. McLean Hospital press release, p. 2.

15. Pollack, "Listening to Boys' Voices," p. 11.

16. Russell D. Clark and Elaine Hatfield, "Gender Differences in Receptivity to Sexual Offers," *Journal of Psychology and Human Sexuality* 2 (1989), pp. 39–55.

17. "Harvard and Yale Restrict Use of Their Names," Associated Press, October 13, 1998. See also www.nytimes.com/library/national/science/.

18. Megan Rosenfeld, "Reexamining the Plight of Young Males," *Washington Post*, March 26, 1998, p. A1.

19. Barbara Kantrowitz and Claudia Kalb, "Boys Will Be Boys," *Newsweek*, May 11, 1998, p. 57. See also www.nytimes.com/library/national/science.

20. "The Difference Between Boys and Girls: Why Boys Hide Their Emotions," ABC, June 5, 1998.

21. Tom Duffy, "Behind the Silence," *People*, September 21, 1998, p. 175.

22. *Saturday Today*, March 28, 1998.

23. Nadya Labi, "Mother of the Accused," *Time*, June 24, 2001, www.time.com/time/magazine/article/0,9171,138917,00.html (accessed January 29, 2013). See also David Koons, "A Boy Killer Speaks," *Arkansas Times*, December 4, 2008, www.arktimes.com/arkansas/a-boy-killer-speaks/Content?oid=934386&storyPage=1 (accessed January 29, 2013).

24. PBS, "Who Is Kip Kinkel?" Last modified 2013, www.pbs.org/wgbh/pages/frontline/shows/kinkel/kip/cron.html (accessed January 30, 2013).

25. FBI Uniform Crime Report: www.fbi.gov/ucr/Cius_97/97crime. See also US Department of Justice, *Juvenile Offenders and Victims: A National Report* (Washington, DC: US Department of Justice, 1995).

26. Some passages in *Real Boys* show that Pollack has genuine understanding for the needs of boys. There is, for example, an excellent discussion of the ways our schools neglect boys and favor girls. He notes that our "coeducational schools . . . have evolved into institutions that are better at satisfying the needs of girls than those of boys . . . not providing the kind of classroom activities that will help most boys to thrive." Unfortunately, such passages are rare. Most of his book is about a male culture that is harming boys, as it harms girls. The demoralization of girls is the paradigm. Even as he is pointing out that our schools are unfairly neglecting boys, Pollack treats girls as the default victims of our culture, adding only that "adolescent boys, *just like adolescent girls*, are suffering from a crisis in self-esteem" (emphasis in original) (p. 239).

27. Pollack, *Real Boys*, p. 6.

28. See, for example, Anne C. Petersen et al., "Depression in Adolescence," *American Psychologist* 48, no. 2 (February 1993), p. 155; and Daniel Offer and Kimberly A. Schonert-Reichl, "Debunking the Myths of Adolescence: Findings from Recent Research," *Journal of the American Academy of Child & Adolescent Psychiatry* 31, no. 6 (November 1992), pp. 1003–1014. See also entry on "Separation Anxiety Disorder" in *Diagnostic and Statistical Manual of Mental Disorders*, 4th ed., p. 112.

29. Susan Faludi, *Stiffed: The Betrayal of the American Man* (New York: Morrow, 1999).

30. Ibid., p. 358.

31. Ibid., p. 9.

32. Ibid., p. 39.

33. David Myers and Ed Diener, "Who Is Happy?," *Psychological Science* 6, no. 1 (January 1995), p. 14. For data from the National Opinion Research Center, see www.icpsr.umich.edu/gss99.

34. Faludi, *Stiffed*, p. 27.

35. Ibid., p. 6. Regier is one of the researchers cited in Faludi's supporting footnote (p. 612, footnote 5).

36. *DSM-IV*, the official desk reference of the American Psychiatric Association, reports that the point prevalence for clinical depression among men is 2 percent to 3 percent.

37. Jim Windolf, "A Nation of Nuts," *Wall Street Journal*, October 22, 1997.

38. Pat Sebranek and Dave Kemper, *Write Source 2000 Teacher's Guide* (Burlington, WI: The Write Source/D.C. Heath, 1995), p. 70. In a 1999 interview, one of the writers, Dave Kemper, told me that in future editions, most of the "feeling" questions and self-esteem exercises will be eliminated.

39. Jack Levin and Arnold Arluke, "An Exploratory Analysis of Sex Differences in Gossip," *Sex Roles* 12 (1985), pp. 281–285.

40. Diane McGuinness and John Symonds, "Sex Differences in Choice Behavior: The Object-Person Dimension," *Perception* 6, no. 6 (1977), pp. 691–694.

41. See, for example, Leslie Brody and Judith Hall, "Gender and Emotion," in *Handbook of Emotions*, eds. Michael Lewis and Jeannette Haviland (New York: Guilford Press, 1993), p. 452.

42. Jane Bybee, "Repress Yourself," *Psychology Today*, September/October 1997, p. 12. See also, Jane Bybee, "Is Repression Adaptive? Relationships to Socioemotional Adjustment, Academic Performance, and Self-Image," *American Journal of Orthopsychiatry* 6, no. 1 (January 1997), pp. 59–69.

43. Amanda Rose et al., "How Girls and Boys Expect Disclosure About Problems Will Make Them Feel: Implications for Friendships," *Child Development*, February 2012.

44. "Males Believe Discussing Problems Is a Waste of Time, MU Study Shows," *MU News Bureau*, August 22, 2011, http://munews.missouri.edu/news-releases/2011/0822-males-believe-discussing-problems-is-a-waste-of-time-mu-study-shows/ (accessed September 21, 2012).

45. Pollack, *Real Boys*, p. 50.

46. Fay Weldon, "Where Women Are Women and So Are Men," *Harper's Magazine*, May 1998, p. 66.

47. At the very end of one of his last books, *Civilization and Its Discontents*, Sigmund Freud sternly cautioned his followers to resist the temptation to talk of whole groups as suffering neurosis brought about by "the culture." Whatever its drawbacks as a

diagnostic and therapeutic technique, Freudian psychology should not be faulted for the way Pipher, Gilligan, and the Pollack group seek to pathologize our children. Freud acknowledged that in important respects the development of civilization shows similarities to the development of individuals. And he noted the temptation to say "that under the influence of cultural urges, some civilizations, or some epochs of civilization—possibly the whole of mankind—have become 'neurotic.'" But he warned "that it is dangerous, not only with men but with concepts [such as neurosis], to tear them from the sphere in which they originate and have been evolved." Freud even predicted that "one day someone will venture to embark upon a pathology of cultural communities" using psychoanalytic concepts. Though he had invented psychoanalysis, he deplored the day it would be used in that way.

48. Nussbaum, "Good Grief," p. 49.

49. Quoted in Sharon Begley, "You're O.K., I'm Terrific: 'Self-Esteem' Backfires," *Newsweek*, July 13, 1998, p. 69. See also Roy F. Baumeister, Laura Smart, and Joseph Boden, "Relation of Threatened Egotism to Violence and Aggression: The Dark Side of High Self-Esteem," *Psychological Review* 103, no. 1 (1996), pp. 5–33; and Kirk Johnson, "Self-Image Is Suffering from Lack of Esteem," *New York Times*, May 5, 1998.

50. John P. Hewitt, *The Myth of Self-Esteem: Finding Happiness and Solving Problems in America* (New York: St. Martin's Press, 1998), p. 51.

51. Ibid., p. 85.

7. *Why Johnny Can't, Like, Read and Write*

1. Story told by Dr. Carl Boyd, president and CEO of the Art of Positive Teaching, an educational foundation in Kansas City (keynote address, National Coalition for Sex Equity Experts, July 1998).

2. Steven Zemelman, Harvey Daniels, and Arthur Hyde, *Best Practice: New Standards for Teaching and Learning in America's Schools* (Portsmouth, NH: Heineman, 1998), p. 51.

3. Alfie Kohn, *What to Look for in a Classroom* (San Francisco: Jossey-Bass, 1998), p. 51.

4. E. D. Hirsch Jr., *The Schools We Need: And Why We Don't Have Them* (New York: Doubleday, 1996), p. 9.

5. National Center for Education Statistics, *Highlights from TIMMS 2007: Mathematics and Science Achievement of US Fourth- and Eighth-Grade Students in an International Context*, US Department of Education, 2009, http://nces.ed.gov/pubs2009/2009001.pdf (accessed July 18, 2012). See also, Harold Stevenson, *A TIMSS Primer* (Washington, DC: Thomas B. Fordham Foundation, 1998). (For full data report, see http://www.csteep.bc.edu/timss).

6. Boys' Reading Commission, *The Report of the All-Party Literacy Commission*, National Literacy Trust, July 2, 2012, p. 5.

7. Larry Hedges and Amy Nowell, "Sex Differences in Mental Test Scores, Variability, and Numbers of High-Scoring Individuals," *Science* 269 (July 7, 1995), p. 45.

8. Center on Education Policy, "Are There Differences in Achievement Between Boys and Girls?," March 2010.

9. Lester Thurow, "Players and Spectators," *Washington Post Book World*, April 18, 1999, p. 5.

10. Charles Hymas and Julie Cohen, "The Trouble with Boys," *Sunday Times* (London), June 19, 1994, p. 14.

11. Barclay McBain, "The Gender Gap That Threatens to Become a Chasm," *The Herald* (Glasgow), September 17, 1996, p. 16.

12. "Tomorrow's Second Sex," *The Economist*, September 28, 1996, p. 23.

13. Robert Bray et al., *Can Boys Do Better?* (Bristol: Secondary Heads Association, 1997).

14. Ibid., p. 17.

15. McBain, "The Gender Gap That Threatens to Become a Chasm."

16. E. Redwood, "Top Marks to the Lads," *Daily Telegraph*, January 17, 1998, p. 19.

17. Ibid.

18. Ibid.

19. Bray et al., *Can Boys Do Better?*, p. 1.

20. Annett MacDonald, Lesley Saunders, and Pauline Benefield, *Boys' Achievement, Progress, Motivation and Participation* (Slough, Berkshire, England: National Foundation for Educational Research, 1999), p. 18.

21. Ibid., p. 13.

22. Boys' Reading Commission, *The Report of the All Party Parliamentary Literacy Group*, National Literary Trust, July 2, 2012, www.literacytrust.org.uk/policy/nlt_policy/boys_reading_commission (accessed July 18, 2012).

23. Ibid., p. 10.

24. Ibid., p. 20.

25. Ibid., p. 15.

26. Ibid.

27. Ibid., p. 22.

28. Ibid., p. 13.

29. Ibid., p. 25.

30. Ibid., p. 76.

31. Ibid.

32. "Success for Boys Outline," www.deewr.gov.au/Schooling/BoysEducation/Pages/success_for_boys.aspx (accessed July 18, 2012).

33. Mark Bauerlein and Sandra Stotsky, "Why Johnny Won't Read," *Washington Post*, January 25, 2005, p. A15, www.washingtonpost.com/wp-dyn/articles/A33956-2005Jan24.html (accessed July 18, 2012).

34. Louisa Moats, *Whole-Language High Jinks: How to Tell When "Scientifically-Based Instruction" Isn't* (New York: Thomas Fordham Institute, 2007).

35. Higher Education Research Institute, *The American Freshman: National Norms for Fall 2010*, pp. 58, 82, http://heri.ucla.edu/PDFs/pubs/TFS/Norms/Monographs/The AmericanFreshman2010 (accessed July 18, 2012).

36. Friedrich Froebel, *The Student's Froebel*, ed. W. H. Herford (Boston: Heath, 1904), pp. 5–6. (The quotation is cited in Hirsch, *The Schools We Need*. See especially Hirsch's chapter 4, "Critique of Thought World," for a thorough and astute analysis of the influence of romanticism on American education, pp. 69–126.)

37. Zemelman et al., *Best Practice*, p. 9.

38. Ibid., book summary on back cover. See Hirsch's chapter 5, "Reality's Revenge," *The Schools We Need*, for his critique of *Best Practice* (pp. 127–76).

39. Zemelman et al., *Best Practice*, p. 4.

40. Ibid., p. 8.

41. Ibid., p. 6.

42. David Brooks, "Honor Code," *New York Times*, July 5, 2012, www.nytimes.com/2012/07/06/opinion/honor-code.html?_r=1&nl=todaysheadlines&emc=edit_th_20120706 (accessed July 18, 2012).

43. Sumitra Rajagopalan, "We Need Tool-Savvy Teachers," *Globe and Mail*, October 20, 2010, www.theglobeandmail.com/news/national/time-to-lead/we-need-tool-savvy-teachers/article1215226/ (accessed July 18, 2012).

44. Harvard Graduate School of Education, *Pathways to Prosperity Report: Meeting the Challenge of Preparing Young Americans for the 21st Century*, February 2011.

45. Ibid., p. 27.

46. *U.S. News & World Report* says it is 44 percent female: www.usnews.com/education/best-high-schools/massachusetts/districts; shblackstone-valley-regional-vocational-technical/blackstone-valley-regional-vocational-technical-high-school-9282 (accessed January 23, 2013).

47. Alison L. Fraser, *Vocational-Technical Education in Massachussetts*, Pioneer Institute White Paper no. 42, October 2008, p. 6.

48. Ibid., p. 14.

49. "Valley Tech Freshmen Get Warm Welcome," *Northbridge Daily Voice*, August 20, 2011, http://northbridge.dailyvoice.com/schools/valley-tech-freshmen-get-warm-welcome (accessed July 18, 2012).

50. Fraser, *Vocational-Technical Education in Massachussetts*, p. 18.

51. Harvard Graduate School of Education, *Pathways*, p. 27.

52. Motoko Rich, "Factory Jobs Return, But Employers Find Skill Shortage," *New York Times*, July 1, 2010, www.nytimes.com/2010/07/02/business/economy/02manufacturing.html?pagewanted=all (accessed July 18, 2012).

53. Harvard Graduate School of Education, *Pathways*, p. 16.

54. National Coalition for Women and Girls in Education, "Title IX at 35: Beyond the Headlines," 2008, www.ncwge.org/PDF/TitleIXat35.pdf (accessed July 18, 2012).

55. Ibid., p. 22.

56. Ibid., p. 22.

57. Ibid., p. 21.

58. Interview with author, July 16, 2012.

59. Arne Duncan in US Department of Education, Office of Vocational and Adult Education, "Investing in America's Future: A Blueprint for Transforming Career and Technical Education," Washington, DC, 2012, p. 4, www2.ed.gov/about/offices/list/ovae/pi/cte/transforming-career-technical-education.pdf (accessed September 23, 2012).

60. Ibid., p. 2.

61. Ibid., p. 11.

62. National Women's Law Center, *Tools of the Trade: Using Law to Address Sex Segregation in High School Career and Technical Education*, Washington, DC, 2005, p. 1.

63. National Women's Law Center, *Tools of the Trade: Using Law to Address Sex Segregation in High School Career and Technical Education: Massachusetts Profile*, Washington, DC, 2005, p. 1.

64. National Women's Law Center, *Tools of the Trade: Using Law to Address Sex Segregation in High School Career and Technical Education: Maryland Profile*, Washington, DC, 2005, p. 1.

65. Ibid., p. 8.

66. Interview with author, July 16, 2012.

67. Jessica Tremayne, "Women in Veterinary Medicine," *Veterinary Practice News*, May 2010, www.veterinarypracticenews.com/vet-cover-stories/women-in-veterinary-medicine.aspx (accessed September 25, 2012).

68. N. Bell, *Graduate Enrollment and Degrees: 2000 to 2010* (Washington, DC: Council of Graduate Schools, 2011), p. 12.

69. http://www.ncwge.org/PDF/TitleIXat40.pdf

70. Bari Weiss, "Life Among the Yakkity-Yaks," *Wall Street Journal Weekend Interview*, February 23, 2010, http://online.wsj.com/article/SB10001424052748703525704575061123564007514.html (accessed July 18, 2012).

71. See, for example, Simon Baron-Cohen, *The Essential Difference: Men, Women and the Extreme Male Brain* (London: Penguin UK, 2003).

72. Sharon Otterman, "Gender Gap for the Gifted in City Schools," *New York Times*, May 31, 2010, www.nytimes.com/2010/06/01/nyregion/01gifted.html?_r=1 (accessed July 18, 2012).

73. Ian J. Deary, Graham Thorpe, Valerie Wilson, John M. Starr, and Lawrence J. Whalley, "Population Sex Differences in IQ at Age 11: The Scottish Mental Survey 1932," *Intelligence* 31, no. 6 (2003), pp. 533–542.

74. Otterman, "Gender Gap."

75. Ibid.

76. Terry Neu, interview with author.

77. National Literacy Trust, Great Britain, www.literacytrust.org.uk/media/4720 (accessed September 20, 2012).

8. The Moral Life of Boys

1. Josephson Institute of Ethics, *2010 Report Card on the Ethics of American Youth* (Marina del Rey, CA: Josephson Institute of Ethics, 2010), p. 26.

2. Ibid., p. 61.

3. Ibid., p. 43.

4. American Psychiatric Association, *Diagnostic and Statistical Manual of Mental Disorders*, p. 85.

5. Ibid., p. 88.

6. Charles Puzzanchera and Benjamin Adams, "Juvenile Arrests 2009," in *Juvenile Offenders and Victims National Report Series* (Pittsburgh, PA: Office of Juvenile Justice and Delinquency Prevention, 2011), p. 4.

7. Alfons Crijnen, Thomas Achenbach, and Frank Verhulst, "Comparisons of Problems Reported by Parents of Children in 12 Cultures: Total Problems, Externalizing, and Internalizing," *Journal of the American Academy of Child & Adolescent Psychiatry* 36, no. 9 (September 1997), pp. 1269–1277.

8. Anna Mundow, "The Child Predators," *Irish Times*, January 27, 1997, p. 8.

9. Janet Daley, "Young Men *Always* Behave Badly," *Daily Telegraph*, July 20, 1998.

10. William Damon, *Bringing in a New Era in Character Education* (Palo Alto, CA: Hoover Institution Press, 2002), p. vii.

11. See Michel Marriot, "A Menacing Ritual Is Called Common in New York Pools," *New York Times*, July 7, 1993, www.nytimes.com/1993/07/07/nyregion/a-menacing-ritual

-is-called-common-in-new-york-pools.html?pagewanted=all&src=pm (accessed July 13, 2012); Robert Handley, "4 Are Convicted in Sexual Abuse of Retarded New Jersey Woman," *New York Times*, March 17, 1993, www.nytimes.com/books/97/08/03/ reviews/glenridge-verdict.html (accessed July 13, 2012); "Scoring with the Spur Posse," *New York Times*, March 30, 1993, www.nytimes.com/1993/03/30/opinion/ scoring-with-the-spur-posse.html (accessed July 13, 2012).

12. Quoted in Bernard Lefkowitz, *Our Guys: The Glen Ridge Rape and the Secret Life of the Perfect Suburb* (Berkeley and Los Angeles: University of California Press, 1997), back cover.

13. Judy Mann, *The Difference: Growing Up Female in America* (New York: Warner, 1994), p. 246.

14. Susan Faludi, *Stiffed: The Betrayal of the American Man* (New York: Morrow, 1999), p. 47.

15. Mann, *The Difference*, p. 243.

16. Lefkowitz, *Our Guys*, pp. 3–4.

17. Ibid., p. 7.

18. Ibid., p. 9.

19. Ibid., pp. 93–94.

20. Ibid., p. 92.

21. Ibid., p. 73.

22. Ibid., p. 95.

23. Jane Gross, "Where 'Boys Will Be Boys,' and Adults Are Befuddled," *New York Times*, March 29, 1993, www.nytimes.com/1993/03/29/us/where-boys-will-be-boys-and -adults-are-befuddled.html?pagewanted=all&src=pm (accessed July 13, 2012).

24. Joan Didion, "Trouble in Lakewood," *The New Yorker*, July 26, 1993, p. 50. See also William Damon, *Greater Expectations: Overcoming the Culture of Indulgence in America's Homes and Schools* (New York: Free Press, 1995), pp. 42–45.

25. *Dateline NBC*, NBC television broadcast, April 6, 1993.

26. Gross, "Where 'Boys Will Be Boys,' and Adults Are Befuddled."

27. WNET Educational Resources Center, *Ethical Choices: Individual Voices*, Thirteen/ WNET (New York, 1997).

28. Ibid.

29. Ibid.

30. Nancy F. Sizer and Theodore R. Sizer, eds., *Moral Education: Five Lectures* (Cambridge, MA: Harvard University Press, 1970).

31. Ibid., pp. 3–7.

32. Ibid., p. 5.

33. Ibid., p. 8–9.

34. Sidney Simon and Howard Kirschenbaum, eds., *Readings in Values Clarification* (Minneapolis: Winston Press, 1973), p. 18.

35. See, for example, Lawrence Kohlberg, "The Cognitive-Developmental Approach," *Phi Delta Kappan*, June 1975, pp. 670–675.

36. Lawrence Kohlberg, "Moral Education Reappraised," *The Humanist*, November/December 1978, pp. 14–15. Kohlberg, renouncing his earlier position, wrote, "Some years of active involvement with the practice of moral education . . . has led me to realize that my notion . . . was mistaken. . . . The educator must be a socializer, teaching

238

value content and behavior and not [merely] a process-facilitator of development. . . .
I no longer hold these negative views of indoctrinative moral education and I believe
that the concepts guiding moral education must be partly 'indoctrinative.' This is true,
by necessity, in a world in which children engage in stealing, cheating and aggression."

37. Pat Sebranek, Dave Kemper, and Randall VanderMey, *Write Source 2000 Sourcebook: Student Workshops, Activities, and Strategies* (Wilmington, MA: Houghton Mifflin, 1995), p. 217.

38. American Psychiatric Association, *Diagnostic and Statistical Manual of Mental Disorders*, p. 85.

39. John Stuart Mill, *On Liberty* (Chicago: Regnery, 1955), pp. 14, 84.

40. *Tinker v. Des Moines School District*, 393 U.S. 503, February 24, 1969.

41. Ibid., Justice Black, dissenting.

42. Abigail Thernstrom, "Where Did All the Order Go? School Discipline and the Law," in Diane Ravitch, ed., *Brookings Papers on Education Policy* (Washington, DC: The Brookings Institution Press, 1999), p. 304.

43. William Damon, *Failing Liberty: How We Are Leaving Young Americans Unprepared for Citizenship in a Free Society* (Palo Alto, CA: Hoover Institution, 2011), p. 46.

44. Quoted in ibid., p. 52.

45. See, for example, Laurence Steinberg in *Beyond the Classroom: Why School Reform Has Failed and What Parents Need to Do* (New York: Simon & Schuster, 1996).

46. Dave Cullen, *Columbine* (New York: Grand Central Publishing, 2010).

47. Ibid., p. 523. See also Michael Kimmel, professor of sociology at Stony Brook University, who explains that the Littleton shooters were "not deviants at all" but "overconformists . . . to traditional notions of masculinity." *Congressional Quarterly*, op. cit. See also, Susan Faludi, "The Rage of the American Male," *Newsweek*, August 16, 1999, p. 31.

48. Jessie Klein, *The Bully Society* (New York: New York University Press, 2012), p. 16.

49. Jessica Portner, "Everybody Wants to Know Why," *Education Week*, April 28, 1999, p. 16; see also Kathleen Kennedy Manzo, "Shootings Spur Move to Police Students' Work," *Education Week*, May 26, 1999, p. 14.

50. Josephson Institute Center for Youth Ethics, "The Aspen Declaration on Character Education," *Josephson Institute of Ethics*, 1992, http://charactercounts.org/overview/aspen.html (accessed July 13, 2012). "Character Education Manifesto," available from the Josephson Institute of Ethics, Marina Del Ray, California, or from Kevin Ryan, director, Boston University Center for the Advancement of Ethics and Character.

51. Josephson Institute Center for Youth Ethics, "How to Get Started with Character Counts!," *Josephson Institute of Ethics*, 2012, http://charactercounts.org/getstarted/index.html (accessed July 13, 2012).

52. Donald Baker, "Bringing Character into the Classroom," *Washington Post*, February 4, 1999, Metro, p. 1.

53. Ibid.

54. Damon, *Failing Liberty*, p. 61.

55. Ibid.

56. Marvin Berkowitz and Melinda Bier, "What Works in Character Education: A Research-Driven Guide for Educators," Character Education Partnership, February 2005, http://www.rucharacter.org/file/practitioners_518.pdf (accessed January 26, 2013).

57. Social and Character Development Research Consortium, *Efficacy of Schoolwide Programs to Promote Social and Character Development and Reduce Problem Behavior in Elementary School Children* (Washington, DC: National Center for Education Research, Institute of Education Sciences, US Department of Education, 2010).

58. Damon, *Failing Liberty*, p. 57.

59. Sarah Sparks, "Character Education Found to Fall Short in Federal Study," *Education Week*, October 21, 2010, www.source.ly/10zH1#.T_oAzvEU4fE (accessed July 13, 2012).

60. US Department of Education, Institute of Education Sciences, "Positive Action," *What Works Clearinghouse Intervention Report*, April, 23, 2007, http://ies.ed.gov/ncee/wwc/pdf/intervention_reports/WWC_Positive_Action_042307.pdf (accessed July 13, 2012).

61. See B. Flay, A. Acock, S. Vuchinich, and M. Beets, "Progress Report of the Randomized Trial of Positive Action in Hawaii: End of Third Year of Intervention," available from Positive Action, Inc., 264 4th Avenue South, Twin Falls, ID 83301, 2006; B. Flay and C. G. Allred, "Long-Term Effects of the Positive Action Program," *American Journal of Healthy Behavior* 27, no. 1 (May–June 2003), pp. S6–S21. Also, see B. Flay, "Randomized Evaluation of the Positive Action Pre-K Program," Virginia Foundation for Healthy Youth and Positive Action, Inc., January 2012; K. Lewis, N. Bavarian, F. Snyder et al., "Direct and Mediated Effects of a Social-Emotional and Character Development Program on Adolescent Substance Use," *International Journal of Emotional Education* 4, no. 1 (April 2012), pp. 56–78; F. J. Snyder, S. Vuchinich, A. Acock, I. J. Washburn, and B. R. Flay, "Improving Elementary School Quality Through the Use of a Social-Emotional and Character Development Program: A Matched-Pair, Cluster-Randomized, Control Trail in Hawai'i," *Journal of School Health* 82 (2012), pp. 11–20; K.-K. Li, I. Washburn, D. L. DuBois et al., "Effects of the Positive Action Program on Problem Behaviors in Elementary School Students: A Matched-Pair, Randomized Control Trial in Chicago," *Psychology & Health* 26, no. 2 (2011), pp. 187–204.

62. US Department of Education, "Positive Action," p. 3.

63. Niloofar Bavarian, Kendra Lewis et al., "Using Social-Emotional and Character Development to Improve Academic Outcomes: A Matched-Pair, Cluster Randomized Controlled Trial in Low-Income, Urban Schools" (submitted for publication).

64. William Herndon, *Abraham Lincoln: The True Story of a Great Life*, vol. 3 (Chicago: Belford-Clark, 1890), p. 439.

65. Epictetus, *The Handbook of Epictetus*, tr. Nicholas White (Indianapolis, IN: Hackett Publishing, 1983).

66. Kim Loop, "Lake County, Michigan Sees Firsthand Effects of Positive Action," *Positive Action*, April 20, 2011, www.positiveaction.net/about/index.asp?ID1=7&ID2=705&ID3=1408 (accessed July 13, 2012).

67. Benjamin DeMott, "Morality Plays," *Harper's Magazine*, December 1994, p. 67.

68. Alfie Kohn, "How Not to Teach Values: A Critical Look at Character Education," *Phi Delta Kappan*, February 1997, p. 431.

69. Ibid., p. 433.

70. Thomas J. Lasley II, "The Missing Ingredient in Character Education," *Phi Delta Kappan*, April 1997, p. 654.

71. The program was developed by a California-based group called the Jefferson Center for Character Education: www.jeffersoncenter.org/.

72. Tim Stafford, "Helping Johnny Be Good," *Christianity Today*, September 11, 1995, p. 34.

73. Ibid.

74. For an excellent practical guide to the moral development of boys, see Michael Gurian, *A Fine Young Man* (New York: Tarcher/Putnam, 1998).

75. Angela Lee Duckworth and Martin Seligman, "Self-Discipline Gives Girls the Edge: Gender in Self-Discipline, Grades, and Achievement Test Scores," *Journal of Education Psychology* 98 (2006), pp. 186–208.

9. War and Peace

1. Peggy Orenstein, *School Girls: Young Women, Self-Esteem, and the Confidence Gap* (New York: Doubleday, 1994), p. 248.

2. The Boys Initiative, www.theboysinitiative.org/ (accessed September 21, 2012).

3. Approximately eight hundred Chicago Public Schools students took part in Becoming a Man—Sports Edition from 2009 to 2011. Researchers at the University of Chicago Crime Lab tracked students and reported a "miraculous change in violent crime arrest rates" (44 percent decrease) and a significant improvement in class attendance among students who had participated in the program. See Frank Main, "Study: Chicago Sports Program Cut Violent Crime, Boosted School Attendance," *Chicago Sun-Times*, July 13, 2012, www.suntimes.com/news/metro/13744284-418/study-chicago-sports -program-cut-violent-crime-boosted-school-attendance.html (accessed July 19, 2012).

4. Tom Wolfe, "The Great Relearning," *Orange County Register*, January 24, 1988, p. J01.

5. Ibid.

6. Patricia Stevens, ed., *Between Mothers and Sons: Women Writers Talk About Having Sons and Raising Men* (New York: Scribner, 1999).

7. Deborah Galyan, "Watching *Star Trek* with Dylan," in *Between Mothers and Sons*, ed. Stevens, p. 50.

8. Ibid., pp. 50–51.

9. Ibid., pp. 51–52.

10. Janet Burroway, "Soldier Son," in *Between Mothers and Sons*, ed. Stevens, p. 37.

11. Ibid., p. 40.

12. Mary Gordon, "Mother and Son," in *Between Mothers and Sons*, ed. Stevens, p. 163.

13. Ibid., p. 164.

14. See Hannah Rosin, "The End of Men," The Atlantic, July/August 2010, www.theatlantic .com/magazine/archive/2010/07/the-end-of-men/8135/ (accessed July 19, 2012). See also Dan Abrams, Man Down: Proof Beyond a Reasonable Doubt That Women Are Better Cops, Drivers, Gamblers, Spies, World Leaders, Beer Tasters, Hedge Fund Managers, and Just About Everything Else (New York: Abrams Image, 2011).

Index

conduct disorders as risk factor in, 63, 173

in girls, 135

lack of moral education and discipline tied to, 173–74, 176, 177, 178, 179–80, 184–85, 187, 189, 240*n*

paternal absence and, 120–21

in schools, 46, 48

zero-tolerance policies in response to rising rates of, 46, 48–49, 50, 51

see also juvenile delinquency; violence

Crosby, Faye, 111

Cub Scouts, 46, 47, 123

Cullen, Dave, 188

Daily Telegraph (London), 173–74

Daley, Janet, 173–74

Damon, William, 174, 191, 192

Darwin, Charles, 113

Dateline NBC, 127, 179

Daugherty, Mrs., 148–49, 151, 171

David Youree Elementary School, 46

Davis, T. Cullen, 53

Debold, Elizabeth, 70, 121

DeFazio, Jackie, 77

DeMott, Benjamin, 195, 197

Denver, University of, 60, 105

depression, 128, 129, 135, 138, 143, 232*n*

Didion, Joan, 175, 179

"difference feminists," 108, 112

DiIulio, John J., Jr., 49, 50, 52, 53

discipline, 3, 8, 63, 146, 177–78, 182, 187, 189

boys as benefiting from, 3, 63, 148–49, 152, 153, 154, 172, 173–74, 181, 193, 194–95, 197, 198

"child-centered" learning and departure from, 149, 150, 185, 186, 187

court decisions and, 185–86

criminal behavior and absence of, 173–74, 176–77, 178, 179–80, 184–85, 189

zero-tolerance policies and, 2, 8, 40, 45–49, 60–62, 174, 186, 190, 198

divorce rates, 86

dodgeball, 40, 44

dolls, 64, 65, 66, 68–70, 72, 90

domestic violence, 54, 220*n*

Dowd, Maureen, 204

Downes, Peter, 152

Drexler, Melissa, 135

drop out rates, 14, 160, 161, 211*n*

DSM-IV, 131, 231*n*, 232*n*

Duncan, Arne, 10, 163

Economist, 152

Edelman, Marian Wright, 191

About the Author

Christina Hoff Sommers is a resident scholar at the American Enterprise Institute in Washington, DC. She has a PhD in philosophy from Brandeis University and was a professor of philosophy at Clark University. Sommers has written for numerous publications and is the author of *Who Stole Feminism? How Women Have Betrayed Women* and coauthor of *One Nation Under Therapy.* She is married with two sons and lives in Washington, DC.